WHEN WAR
PLAYED THROUGH

ALSO BY JOHN STREGE

Tiger: A Biography of Tiger Woods

Tiptoeing Through Hell

Tournament Week

Off the Record

WHEN WAR PLAYED THROUGH

Golf During World War II

•

JOHN STREGE

GOTHAM BOOKS

GOTHAM BOOKS
Published by Penguin Group (USA) Inc.
375 Hudson Street, New York, New York 10014, U.S.A.
Penguin Group (Canada), 90 Eglinton Avenue East, Toronto, Ontario, Canada M4P
2Y3 (a division of Pearson Penguin Canada Inc.); Penguin Books Ltd, 80 Strand,
London WC2R 0RL, England; Penguin Ireland, 25 St Stephen's Green, Dublin 2,
Ireland (a division of Penguin Books Ltd); Penguin Group (Australia), 250 Camberwell
Road, Camberwell, Victoria 3124, Australia (a division of Pearson Australia Group Pty
Ltd); Penguin Books India Pvt Ltd, 11 Community Centre, Panchsheel Park, New
Delhi - 110 017, India; Penguin Group (NZ), cnr Airborne and Rosedale Roads,
Albany, Auckland 1310, New Zealand (a division of Pearson New Zealand Ltd);
Penguin Books (South Africa) (Pty) Ltd, 24 Sturdee Avenue,
Rosebank, Johannesburg 2196, South Africa

Penguin Books Ltd, Registered Offices: 80 Strand, London WC2R 0RL, England

Published by Gotham Books, a division of Penguin Group (USA) Inc.

First printing, October 2005
10 9 8 7 6 5 4 3 2 1
Copyright © 2005 by John Strege
All rights reserved

LIBRARY OF CONGRESS CATALOGING-IN-PUBLICATION DATA
Strege, John.
When war played through: golf during world war II / John Strege.
p. cm.
ISBN 1-59240-154-6
1. Golf and war—United States—History. 2. World War,
1939-1945—Social aspects—United States. 3. United States—
Social life and customs—1918-1945. I. Title.
GV963.S77 2005
796.352'0973'09044 dc22   2005011228.

Printed in the United States of America
Set in New Baskerville
Designed by Mia Risberg

For Marlene and Hannah
who brighten every day

CONTENTS

PREFACE

On the eve of World War II, golf was foundering. The Great Depression had deprived families of the wherewithal to pursue frivolous activities, including golf. One million players, one of every five golfers in America, had abandoned the game. Hundreds of country clubs had been unable to endure the financial hardship and folded. It was largely considered an elitist sport before the Depression, more so when unemployment ravaged the working class. Even spectator interest in the game had waned since Bobby Jones had retired from competitive golf in 1930, the game's lone transcending star virtually abandoning the public stage for good.

Then came the war. A crisis diminishes sports' relevancy, even exposes their irrelevancy. When bombs drop, does it matter whether putts do too? There were those for whom yes would have been the response, perhaps those for whom editors at the

Associated Press intended their message when they dispatched a memo to their sportswriters shortly after World War II began, asking that they refrain from employing war terminology in their sportswriting. A football grid is not a battlefield, whatever the extent of the animus one side has for the other.

It was no surprise, then, that when the United States Golf Association canceled its showcase event, the U.S. Open, in response to America's entrance into World War II, it was not a universally popular decision. The noted golf writer Herb Graffis recounted the protestations of more than a few of his colleagues in the press room. "But in gentlemanly Ivy League accents," Graffis wrote, "the USGA silenced criticism by the rebuttal, 'What to hell, don't you guys know your country is in a war?'"

As a scolding goes, this was a watershed moment for a game that tended to take itself too seriously, as its heritage—royal and ancient—suggests. It would soon become apparent that the game and its devotees understood the dire nature of the crisis and their obligation to assist.

When Winston Churchill delivered his speech at the Lord Mayor's Day Luncheon in London on November 10, 1942, he was not thinking about golf, precisely. Then again, neither was he dismissing it.

"In this strange, terrible world war," Churchill told the audience, "there is a place for everyone, man and woman, old and young, hale and halt; service in a thousand forms is open. There is room now for the dilettante, the weakling, for the shirker, or the sluggard. The mine, the factory, the dockyard, the salt sea waves, the fields to till, the home, the hospital, the chair of the scientist, the pulpit of the preacher—from the highest to the humblest tasks, all are of equal honor; all have their part to play."

Even golf, he could have added.

1

GOLF ON
A DAY OF INFAMY

The Pearl Harbor Attack

The rising sun was a reliable ally for off-duty sailors and soldiers looking for the weather to cooperate with their golf habits. On the Hawaiian island of Oahu, sunny and warm is less a forecast than a reasonable expectation. On Sunday morning, December 7, 1941, the sun arrived on cue over the clouds that were shrouding the Koolau Range on the eastern end of Oahu. Its radiance poured through the open windows of the new four-bedroom, two-story home on Makalapa Drive that had been constructed on a patch of an old sugar plantation on the southwestern slope of Oahu's Makalapa Crater, overlooking Pearl Harbor. The home was built to quarter the commander in chief of the United States Navy's Pacific Fleet. Admiral Husband E. Kimmel was its first resident, and on virtually every Sunday morning there, the sun was his wake-up call, luring him eagerly from bed and to the first tee.

Mornings ritually allay fears that flourish in the dark of night. Admiral Kimmel's sunrise reverie on December 7 belied the concern that had accompanied him the night before to a party hosted by Rear Admiral H. Fairfax Leary at the Halekulani, on Waikiki Beach. A Saturday evening at the Halekulani, "House Befitting Heaven," was where worries ordinarily vanished. Warm, gentle trade winds set a laid-back tempo, and the sun colorfully and gracefully bade adieu to another day in paradise. Waiters served platters of fresh fish from local waters, wrapped in ti leaves and steamed, while a dulcet-toned crooner coaxed Hawaiian standards from his heart.

The tranquility in this setting was palpable. For Admiral Kimmel it was also deceptive, which helped cast a pall over the quiet dinner party. Kimmel's own worries were too durable to succumb to the hypnotic virtues of a Hawaiian sunset; he had read War Department communiqués that buttressed a growing uneasiness that a Japanese attack was imminent. On this night, worries prevailed and a party died.

Kimmel's title, Commander in Chief of the Pacific Fleet (CINCPAC, in the shorthand of the Navy), was a sobering accomplice. He was the boss, and he was a stern, serious man who was inherently unlikely to salvage a listless party. He was not a raconteur, nor was he disposed to consume a quantity of alcohol necessary to his becoming one. He typically had no more than a single drink, as was the case on this night. He left the party at ten.

Golf was Kimmel's only vice in these uncertain times. Indeed, the only certainty from his standpoint was that a Japanese attack was not so imminent as to prevent his being on the first tee at Fort Shafter Golf Course. He was scheduled to play with Lieutenant General Walter C. Short, his Army counterpart on the islands, the commanding general. Short's own Saturday evening was similarly dampened by the pervasive notion that Oahu would soon be in Japanese crosshairs. General Short and his wife, accompanied by Lieutenant Colonel and Mrs. Kendall Fielder, had attended a charity dinner dance at the Schofield Barracks fifteen miles from his quarters at Fort Shafter. The general never had more than a single drink, either, whiskey, usually, which allowed him to gracefully bow out early from any social function, as he did from this one.

Their thirty-minute drive back to Fort Shafter took them along the coast highway overlooking Pearl Harbor. Nearing home, Short gazed pensively at the glittering lights of the harbor, a luminous demonstration of America's sea power, its fleet of warships tethered majestically along Battleship Row.

"Isn't that a beautiful sight?" Short said to the passengers in the car.

"And what a target it would make," he added, unable to suppress a terrifying afterthought.

If an attack were imminent, General Short was confident only that it would not occur before his appointed round with the admiral at Fort Shafter Golf Course.

ADMIRAL KIMMEL BEGAN CONSIDERING whether this was the day that he might finally solve the insoluble, the riddle called golf. This was part of his Sunday-morning ritual. The typical golfer brings more hope than skill to the first tee, and the admiral was always more likely to break a sweat than ninety, however elevated his optimism. His handicap was in the twenties and disinclined to descend, even though a Sunday morning game had become part of his weekly regimen on the advice of his doctor, who had prescribed more exercise.

Kimmel's skill was at least of sufficient strength to challenge his regular playing partner. General Short's handicap was also in the twenties, despite his proximity to the Fort Shafter Golf Course. A quick nine was never more than three hundred yards away, the distance between Quarters 5, the commander general's house in which he lived on Palm Circle at Fort Shafter, and the first tee of the fort's golf course.

This was literally a stars-and-stripes pairing, Short and Kimmel, their collective mélange of silver and gold Army and Navy insignia surely a deterrent to players with more skill and less rank who might have considered (for no more than a fleeting moment) the possibility of asking to play through. Short and Kimmel were the highest-ranking officers on Oahu, each responsible for the defense of the Hawaiian Islands and the preparedness of his branch of the military.

Louis Truman, a respected captain who would eventually earn his own general's silver stars, had been invited to join them. A second cousin to Senator Harry S. Truman, Captain Truman was Short's aide-de-camp and the only accomplished golfer in the threesome. Two weeks earlier, Truman had won the Navy Cup at Fort Shafter Golf Course, an achievement he modestly attributed to the fact that the better players had all been out on maneuvers with Admiral William Halsey. Truman's seven handicap probably would have allowed him to contend even without anchors aweigh.

This was a stoic threesome, a group for which frivolity was a luxury it could not afford in these uncertain times. Each of the men took his work seriously; with war apparently imminent, anything less would have been unacceptable. They worked hard, slept fast, and shouldered the burden of responsibility without complaint. They approached their golf with no less seriousness. A tee time represented a blessed break from their workaday routine, a diversion to which each of them looked forward, once a week. A round of golf was not a trivial pursuit.

Admiral Kimmel accordingly winced when the phone rang at his Makalapa home as he was dressing for his golf match. On a Sunday morning, a ringing phone tended to signal only bad news. Captain James Murphy was calling to inform him of an encounter between the USS *Ward,* a destroyer on port patrol, and a Japanese midget submarine that had encroached on Pearl Harbor.

Kimmel and his staff were certain that it was another of several false alarms, each of them requiring his attention nonetheless. To confirm his intuition, he planned to stop by his headquarters on the way to the golf course. Moments later, his phone rang again. This time, Captain Murphy was calling to inform him that the *Ward* was towing a sampan into Honolulu Harbor.

In the midst of their conversation, Murphy was interrupted by a panicked yeoman, who breathlessly told him that the Japanese were attacking Pearl Harbor. Murphy quickly relayed the message to Kimmel, who bounded out of his home and onto the lawn of the home of his neighbor, Captain John Earle. The Earle home afforded an unobstructed view of Battleship Row, a balcony seat to a stage on which history was beginning to play out in a cacophony of explosions and horror. Still buttoning his white uniform top, an ashen Kimmel looked on aghast at the drama unfolding before him. Overhead, Japanese planes were so dense they nearly blotted out the sun. Beneath him, one end of a battleship lifted from the water, a final futile act of defiance before it began its descent to the bottom of the harbor.

Captain Earle's wife stood alongside Kimmel, witnessing the carnage. She cast a glance at Kimmel, whose face, she noted to herself, was as white as the uniform he wore. She returned her gaze to the harbor in time to see another battleship being destroyed.

"Looks like they've got the *Oklahoma,*" Mrs. Earle said.

"Yes, I can see they have," Kimmel replied, his mind racing and his spirits sinking.

At Fort Shafter, General Short was stricken with horror as he entered his headquarters and encountered a bewildered intelligence officer.

"What's going on out there?" Short asked, the rising volume of his voice exposing his impending panic.

"I'm not sure, General," the officer replied. "But I just saw two battleships sunk."

"That's ridiculous," Short said, desperately denying what he already knew to be the painful truth, that his premonition on the drive home the evening before had been correct.

Captain Truman was already attired in his golf togs and was virtually out the door and on his way to the course when the attack began. He ran next door to department headquarters for a briefing, then emerged back into daylight. He glanced skyward, just as an enemy plane approached, a Japanese Zero, flying so low that he could see the pilot's resolute face. On the fuselage beneath him, Truman saw "the great big round red circle on the plane," he said.

Only an hour earlier, the rising sun had been the equivalent of a starter's call to report to the first tee, warm and inviting. Emblematically represented on the sides of enemy aircraft, it had become a chilling symbol of the epic assignment awaiting the United States, a nation now at war, pending the formality of an official declaration.

Admiral Kimmel and General Short, meanwhile, were held accountable—initially, at least—for Pearl Harbor's general state of unreadiness and the burning armada of tethered United States warships. Mercifully (if any mercy could have been culled from the wreckage), their confessionals did not have to include an admission that they were out playing golf at the time.

SAN ANTONIO, TEXAS, was akin to a dusty outpost, for those who weren't born under the Lone Star. Those asking directions to San Antonio might have been told that once they arrived in the middle of nowhere, they would be close. It was the kind of place in which a soldier was not likely to find anything remarkable by way of amusement, other than tumbledown cowboy bars and, curiously, world-class golf. In 1921, the legendary course architect A. W. Tillinghast put his rather imposing imprint on San Antonio. A reformed ruffian once known as Tillie the Terror, Tillinghast took his first golf lesson from Old Tom Morris at St. Andrews in the 1890s and returned frequently to study under the four-time British Open champion. He also coined the word *birdie* for playing a hole in one under par. Tillie had a noble golf pedigree.

By the time he arrived in San Antonio, Tillinghast had already constructed an impressive architectural resume, which included the Philadelphia Cricket Club and the San Francisco Golf Club. In the Texas hill country of San Antonio, he opened a trio of courses in 1921—Brook Hollow Golf Course, Alamo Country Club, and Fort Sam Houston Golf Course.

The last was one of the finest military courses in the country, an unexpected treasure for the uniformed golfers sentenced to a tour of duty at Fort Sam Houston. By 1941, the course had the additional aura of having been built by the same designer who in 1923 had produced Winged Foot and Baltusrol, two of the finest courses in the world, each of which had already hosted the U.S. Open.

Among the golf enthusiasts stationed at Fort Sam Houston in 1941 was Brigadier General Dwight D. Eisenhower, chief of staff to General Walter Krueger, the commanding general of the Third Army. Eisenhower had discovered golf in 1927, when he was thirty-seven and attending an army command school in Fort

Leavenworth, Kansas. The game immediately entered his blood-stream and went straight to his heart. He was smitten.

In the ensuing years, he pursued the game as religiously as he could for a military officer bent on promotion. His Army duties precluded him from devoting the time and effort required to refine his game. Those who entered the service without golf skills weren't likely to find them anywhere along the military trail.

His lack of proficiency failed to stifle his enthusiasm for the game. A poor shot might elicit an epithet he used not infrequently, nor without emphasis. "Goddammit!" he said in response to a wayward effort. Other times he would mutter, "There's a typical Eisenhower," evoking the time-honored tradition of allowing the game to eviscerate your self-esteem. Still, he played on, eager for another opportunity to attempt to pull rank on an egalitarian game that, alas, treated privates and generals with equal contempt.

In the five months of 1941 that Eisenhower and his wife, Mamie, had lived at Quarters 219 on the Artillery Post at Fort Sam Houston, Ike whiled away available idle hours on the rolling hills of Fort Sam Houston Golf Course, alternately pondering the shot at hand and his military future. The prevailing opinion was that somehow, someday, the United States would be required to join the war already under way in Europe, and should that be the case, he longed to play a substantive role.

In the meantime, the Japanese threat seemed to have waned, according to what Eisenhower was hearing. On December 4, 1941, he had read a newspaper editorial that emphatically stated that the Japanese weren't interested in engaging the U.S. in war. Two days later, he noted that a newspaper columnist echoed the Washington consensus that the crisis in the Pacific had passed for the time being.

The order of the day at Fort Sam Houston on December 7, 1941, was business as usual. For Eisenhower, it meant completing the analysis of the recent Louisiana maneuvers that had earned him his promotion to brigadier general. It was a particularly gratifying promotion, because it was the result of his having maneuvered the Third Army to a victory over another inveterate golfer, General Ben Lear, also known as Yoo-hoo Lear. In the summer of 1940, General Lear had been wearing civilian attire, shorts and a golf shirt, while playing a round at Memphis Country Club in Memphis, Tennessee, when a couple of truckloads of soldiers drove by the course en route to the base after maneuvers. Meanwhile, a couple of pretty women were walking along the road adjacent to the fairway, when the men opened with a series of "yoo-hoos," followed by lewd catcalls and even some jabs at the old man, whom they failed to recognize in his civvies. An enraged Lear ordered his playing partner, Colonel Richmond, to venture onto the road and stop the trucks. The colonel dressed down the officers in charge and warned of further repercussions. The next day, the offending troops were ordered on a fourteen-mile hike through the heat and humidity of a Memphis day. News leaked of the discipline that Lear had meted out, even reaching a senator, Bennett Clark, who in an interview called Lear "a superannuated old goat who should be relieved of his duties."

Beating Yoo-hoo on the battlefield was better than beating him on the golf course, but the months-long endeavor had left Eisenhower exhausted. Shortly after noon, Central Standard Time, he fell into his bed at Quarters 219 after leaving word for his assistants that he was not to be disturbed under any circumstance. A long nap was on his agenda, and sleep came easily. He may have dreamed of his impending two-week leave, during which time he and Mrs. Eisenhower had plans to travel to West Point to celebrate Christmas with their son, John, a military academy plebe. When word of the Japanese attack on Pearl Harbor reached Fort Sam Houston, Eisenhower was immediately awakened and given a quick briefing. Within an hour of the attack, the Third Army brass was besieged with orders issued by the War Department. Among them was to dispatch antiaircraft units to the West Coast in the event of Japanese attacks on the mainland. Phantom Japanese Zero sightings were already being routinely reported. Troops were ordered transferred to the coast in the event of a Japanese ground assault.

Eisenhower, meanwhile, would soon be heading back to Washington, D.C., summoned there by General George Marshall. Ike was certain that another desk job was his destiny, and the thought depressed him. The only possible upside—a sliver of consolation—was that in pursuit of a quick nine, it was easier to sneak out of the office than out of a war zone.

THE PACE AT WHICH news traveled in December of 1941 was languid, which tended to bleach some of the bold from the banner headlines trumpeting breaking news. Word of the Japanese attack on a remote island somewhere in the Pacific eventually reached the Miami Springs Golf Course, where it was disseminated largely in whispers through the crowd of seven hundred. It failed to resonate. There was no panic, nor even the urgency to hurry home.

The world was not yet a terrifying place to those who were sharing a small corner of it with a famous foursome on the afternoon of December 7, 1941. So long as the Japanese bombers weren't en route to Miami at that moment, whatever damage they had inflicted in a faraway place was of minimal concern to those lining the fairways at Miami Springs. They were there to watch Ben Hogan and Byron Nelson engaged in a friendly, though spirited, exhibition match with Sam Snead and Clayton

Heafner. The stakes were considerable: they were playing for pride. A gratified ego, of course, would not spend in the manner of a thousand dollars, the winner-take-all sum for which they were to have played before the PGA intervened on the grounds that it too closely resembled gambling. Still, the greater prize at this level was dominion over one's peers. In this foursome, Heafner was the intruder. The other three—Snead, Hogan, and Nelson—were emerging as the best players of their generation, and an opportunity to gain an advantage, or the possibility of surrendering one, elevated the pressure in this exhibition.

Accordingly, they were absorbed in their four-ball match when word of the attack arrived. Hogan was already developing a reputation for playing in a vacuum of his own creation, by blocking out anything that might be a distraction to his perpetual quest to play the perfect round of golf. The other three players barely took notice either. It's not that the foursome was oblivious; indeed, each of the players was of an age that might subject them to service in some form in the event of an extended, multi-front conflict. But here and now, the more important matter was beating an opponent to the hole. So they played on.

The crowd was only marginally more engaged in the war news. Among those in the gallery was George A. Smathers, an ambitious assistant U.S. attorney with higher political aspirations. Smathers was standing with Dan Mahoney, the editor of the *Miami Daily News*. One of Mahoney's reporters approached them with the news of the Japanese attack on U.S. forces in Pearl Harbor.

"Where is Pearl Harbor?" the *Daily News* reporter finally asked, his question instantly considered by everyone within earshot as well.

Neither Smathers nor Mahoney knew. Others in the crowd shook their heads in bewilderment. Finally, someone ventured a guess.

"I think it's in the Hawaiian Islands," he said.

This was the pervasive tenor of the week in Miami, not indifference, precisely, but neither a comprehensive understanding of the enormity of the task ahead for the nation. The foursome of golf stars was in town in advance of the $10,000 Miami Open, a seventy-two-hole affair scheduled to start on the following Thursday at Miami Springs. The community gave no thought to canceling the event in the wake of the Japanese attack and President Roosevelt's declaration of war.

Bookmakers went about their business too. Nelson and Hogan had come from behind to defeat Snead and Heafner, 3 and 2 (three holes up, with two to play), in their exhibition match to establish themselves as cofavorites to win the Miami Open, according to the local sporting literati, whose golf coverage was paying scant attention to the real world that existed beyond the confines of the playgrounds they mined for material. References to the war were minimal. One writer mentioned that Gene Sarazen was of the opinion that the manufacturing of golf equipment should continue unabated, that recreation in general and golf in particular were imperative to keeping morale elevated. Another story noted that British star Henry Cotton had written to Fred Corcoran, the PGA Tournament Bureau manager, informing him that he had joined the Royal Air Force, and that during downtime he was participating in exhibitions on behalf of the British Red Cross.

An editorial in *The Miami Herald* even attempted to keep the Miami Open's relevance from being diminished by the war. It read in part:

> The Miami Open is competing with the greatest news of the generation—the war with Japan. But its value will not be lost, its interest for the public entirely blotted out by the clouds of war.

Your golf addict will be watching the daily reports of the play from coast to coast. The American sports fan never quite loses interest in athletic battles, come war or high water.

The Professional Golfers Association of America, to its credit, recognized immediately that its franchise needed to abandon the status quo, that it had to be malleable to exist in a changed world. Among the PGA's first orders of business was to announce that in lieu of paying Miami Open participants in cash, it would pay them in war bonds. Byron Nelson was joined by Tony Penna, Heafner, Henry Picard, Lloyd Mangrum, and PGA president Ed Dudley, among others, in a pretournament ceremony in which ten thousand silver dollars were exchanged for war bonds. They stood behind a sign that read:

ATTENTION, U.S.A.! VICTORY OR BUST!
WE'RE BUYING U.S. DEFENSE BONDS WITH OUR . . .
$10,000 PRIZE MONEY

The gesture was a means by which the association could immediately begin to contribute to war relief, and it set a benevolent example for the populace. It also staved off a potential public relations gaffe, the imprudence of doling out $10,000 to golfers, whose fans were starting to brace themselves and their families for the inevitable sacrifices the war would require of them.

THE MIAMI OPEN marked the debut of the PGA's winter tour, and it was evident that the nation's best golfers were yearning for warm weather and tournament golf. The field was flush—two hundred thirteen professionals and amateurs filing their entry fee, the largest number ever for a medal-play tournament. Hogan,

Nelson, and Snead were the tournament's headliners on a marquee that also included Craig Wood, Gene Sarazen, Paul Runyan, and Henry Picard.

Hogan opened by equaling the course record of 64 and retained his lead at the end of three rounds, a stroke ahead of Nelson, the defending champion, who was determined to leave nothing to chance. For the final round, Nelson chose the identical clothes he had worn for the final round a year earlier: light brown slacks, tan shirt, brown shoes, white eyeshade. "It's one of my pet superstitions," he said.

His caddie, Livingston Wildgose Knowles, better known as Winky as a result of a twitching eye, was equally determined not to disturb the alignment of the stars. He also wore the same clothes he'd had on the year before. Moreover, he chose not to shave throughout the tournament and by Sunday displayed a generous down payment on a beard. "Can't take no chances," he said. "If I shave I might shave us out of the championship."

The two of them overlooked the fact that talent is a worthy adversary to superstition and usually is the overriding factor. Nelson's formidable skills were in full flower in the final round, notwithstanding an errant tee shot that struck a female spectator and led to a rare bogey, what Nelson defined as his worst break of the tournament. "Of course, it was a tough break for her too," he said. The woman was not hurt, and neither was Nelson's quest for victory. He closed with a second consecutive round of 66 to win by five, the first time in his career he had successfully defended a championship.

Nelson's and Winky's superstitions would have no bearing on whether they'd even have an opportunity to win another Miami Open. Only the war would determine whether they'd be back to try for a third. The PGA of America understood this implicitly. It drafted a letter to President Franklin D. Roosevelt, pledging whatever assistance it could. The letter read:

My dear Mr. President:

The Professional Golfers' Association of America is solidly behind you in the present crisis and we stand ready to provide any service you may ask of us. Already we are planning a nationwide Golf War Relief Day, the entire proceeds to be used for war relief agencies or in any other way in which you may direct. This program will be participated in by sections of the P.G.A. throughout the United States. You may be sure that we will continue our policy of aiding and assisting in the present war program wherever and whenever we are called upon.

Very sincerely yours,
Ed Dudley, President
Professional Golfers' Association of America

2

IT'S YOUR DUTY TO PLAY MORE GOLF

The Game's First Response

Among the questions that arose in the wake of America's entry into the Second World War was whether playing golf was even an appropriate activity in such sobering times. The question was a vitally important one for a sport trying to regain its equilibrium. The answer fell to John B. Kelly, a Philadelphian whose title was assistant U.S. director of civilian defense in charge of physical fitness. Kelly was a former Olympic rower, a gold medalist in both the 1920 Olympic Games in Antwerp, Belgium, and in the 1924 Games in Paris. Even at fifty-three he appeared capable of rowing a scull to Olympic glory. On land he was a winner as well; he was a successful businessman, having made his fortune in the construction business in Philadelphia, where he owned a brickworks that was responsible for several federal buildings in Washington, D.C. He had also fathered two children, one of them Grace Kelly, a precocious twelve-year-old girl with an eye on the theater.

Whether golf should continue was no trivial question either. The Office of Civilian Defense was an official government agency. It had been established on May 20, 1941, by President Franklin D. Roosevelt, as a means of coordinating efforts between local and state governments and the federal government to protect the civilian population, and to maintain morale and promote volunteerism. Roosevelt asked New York City mayor Fiorello H. La Guardia to direct the Office of Civilian Defense. La Guardia in turn appointed Kelly to the post of assistant U.S. director of civilian defense in charge of physical fitness.

Kelly's mandate was to convince the citizenry that its physical fitness was imperative to the war effort. Even those who weren't directly involved in the war were certain to be indirectly involved, perhaps in war-related industries that were likely to find themselves short of manpower, requiring that available bodies routinely work overtime. A physically fit populace would be better equipped to deal with the energy-sapping demands of a nation at war.

A member of the Bala Golf Club in Philadelphia, Kelly played golf sparingly and usually with former Philadelphia Athletics infielder Jimmy Dykes. The two of them went around a course as though they understood that the object of the game was to complete eighteen holes in the fewest number of minutes, rather than strokes. They regarded it more a test of speed, not one of skill, a miscalculation they never would have made had Kelly been aware that Porky Oliver was among the game's stars. One might accurately surmise that Porky Oliver did not acquire his sobriquet by virtue of his chiseled physique. It was evident at a glance that he was more kneaded than chiseled, that his favorite club was not the niblick or the mashie, but the spoon, especially when it worked in cahoots with the fork. When Porky was soon inducted into the Army, he redefined the term *doughboy*.

Kelly's knowledge of the game was not gleaned from Porky Oliver's example, which consequently may have formed the lifeline of which the game was desperately in need. Kelly surely would have rethought his position had he accurately gauged the amount of energy expended on a course by those who play golf every day and still answer to Porky.

Instead, Kelly's view of the game was shaped by his own periodic sprints around a course. It suggested to him that golf was a useful device to get the legs moving and the heart pumping, and that a citizenry that collectively needed to improve its conditioning and stamina in the event of an enemy invasion could do so by taking to the golf course.

He even lectured the USGA on the importance of its constituency continuing to play golf, and in the process invoked the plight of the French as proof, as though France might have avoided being overrun by the Germans had its people only put aside their *vin et fromage* and taken up golf.

"Eight million people will be going into the armed forces," Kelly said to the USGA. "My job is to look after the one hundred twenty-four million who won't or can't go. They can keep fit by playing golf. France was the most physically inactive country in the world, and look what happened to it."

Among Kelly's first orders of business was to create the position of golf deputy. He offered the post to Fred Corcoran, the manager of the PGA Tournament Bureau. Kelly then proposed that the USGA encourage its member clubs to conduct a patriotic series of tournaments that would coincide with national holidays—Memorial Day, the Fourth of July, and Labor Day—as fund-raisers for war relief. He suggested that they be called Hale America tournaments.

Corcoran, meanwhile, had accepted Kelly's offer and in turn recommended that Bobby Jones, reigning U.S. Open champion

Craig Wood, and PGA of America president Ed Dudley be brought aboard as advisors for the Hale America events. Jones was a logical choice, given his stature in the world of golf. Moreover, he shared Kelly's view that golf had a place in wartime America, a point he emphasized in a letter he wrote to the prominent Atlanta sportswriter and Jones biographer O. B. Keeler. Jones was responding to a letter he had received from Keeler, asking him to weigh in on the future of golf during a time of war. Jones's perspective had been shaped in part by World War I; though he was only fifteen when the United States entered that war, he played a series of exhibitions around the country on behalf of war charities, travels that provided him an opportunity to gauge the impact of war on golf and the game's role in contributing to the war effort.

Jones's letter was written on the stationery of the American Golf Institute, an organization formed by the sporting goods manufacturer A. G. Spalding & Brothers to expand the game. It read:

Dear O.B.:

During the last war golf did what it could, as it will do in this one. Perhaps it can do less this time; at least less of a tangible nature. On the imponderable side, it may do more because the need is greater.

I told you, the Red Cross and other War Relief matches in which I played in 1917–18 netted over $150,000. There were many other such matches. But taxes were not so high then and voluntary giving could be more generous. The accepted practice involved an auction for the privilege(?) of carrying the bag of each player. This produced an excuse for wealthier spectators to kick in from $500 up in exchange for a few handclaps. You couldn't do this today, so that in this and other ways the take would be smaller.

Of course, you will recall that I was barely fifteen when we entered World War I. Naturally, my memory is not too clear, and I have not the history or statistics before me. But George Sargent tells me there was a lull in the playing of golf for a couple of months after he went in. After this, according to George, there was more play than before. I should expect the same thing again, after people learn that the cobwebs have to be cleared and that too much work can be a loss rather than a gain.

You will recall that Bevan, or Bevin, in England, last spring asked British industry to arrange for certain periods of rest during each shift. Studies had revealed that these breaks tended to increase output.

The production job we face now is far greater than that of the previous war. It is going to require the most efficient use of all the resources we possess. The men who work with their hands are of vast importance, but the real McCoys are the fellows who know how to set up a production schedule and make it click—in short, the managers. And they need breathing spells in their thinking as much as the workmen need rest for their hands. They can take a walk, or pull the weights, or ride a bike for physical exercise. But the best way for them to get exercise, fresh air, and mental relaxation at the same time is to play golf. They can't do much worrying on a golf course. I think a judicious use of the game can prevent a lot of jitters and nervous breakdowns. I wish you would check this angle with some of your psychologist friends. It might be a sale you ought to make.

Of course no one would suggest that a sport should compete with War production for materials, facilities, time, or energy. But if the playing of a little golf can replenish energy and revive the spirit, it should be continued.

Another thing different in this war is our rubber supply. Last time the East Indies were never threatened, and so we had plenty of rubber for golf, tennis, and inflated balls. The requirements of all manufacturers for these purposes, according to my understanding, is less than one tenth of one percent of the nation's annual requirements. Yet since war production comes first, even this may not be available. But there is a backlog of golf balls which will last, at a reduced, but reasonable, rate of consumption, for several months. After that, it is likely that some way will be found to keep 'em playing. There may not be as many or as good balls, but everybody will have the same kind. It'll still be a great game.

From the standpoint of the tournaments, I can see reason in the decision to abandon the major championships. If they are not representative they lose their point, and they could not be representative under war conditions. The winter tournaments are somewhat different. Where local conditions are not unfavorable, and enough good players are to hand, they offer a diversion which might do some good.

It seems to me that the whole question here, as elsewhere, is to keep as much of everything as nearly normal as may be so long as it takes nothing in men, materials, or time from our war effort.

Hope this helps a little.

Sincerely,
Robt. T. Jones, Jr.

Kelly's most important decree, meanwhile, was to a wider audience that did not necessarily play tournament golf, even at the local level. Kelly wrote on Office of Civilian Defense letterhead, in a missive dated December 24, 1941, the following letter to golf associations and golf writers:

Dear Sir:

This is the time when golf really must score for the physical and mental conditioning of American citizens under wartime pressure.

The wealth of a nation is in the strength of its people. High pressure of emergency effort demands planned balance of recreation for

*top efficiency. Without good food, plenty of recreation, and suffi-
cient sleep, the workers of America will not have the strength to
carry on their great defense program.*

*Golf's strong attraction as a sport in which more than 2 1/4
million of our citizens exercise regularly in the open air qualifies
the game for national service of a vital character.*

*Therefore we are urging the golf clubs and organizations of
America to exert themselves to the limit in expanding and en-
larging their present programs to the point where their facilities
for recreation can be utilized on a 100% efficiency basis to meet
the requirements of individual and collective physical fitness.*

*No work can operate efficiently without regular periods of recre-
ation. And America, now more than ever, cannot risk inefficiency
when wartime production requires peak performance.*

Very truly yours,
John B. Kelly
*Assistant U.S. Director of Civilian Defense in
charge of physical fitness*

There it was, a direct order to play on, and to do so with a new-
found sense of purpose, no doubt to the chagrin of the nation's
golf widows. Their husbands had become empowered to argue
honestly that their Saturday golf games were government sanctioned. It may have been the most important endorsement the
game ever received, a government seal of approval, framed in
red, white, and blue.

IF ONLY IT WERE as simple as a government endorsement. The
continuation of the game could not be guaranteed so easily. In
fact, Kelly's letter probably ought to have included a golf lesson

designed to improve golfers' accuracy and ball-striking abilities, to reduce the likelihood of their losing or disfiguring a ball, either of which would require a replacement ball. Finding one was going to prove problematic, as golfers had already been discovering.

On the morning of December 18, the sales staff at Abercrombie & Fitch in New York City was preparing for a day of business as usual. When they unlocked the doors to open for business, *as usual* was trampled in a stampede to the sporting goods department. Only the day before, Leon Henderson, administrator for the Office of Price Administration, had announced a rationing plan for the civilian consumption of rubber products. Henderson was calling for a reduction of nearly eighty percent and said the plan would be enacted on January 4, 1942.

The immediate and logical concern: tires, which accounted for seventy-five percent of crude rubber consumed by Americans. An existing prohibition against retail sales of new tires, set to expire on December 22, was extended indefinitely. The OPA edict was going to restrict the supply of reclaimed rubber as well.

"Substantial amounts of reclaimed rubber are available, but will have to be used in large part to replace crude rubber in the manufacture of mechanical goods and other products," Henderson said. "Likewise, a substantial part of the ten thousand tons of crude rubber available per month for civilian goods will have to be used in the manufacture of such products. Amounts of synthetic rubber available in the near future will be very small. This means that only a part of the ten thousand tons a month of residual supply will be available for tire production."

A headline in *The New York Times* stated, RATIONING OF TIRES TO START ON JAN. 4. Clearly, a shortage of tires would have the greatest impact, and no doubt millions considered the ramification of their growing inability to adequately equip their automobiles. Public transportation, bicycling, and walking received immediate boosts.

Golfers read the text of the story, but ultimately they were more interested in the subtext. The *Times* article read: "While production of a few products considered essential for civilian and industrial use will continue, golf and tennis balls, bathing apparel, toy balloons, and similar items will be virtually eliminated."

Tires, yes, they were a concern, but transportation to the golf course was a surmountable problem. The horse and buggy, for instance, was not too far into the past that it could not be resurrected in a pinch. An insurmountable problem was a dearth of golf balls, which for golfers represented the shared sacrifice to which radio broadcasters were referring when speaking about the war and its demands on those on the home front.

Ball conservation was the only defense against a scarcity, and it was virtually impossible, short of giving up the game. The covers of golf balls in 1942 were made from balata, a soft material similar to rubber that responded favorably to shots struck perfectly, on the imaginary dime-sized circle known as the sweet spot, located just above the leading edge of an iron and equidistant between heel and toe. Balata did not respond favorably to shots hit thin; when the leading edge of an iron struck the middle of a ball, it lacerated the cover, leaving what golfers referred to as a smile, though in reality it was more of a smirk. At that point, the ball was worthless, an aerodynamically challenged, out-of-round lump ready for the trash heap.

The short life span of a golf ball required a replenishing supply, which was now threatened by the rubber shortage, the subtext that triggered the stampede at Abercrombie & Fitch. By eleven a.m. on the morning of the eighteenth, the store had sold its entire inventory of golf balls, more than twenty-four thousand of them. Sales staff then began taking orders against future shipments that weren't likely to come.

Amateur and professional players alike descended on the offices of A. G. Spalding & Brothers, a prominent sporting goods company that produced the top-shelf Spalding Dot preferred by many touring pros. Many of the customers sought to buy balls by the gross, requiring company officials to restrict sales to two or three dozen lots. The Spalding store on Fifth Avenue moved more than fourteen hundred dozen balls in the morning. Modell's Sporting Goods Company began selling its supply of balls without restricting the number per customer. When the supply rapidly dwindled, owner Henry Modell imposed a limit of a dozen balls per customer. By the end of the day, he had exhausted his supply of two thousand dozen balls. A rush on balls at Macy's forced management to restrict sales to a dozen balls per customer.

The story was identical from coast to coast. At the A. G. Spalding & Brothers Loop office in Chicago, wire and mail orders for balls arrived in such numbers that a majority of them were refused. In Los Angeles, U.S. Rubber received orders from its New York office to cease sales of balls entirely, to discourage a stampede.

U.S. Rubber was a major supplier of golf balls to a variety of companies, among them Wilson Sporting Goods. Wilson's supply of balls at its Los Angeles office had already been largely depleted by country clubs and public courses, which had previously stockpiled balls in advance of a price increase. Some bought balls by the hundred dozen, rather than the gross, according to the *Los Angeles Times*. A Wilson sales rep told the *Times* that anyone asking for a hundred dozen balls now "would be given nothing but a cold stare in return."

Some saw the hoarding as boorish behavior, the worst of humankind emanating from a crisis that, with the world at war, was not especially important. Among the critics was Randal Heymanson, who voiced his displeasure in a letter to the editor of *The New York Times*. Heymanson wrote:

> The scramble for golf balls, reported in your columns today, reveals an attitude of mind which is distinctly anti-social. It needs little imagination to see that such selfish conduct, if widespread, could create a dangerous shortage even of materials which are plentiful enough to be enjoyed by everybody. Any one buying beyond his immediate needs steals from his fellow-citizens and deserves their contempt.

The number of buyers wasn't small. The rush continued into the next day, though stores that still had supplies of balls restricted sales to a dozen per customer. One New York City store dispatched six employees on a scavenger hunt, assigning them the task of scouring stores in Westchester, Nassau, and New Jersey counties for balls, new and used.

The resourceful Henry Modell, sensing an impending need for used, rewashed, or repainted balls, put out an alert to fifty head caddies and greenkeepers at Eastern seaboard golf clubs, asking that they send him salvaged balls, ASAP.

Macy's in New York City even began running ads soliciting used balls. "Since the early 1900's," the ad read, "we've been selling YOU golf balls. Now it's your turn."

Golf ball manufacturers immediately began devoting research-and-development capital to producing balls made from artificial substances. This was an idea, incidentally, first hatched by the enemy, despite the fact that it had never fully embraced the game. Germany was offering free golf for life on German courses to anyone who developed an ersatz ball.

In the event that German troops ever brought the war to U.S. shores, Americans who followed John B. Kelly's orders would at least be physically fit enough to mount a defense. An advancing enemy would even give them something to swing at in lieu of a diminishing supply of golf balls.

THE LUNCH DINERS at New York City's most popular saloon, Toots Shor's on West Fifty-first Street, were not discussing golf. If anyone mentioned a hook, they were surely referring to Joe Louis's powerful left. The topic of the day on January 9, 1942, was the heavyweight championship fight that night at Madison Square Garden just down the street. Louis, the Brown Bomber, was in town to defend his heavyweight crown against challenger Buddy Baer, and the town was abuzz. Seventeen thousand tickets had been sold for the fight, which was serving two purposes, the least of them to identify the world heavyweight champion; it was virtually a given that Louis would retain his title. More important was the fact that it was a wartime fund-raiser, proceeds going to the Navy Relief Society. Louis had pledged to add to the evening's take, by donating his entire purse, $100,000, to families of victims of the Pearl Harbor attack.

On the same day, seventeen men who would have preferred that the world revolve around their sport, but knew that that would never be the case, filed into the Executive Office of the United States Golf Association at 73 East Fifty-seventh Street, only a few blocks from Toots Shor's. The USGA, an entity separate from the PGA, is the governing body of golf in America, the group that writes the rules and sets the game's agenda. The charity bout that night and Louis's own benevolence were not lost on these men who formed the USGA's Executive Committee, which had been scrutinizing how other sports and organizations were responding to the onset of war.

For the USGA, as for Louis (notwithstanding the odds in his favor), the stakes were considerable. Louis was risking his title without recompense. The USGA, meanwhile, had to respond in a responsible manner that was consistent with its role as the governing body of a sport with millions of constituents, and to do so in consideration of its unflattering reputation as an elitist sport. The worst decision it could make would be any that invited the perception that it thought itself above the fray.

This was among the most important Executive Committee meetings in the history of the USGA. As the governing body of golf in the United States, the USGA had an enormous responsibility to golfers, golf clubs, and local associations, all of whom were looking for guidance in the aftermath of the outbreak of war. There were those among the populace who argued that the simple act of playing a game in these serious times represented a breach of proper conduct, that whatever efforts were ordinarily devoted to golf ought to be redirected toward the war effort.

Recommending the cessation of play at any level was not a viable option; those who weren't directly involved in fighting the war were going to continue to pursue diversions that appealed to them, be it golf or chess. Still, the USGA had to tread carefully and set a tone that reflected the gravity of the times.

USGA President Harold Pierce was presiding over the meeting. Also in attendance were his successor, George Blossom Jr. (for whom ascending to the presidency was but a formality, scheduled to come at the USGA's annual meeting, which was set to begin the following day), and legendary Francis Ouimet, who at twenty and an amateur won the U.S. Open in 1913, a victory that began transforming golf from largely a British game to an American one. When the meeting was called to order, the members elected to forgo the reading of the minutes of the previous session of the Executive Committee, so that it could move directly to the issue at hand. Pierce did not broach the subject in a circuitous way either; he went straight to the heart of the matter. "With the nation at war," he said, "the association is faced with a major question of policy. I feel the association should cancel its championships and devote its efforts to war relief."

Pierce cited precedent: The association had canceled the U.S. Open, the U.S. Amateur, and the U.S. Women's Amateur in 1917 and 1918 as a result of the First World War. The USGA's roster of national championships had expanded to include the U.S. Amateur Public Links, and Pierce argued that all of them should be scrapped for 1942 and perhaps beyond. The most forceful argument in support of Pierce was that the strength of the fields would be depleted by golfers serving in the armed forces, depriving each event of a representative field. Reigning U.S. Amateur champion Bud Ward was among a legion of golfers who had already enlisted, and his military service would probably preclude him from defending his championship. When you're conducting a national championship, inherently designed to identify the best player in the country, how do you do so when so many otherwise worthy players will not be there to compete?

The suggestion was floated that the USGA should wait to take its lead from the government. This was countered by the argument that it was the association's duty to lead, rather than to follow, and to move posthaste in the event that the committeemen agreed that the championships should be canceled, so that clubs scheduled to host the respective championships and already in the planning process could be alerted immediately. Eventually, it was suggested that the association's energies be devoted to something more useful than tournament golf, that the staging of national championships in wartime "would be hollow and perhaps improper."

Once the discussion had run its course, Fielding Wallace, a committeeman from Augusta, Georgia, spoke.

"I move that the USGA cancel its championships and devote its efforts to war relief."

"Second," Ouimet said.

"All in favor, say aye," President Pierce said.

There was a chorus of them.

"All opposed?"

Silence.

"The motion is carried, unanimously," Pierce said.

With that simple aye or nay vote a game steeped in elitism was allowed to descend from its pedestal and join the masses in helping to win a war. The Executive Committee drafted a resolution in which it outlined its position:

> Resolved, that it is the sense of the Executive Committee of the United States Golf Association that the main aim of golfers and golf organizations should be to contribute the greatest possible service to the nation for the duration of the war.
>
> Therefore, be it further resolved, that the Executive Committee of the United States Golf Association hereby cancels the four championships which it has scheduled for 1942—namely, the open, the amateur, the women's amateur, and the amateur public links championship.

The USGA announced its decision at the annual meeting of the organization the following day at the Waldorf-Astoria. Several members of the Executive Committee, in support of the cancellations, individually expressed the view that a victory against a field depleted by calls to service would be tainted.

The association stopped short of encouraging other associations to follow its lead, including the PGA. Pierce even issued a statement that clearly signaled the USGA's approval to any organization that chose to play on:

> The United States Golf Association has been asked for its views regarding the status of the various open tournaments scheduled on the Winter circuit and later in the 1942 season. The U.S.G.A sees no reason for there to be any disturbance of this program (which primarily is conducted by the tournament bureau of the Professional Golfers Association of America) unless, of course, there is interference with the general national welfare.

The USGA's decision was not popular in all precincts. Ed Dudley, president of the PGA, was among those who expressed regret over the USGA's decision. His tour had already decided to play on and was in the process of planning the PGA Championship scheduled for May. The USGA's position was also out of step with that embraced by America's national pastime, baseball. Five days after the USGA's decision to cancel its events, Judge Kenesaw Mountain Landis, baseball's commissioner, wrote a letter to President Roosevelt, asking "what you have in mind as to whether professional baseball should continue to operate."

The following day, President Roosevelt sent his reply, which quickly came to be known as "the Green Light Letter." It read in part:

> *My dear Judge:*
>
> *Thank you for yours of January fourteenth. As you will, of course, realize the final decision about the baseball season must rest with*

you and the Baseball Club owners—so what I am going to say is solely a personal and not an official point of view.

I honestly feel that it would be best for the country to keep baseball going. There will be fewer people unemployed and everybody will work longer hours and harder than ever before. And that means that they ought to have a chance for recreation and for taking their minds off their work even more than before . . . .

As to the players themselves I know you agree with me that individual players who are of active duty or naval age should go, without question, into the services. Even if the actual quality of the teams is lowered by the greater use of older players, this will not dampen the popularity of the sport. Of course, if any individual has some particular aptitude in a trade or profession, he ought to serve the Government. That, however, is a matter which I know you can handle with complete justice. Here is another way of looking at it—if 300 teams use 5,000 or 6,000 players, these players are a definite recreational asset to at least 20,000,000 of their fellow citizens—and that in my judgment is thoroughly worthwhile.

> *With every best wish,*
> *Very sincerely yours,*
> *Franklin D. Roosevelt*

Baseball elected to defer to the President, perhaps with relative certainty that he would indeed give the green light to America's most popular sport. The USGA had no such luxury; its game had never appealed to the masses and had no reservoir of goodwill on which to rely. The USGA was actually determined to do the right thing on behalf of the country, without regard to its standing. If along the way it altered the perception of the game as an elitist one, all the better.

Most Americans considered the war effort central to their lives, and the USGA was striving to avoid being out of step. Executive Committee member Edward Cheyney suggested that the USGA urge every golf course in the country to put a Red Cross box by the first tee as part of a campaign to appeal to golfers to donate a dime a round. He noted that sixty-three million rounds were played in the U.S. in 1941; were the number duplicated in '42, the idea represented a potential windfall of $6.3 million.

The committee agreed to promote John B. Kelly's suggestion that each club stage a series of Hale America tournaments, commencing with one on Memorial Day weekend. It would also encourage all state associations to cooperate in any relief enterprises with which it was presented. The USGA even went so far as to offer to the War Department the services of Dr. John Montieth, for fourteen years its director of turf investigations for the association's Green Section. The U.S. Army Corps of Engineers was assembling a Turf Unit for the purpose of developing a strong, wear-resistant turf to be used for airfields. The War Department accepted the USGA's offer, and Dr. Montieth became the chief of the Turf Unit of the Construction Branch of the U.S. Army Corps of Engineers.

The USGA, which the summer before had presented St. Andrews, Scotland, with a new ambulance, used the occasion of its annual meeting to reaffirm support of its beleaguered brethren at the Royal and Ancient Golf Club of St. Andrews. It drafted a note to the members there:

The United States Golf Association sends from its annual meeting its sincere expression of goodwill to the Royal and Ancient Golf Club and its renewed hopes for a just peace for the world.

The USGA was willing to consider any idea that might enable it and its constituents to contribute to the war effort. One came from Bobby Jones, who a few weeks after the annual meeting wrote a letter to new USGA President George Blossom, Jr., informing him of Augusta National Golf Club's plans to build and maintain a driving range at Camp Gordon in Augusta, Georgia.

We are going to allocate whatever amount may be necessary from the proceeds of the Masters' Tournament to construct a full-sized driving range and a large practice putting green in the Service Men's Recreation Center of Camp Gordon, near Augusta. The Club's organization will do the designing, seed the fairways, tees, and putting greens, make whatever use is necessary of its turf nurseries, and supply greenkeeping supervision necessary to upkeep. Floodlighting will be provided if it can be had, which I understand is possible. We will also equip the range with a sufficient number of assorted clubs and an adequate supply of golf balls.

We have spent a good bit of time with the Post Commander at Camp Gordon, and the Recreation Officer, and they both are apparently quite enthusiastic over the prospect. They state that 85% of this Army is made up of selectees, and that in their opinion there will be a much higher percentage of golfers in the crowd than would be the case with the regular Army. It is our notion that when the pros come through we can have the range in good enough shape to give them an exhibition, and that from the men in the Camp there will be found numbers who are familiar with golf and will use the range, and at the same time introduce the activities to others to whom it may be a bit strange.

This sort of thing is frankly an experiment because we don't know how the boys are going to take to golf, but it seems to us to have a good many possibilities. In the first place, it goes right on to the Camp with the men, so that no transportation at all is needed to reach it. In the second place, it offers an opportunity for the specialized knowledge of golfers and golf clubs to be used for the benefit of the service men. It seems to us that this is a more direct relationship and a service of greater value than the bare contributions of the same amount of money. We have made a guess that probably 5 % of the men in a camp like Gordon would have at least an elementary acquaintance with golf.

It occurs to me that if this experiment proves successful and the range provides something useful to the men, the United States Golf Association might suggest to clubs, or groups of clubs, in camp areas, that they provide similar facilities. In addition to the service which could be done the men in the Army, a widespread movement of this kind I think could do much for golf at the end of the war. When this thing is over it is entirely possible that many boys first introduced to the game in this way will be instrumental in keeping our game facilities in use.

When Jones spoke, the USGA listened intently. He was its beau ideal, a champion (a four-time U.S. Open and five-time U.S. Amateur winner) who espoused humility and embodied the USGA's de facto position, that the game was meant to be played for enjoyment rather than pay, as an amateur rather than a professional.

The USGA enthusiastically embraced Jones's suggestion. It surveyed a range of Army officers, to gauge their opinion as to whether introducing golf to their bases was a viable and valuable undertaking. It received its answer in a missive from Brigadier General F. H. Osborn, chief of the Special Services Branch of the War Department, who wrote in a letter to the USGA:

The offer to introduce one of the country's most popular sports wherever possible throughout the military establishment is sin-

cerely appreciated and is in conformity with the Army's desire to
maintain and develop fitness among the men in ranks.

That was the only impetus the USGA required. It dashed off a
letter to golf associations and clubs around the country, imploring them to follow Augusta National's lead in exposing the
armed forces to the game. Now dedicated to bringing the game to
those in the service of their country, the USGA set out to collect
the necessary balls and "implements," as the USGA referred to
clubs. The Women's Golf Association of Philadelphia was its
model. An eight-woman committee representing the association
collected 1,352 golf clubs, 200 golf balls, and 138 golf bags in a
single week. "The Motor Corps of an American Red Cross Chap-
ter assisted Mrs. E. G. Betz as Chairman of the Committee, and
covered 649 miles and was credited with 39 hours 55 minutes. It
is obvious that the ladies can be a tremendous help," a WGA report stated.

In summary, the USGA wrote: "During the last war many
clubs and associations cooperated with the United States Golf Association in a campaign in which hundreds of sets of clubs and
hundreds of golf balls were sent to Army camps. The War Department was most grateful. Today all of us in golf can do a similar patriotic job. It's one of the least things we can do for the
boys."

The bluebloods running the USGA (and by extension much of
the golf world) were stepping away from their elitist traditions on
behalf of the greater good. It was a defining moment for golf and
for those governing it, who acknowledged without reluctance—
some, perhaps for the first time—that as Americans they were all
in this together.

3

WAR COMES TO AUGUSTA

Curtain Calls for the Masters and PGA Championship

Uncertainty permeated the Augusta National Golf Club and the Masters in April of 1942, inviting nostalgia to overwhelm a man. When he arrived, Grantland Rice, the poet laureate of American sportswriting, gazed pensively at the flora that ushered in the spring there—the flowering dogwood, pink and white, the azaleas and camellias and purple wisteria—and was inspired to craft an ode to old friends and better days:

> *Back to the red clay hills again,*
>   *back to a trail I know,*
> *Where the ghostly tramp of the years returns*
>   *to a spring in the long ago.*
> *When a mockingbird and a bluebird call,*
>   *"Don't you remember the day*

When Bobby Jones was the Grand Slam kid
* and Ty had the right of way?"*
Back to the red clay hills again,
* back where the years were young,*
When Uncle Remus was still around
* and Stanton's songs were sung.*
And a mockingbird calls from a dogwood flame,
* "Here's to an ancient toast—*
When Bobby Jones was the king of golf
* and Ty was the Georgia Ghost!"*

Jones vying for first, Cobb breaking for second—these were memories that for Rice provided a measure of warmth against the chilling reality that encompassed the Augusta landscape. They couldn't smell the war in Augusta, but they could feel it. Augusta was a military town, ninety miles due east of Atlanta, the home to the United States Army's Camp Gordon, and already it was on its war footing. Military planes passed overhead every couple of minutes. In town, uniformed personnel seemingly outnumbered civilians.

Augusta was also home to the Augusta National Golf Club, a private sanctuary created by the renowned Atlanta lawyer and Rice's dear friend, the inestimable Bobby Jones. Jones's involvement in founding the club, as well as the annual exercise that had come to be known as the Masters, had restored Augusta's prominence, which had largely been moribund since it had relinquished its role as the capital of Georgia nearly one hundred fifty years earlier.

The war had caused Camp Gordon to eclipse the Masters on the scale of importance there. The tenor and the time were wrong for a rite of spring, as the Masters had become. Now, as the ninth playing of the Masters approached, there was a foreboding sense that it would be the last for a while. The U.S. Open had already been canceled. Gasoline rationing and Augusta's isolation challenged the logic of keeping the course open over the duration of the war. Each week, the ranks of professional golf were thinned by the call to serve. The Masters this time around seemed not so much an opportunity to say hello to old friends as it was as an occasion to say good-bye to them.

The press sensed it too. It was determined to elevate the stature of the 1942 Masters to a degree that it would be regarded an appropriate send-off, if indeed this was its farewell pending the return of peace in the world. Writers were selling it as the de facto national championship. "This year, with the U.S. Open tournament canceled by war, the Masters' title will be regarded by many as equivalent to a national championship," *The Atlanta Constitution* wrote.

The membership at Augusta National did not summarily reject the media's hyperbole. Indeed, it helped reinforce what Clifford Roberts, the cofounder of the club and the tournament chairman, had come to believe about the tournament. Roberts wrote, "While we may not have expected it originally, we have created a tournament of such importance that we are bound to see that it continues."

Another reason for the welcome injection of hype was that it introduced the possibility of an attendance spike. To its credit, the club had earmarked the Masters gate receipts for a worthy cause that demonstrated on behalf of the membership a greater concern for the plight of its country than its country club: Augusta National had offered to bankroll and build a practice facility at Camp Gordon, to stock it with equipment, and to periodically supply renowned tour pros to conduct clinics for the soldiers.

Jones and Roberts had considered a variety of suggestions of ways in which the club and its members might assist in the war effort, including one culled from the radio program *Information, Please.* A tobacco company that sponsored the show donated twenty-five dollars to charity for every question that was answered incorrectly. Roberts and Jones concocted the idea of soliciting pledges from the members, who would donate to the Red Cross each time a Masters contestant made a birdie.

That idea gave way to Jones and Roberts deciding that proceeds from the Masters would go for a golf facility at Camp Gordon. The club's news release announcing the project began: "A man in an Army training camp can't come to a golf course—at least, not often. So golf is coming to him."

Officers at Camp Gordon were thrilled with Augusta National's benevolence and pledged their support. Jones was enlisted as the club's emissary, and he met with Camp Gordon officers and an architect whom the camp was employing and drew up a design, which began with a putting green large enough to accommodate seventy-five players. Adjacent to the green was a large, gradual slope that overlooked the practice range and was capable of holding as many as two thousand spectators for those occasions when Augusta National would send over marquee professionals to conduct clinics.

The range itself would have room enough for fifty golfers, most of whom would never be able to reach the far end of the range, two hundred fifty yards off. Four greens (made from sand, actually) would be situated at intervals from one hundred to one hundred seventy-five yards away, providing a series of targets. Augusta National also intended to supply the camp with seventy-five woods and irons and fifty putters, as well as upwards of a thousand golf balls. It even intended to install floodlighting, for night practice, at a cost of about a thousand dollars.

Roberts concluded that it would be money well spent on soldiers otherwise unable to entertain themselves during downtime.

"To my mind," Roberts wrote in a letter to the United States Golf Association, "the one controlling thought to keep in mind about this whole thing is the fact that a great deal of money is being raised to entertain soldiers and sailors in the cities and in the towns, but for every soldier boy seen on the streets of our cities, there are probably ten out at some camp who cannot get a pass to leave the camp or who haven't the money to go outside."

The Bobby Jones Driving Range at Camp Gordon was finished in time for players from the Masters field to participate in its inauguration. The bill came to $2,669, while the equipment was donated by club members and the Augusta National pro shop. The facility was dedicated on the eve of the Masters, a five o'clock ceremony that allowed the players to complete practice rounds and still make their way over to the camp.

Practice rounds were not trivial affairs. Newspapers covered them as though information might be gleaned that could help them with their tournament form charts, disregarding the fact that what a player scores on Tuesday has no bearing on what he'll shoot on Thursday. Still, their diligence in reporting on practice rounds often turned up, if not useful intelligence, at least amusing asides. Two days before the Masters was to begin, Sam Snead was at the first tee, ready to play a practice round. Also there were Fred Corcoran, the PGA tournament manager, and a couple of sportswriters. Corcoran had a keen eye for promotion, and he began boasting about Snead's talent, even suggesting that he could win the Masters playing barefoot.

"You should kick off those shoes," Corcoran said. "Remember, you played five holes in practice in your socks before the Canadian Open last year and won it."

The writers similarly urged him to remove his shoes and socks. Snead pondered whether it might be bad form to do so at an upscale club, but eventually he succumbed to the challenge.

He rolled up his pants and removed his shoes and socks, then playfully wiggled his toes in the grass.

"You know," he said, "it sure feels good to get your feet on the ground. I used to play barefoot all the time back home on the goat course at Hot Springs, Virginia."

He stepped up to the tee and hit a perfect drive, long and straight. He followed with a perfect second, the ball stopping three feet from the hole. He made the birdie putt.

"Honestly, I'm telling you the truth," he said. "I feel better when I stand up to the ball in my bare feet. Those thick-soled shoes keep you too far off the ground."

Snead went around Augusta National in 68 strokes and even hinted that he might play the tournament sans shoes. Word of Snead's escapade, meanwhile, had traveled all the way back to the clubhouse, where Gene Sarazen was waiting for him. Sarazen was spitting angry at Snead, whom he accused of acting like a "barefoot hillbilly" on this hallowed course. "Can you imagine Walter Hagen or Henry Cotton playing barefoot on this course?" Sarazen asked.

Corcoran predictably sided with Snead; he told Sarazen that he'd bet on Snead barefoot in a match with Sarazen, who went off again, reciting his record and contrasting it with that of Snead, who had won nothing of substance to that point in his career.

To Sarazen's chagrin, the media generally sided with Snead as well. "Wild man Walter Hagen not play barefoot?" Bill Corum wrote in the *New York Journal.* "Hagen would play in a bathing suit if the mood struck him. Sarazen would, too, if he thought it'd help win. Gene should be the last to squawk—all golfers remember his weird proposal to enlarge the cups to eight inches." The California Golf Writers Association, coming down on the side of "barefoot hillbillies" over the game's elitism, made Snead an honorary member "for putting the game back on its feet."

Another practice round produced some of the finest, most spirited golf of the week. Bobby Jones had been retired from competitive golf for nearly twelve years, though once a year he pulled his rusty skills out of storage and allowed himself to play in the Masters. In the practice round, he paired with Byron Nelson in a match with Gene Sarazen and Henry Picard, and he showed that on a given day he could still provide a reasonable impersonation of Bobby Jones. Even with a ball in the water at the thirteenth hole, Jones shot a five-under-par 31 on the back nine for a round of 68 that enabled him and his partner to halve their match.

"What do you think of that?" Sarazen said. "Picard and I scored seven birdies in the last nine holes and didn't win a hole."

After their practice rounds, Jones and another thirty players from the field of forty-two made their way to Camp Gordon for the dedication ceremony. Craig Wood was there, as were Ed Dudley, the host pro and the PGA president, Nelson, Sam Snead, and Ben Hogan. The master of ceremonics was Grantland Rice, who opened his remarks with a lighthearted apology: "We're sorry we can't offer you soldier boys a better bunch of golfers for this show, but there aren't any better golfers in this world today."

An assortment of military dignitaries was there, including the camp's commanding officer, which ensured that the hundreds of enlisted men in the crowd behaved in an orderly manner. Eventually, Jones was introduced to a standing ovation.

"I hope you boys find sport, relaxation, and a lot of fun in the range and putting green," he said.

The microphone worked its way to Horton Smith, a successful tour pro who could talk as good a game as he played. Smith emceed the clinic and brought on Jones to strike the ceremonial first shots.

"Bobby Jones led off with three dedicatory wallops, all beautifully struck," his friend and biographer, O. B. Keeler, wrote in *The Atlanta Journal* the next day.

FOR THE NEXT FOUR DAYS, golf moved to the fore, a brief respite from the real world represented by the uniformed spectators lining the fairways, as well as the military cadets, more than a hundred of them, recruited from a dozen academies to control and direct the galleries. If the uniforms provided a visible reminder of the challenges ahead, the golfers delivered an oral reminder that they were going about their business as usual. It manifested itself in the obligatory whining about the difficulty of the course, specifically the speed of the greens, unduly fast, an Augusta tradition.

The year before, a couple of pros complained about the speed of the greens within earshot of Ed Dudley, Augusta National's head professional. "If you don't like them that way," Dudley replied, "I'll put the blades down on those mowers in the morning and you'll think you're on a billiard table."

Al Sharp wrote in his column "Sharp Shootin" in *The Atlanta Constitution,* "It isn't true that men with razor blades manicure the greens to make them so perfect . . . but it does look as if that's what happens."

Golfer Henry Picard noted, "We aren't used to tapping six-foot putts, and that's what you have to do here. Stroke a short one and it'll end up in the fairway."

One particular habitual whiner, who built his reputation complaint by complaint, entered the clubhouse and headed for the bar, grumbling all the way about how unfair the layout was. Tommy Armour, the Silver Scot and the preeminent raconteur in the field, listened to the diatribe, accompanied by the tinkling of ice in his own cocktail. Armour took a drink, while considering the man's complaint and weighing it against the difficulty quotient experienced by Americans and Brits required to carry weapons more lethal than irons. Finally, he felt compelled to issue a rejoinder.

"There weren't any bombs out there, were there?" Armour said.

The quality of the competition was high, as the war had not yet appreciably thinned the talent—Hogan and Nelson were entered, as was Snead, and defending champion Craig Wood. The Navy was generously allowing Ensign Charles Yates, a former British Amateur champion and an Augusta National member, to participate. The Army gave a pass to Corporal Bud Ward, the reigning U.S. Amateur champion, to participate.

Players polled in the run-up to the Masters established Nelson, Hogan, and Snead as the favorites. It was a demonstration of sound judgment; they were the three best players in the world. Still, the year before the players had established Wood as the favorite, and he delivered on their behalf.

The tournament actually delivered on behalf of those in the press who were determined that it should be special. Jones was in contention briefly—he was tied for fifth after the first round. Sam Byrd, the former New York Yankees outfielder, was the first-round leader. Nelson opened with rounds of 68 and 67 to take the lead after thirty-six holes, while Ben Hogan, the pretournament betting favorite at five to one, was eight shots in arrears at the halfway mark. "The impossible impediment," Grantland Rice called the deficit, for once choosing the wrong words.

Hogan erased five shots of Nelson's advantage in the third round, and whittled away two more shots on the first seventeen holes of the final round. On the difficult par-four eighteenth hole, Hogan hit his second to three feet of the hole and made the birdie putt to pull even with Nelson, forcing an eighteen-hole play-off the following day.

"When the showdown came on the final green," Rice wrote, "with Army men helping to check the human surge, Ben Hogan and Byron Nelson, the two star Texans, were all snarled up at 280 in a tie for first place. . . . Hogan cleared away the killing margin with one of the greatest finishes I've ever seen in golf."

The play-off was not anticlimactic either. The crowd was two thousand—"many of them in the khaki and blue of the armed forces," the *Constitution* wrote—forming a horde crowding around the only hole on which there were players. Among them was virtually every player who had competed in the Masters, each of them staying in town one more day to bear witness to a duel between the two best players in the game. Tommy Armour, Jimmy Demaret, Henry Picard, Jug McSpaden, Ralph Guldahl—they were there as well to pay tribute to the men who were selling their sport better than anyone else.

Hogan opened a three-stroke lead through four holes. By the eighth hole, Nelson had erased the deficit and had taken a one-stroke lead that he never relinquished. Nelson shot 69 to Hogan's 70, to win the tournament for the second time in six years.

The show that Nelson and Hogan put on over five days elevated the stature of the Masters, stamping it distinctive, a cut above the endless succession of *opens* that more or less followed a road map from town to town. Clifford Roberts considered that the 1942 Masters had two winners—two champions, certainly—and he expressed his thanks in a letter to each of them, enclosing as well checks for two hundred dollars, extra prize money, he told them. The four hundred dollars erased the net profit the club realized from the additional day of revenues, but the sum was less important than the gesture, one of profound gratitude.

O. B. Keeler saw Nelson's victory as possibly preordained. At the beginning of the week, a package had arrived at the club at about the same time that Nelson did. The package contained plaques, individually wrapped, each with a name and a year etched onto it. The plaques were to be awarded to each of the past Masters champions.

"Open it up," Clifford Roberts said to Nelson.

Nelson obliged.

"Draw one," Roberts said.

Nelson selected one, unwrapped it, and saw that it had been emblazoned with the name *Byron Nelson* and the year *1937*, representing his Masters victory five years earlier.

"It's an omen," Roberts said elatedly. "If there's anything in hunches, you're going to win this tournament."

Roberts noted that were Nelson to win, the club would only have to add *1942* to the plaque, absolving it from having to spend money on another one.

"I'll show you," Roberts said. "Draw another one."

Nelson unwrapped a second plaque. The name on it was *Horton Smith*, under which the years *1934* and *1936* were etched.

"See?" Roberts said. "You can't miss. It's your tournament."

Keeler considered the evidence. "Golf," he wrote, "is a Scottish game, and Scots run largely to Presbyterians, and Presbyterians have always stuck more or less to the plan of predestination; it's all in the Book, they say, before ever a ball is struck off the first tee, in the game of golf, or in that other game we call Life."

The diversion known as the Masters was over and "that other game" reappeared, in all its myriad forms. For some of those who played in the Masters, it appeared as a draft notice. In the back rooms of the Augusta National Golf Club, it appeared as a challenge: Which way to turn? Jones and Roberts began the year with the idea that they would keep the club and the tournament operating until circumstances erected an obstacle that was simply too considerable to overcome. In the aftermath of the Masters,

Jones and Roberts each concluded that moving forward was going to be problematic, though they at least had time to contemplate alternatives—the club would soon close for the summer and was not scheduled to reopen until October.

The outlook was bleak at any rate. The war raged on, hinting at an epic struggle rather than an abbreviated one. Indeed, there was nothing to look forward to in the near term at Augusta National. Grantland Rice, of course, had already recognized the dearth of options and chosen a convenient one. He took comfort in his nostalgia, destined as it was to return him to Georgia's red clay hills and the bygone era that he cherished most . . .

When Bobby Jones was the king of golf
and Ty was the Georgia Ghost!

Sam Snead was not a rube, though he often played one. He fancied himself a hillbilly, invoking his roots—he grew up near Bald Knob in the Back Creek Mountains of Virginia, in the Appalachians, sandwiched between the Blue Ridge and the Alleghenies. There was the episode at Augusta National in April of 1942, when he threatened to play barefoot, citing his history of having played without shoes as a youngster. Generally, Snead did nothing to dispel the perception that he was a hayseed. For instance, he was reputedly frugal in the way of those who never had much money. He was rumored to have buried his money in tomato cans in his backyard, a work of fiction, he said unconvincingly, that had been written in the aftermath of his having once asked that a tournament pay him with a certified check. He was also heard to say that you should put all your eggs in one basket, then watch the basket.

There was no doubt that he appreciated the value of a hard-earned dollar, or even one acquired through dubious means. He enjoyed the friendly wager, so long as he was able to dictate the terms. He knew it wasn't gambling when you stacked the deck. Accordingly, he was adept at the art of negotiation, and he had developed an innate ability to recognize when he was on the wrong side of a hustle.

So it was that an alarm sounded when a Navy recruiter attempted to sign him up for a tour of duty a few days before the PGA Championship in 1942. Snead had received his draft notice and intended to join the Navy after the tournament. After he had completed his physical examination, the recruitment officer tried to convince him that delaying his enlistment was unnecessary.

"Sign right here," the Navy recruiter said, his gallows-humor punch line at the ready, "and we'll ship the body."

Snead hesitated. He was thinking that were he to sign he might be ordered to report right then and there, precluding him from playing in the PGA Championship.

"I have a big golf meet next week," Snead said. "I want one more shot at a title before I go."

"Oh, we'll give you a pass for that," the recruiter said. "Don't you worry. Sign here."

Snead pondered the potential windfall on which he'd be passing if the man was lying, including the $2,000 bonus that his equipment company, Wilson Sporting Goods, would provide him were he to win the PGA Championship. First-place money was $3,000. A chance at $5,000 was not worth wagering on the word of a stranger who was paid to get men into uniforms. Snead concluded that he was on the wrong side of a hustle and declined to sign up until after the tournament.

The odds on his winning were stacking up against him, however. An established champion of lesser events, Snead had never won a major championship, a distinction for which he was called "a hex-haunted hillbilly" by one writer. The tournament site was Seaview Country Club in Atlantic City, New Jersey, less than an hour away from Fort Dix. The soldiers who would form the bulk of the gallery were unlikely to look kindly on a seemingly healthy young man who was not in the service of his country.

There were also several Army men playing for whom it would be akin to a home game. The defending champion was Vic Ghezzi, an Army corporal on leave from Fort Monmouth, another New Jersey military base. Also playing was Corporal Jimmy Turnesa, who was stationed at Fort Dix and was particularly popular among the soldiers who descended on Seaview each day. The oddsmaker had failed to consider the effect the overzealous soldiers would have on Turnesa's opponents in the match-play event; he had established Turnesa as a fifty-to-one long shot to win.

Once the tournament began, Turnesa played like a brigadier general. He defeated Ben Hogan one day, then came from behind to defeat tournament favorite Byron Nelson on the nineteenth hole the next day to advance to the thirty-six-hole final.

"I just saw the best putter in the world," a dazed Nelson said, coming off the course.

Snead, meanwhile, steadfastly moved through his bracket, dispatching Jimmy Demaret, 3 and 2, in their semifinal match. Snead was cheered in that one; Demaret was the scoundrel who had sent Corporal Ghezzi back to Fort Monmouth the day before.

For the final, the stage was set: An Army corporal, Jimmy Turnesa, versus a worthless civilian, Sam Snead—thirty-six holes to determine the championship of professional golf, on a swath of green framed by khaki. Upwards of seven thousand soldiers from Fort Dix made the trek southeast on the highway to Sea-

view Country Club to cheer their colleague and jeer his opponent. Snead had to maneuver through an Army obstacle course
just to get to the first tee, where Ed Dudley, the president of the
PGA and the marshal for the match, was waiting.

"This crowd isn't exactly pulling for you, Sam," Dudley said.

"Pulling for me?" Snead replied. "I'll settle for less pushing.
They almost knocked me down twice."

Dudley observed that the soldiers were unaware that Snead
was enlisting in the Navy, although newspaper accounts of the
tournament had noted his plans. "You know how it is, Sam," he
said. "They hate the man out of uniform."

"Well, don't tell them a thing," Snead replied.

Snead had never experienced a gallery so hostile. Dudley was
right; its enmity was fueled by the premise that the corporal's opponent was a civilian. Again relying on his ability to calculate
odds, Snead concluded that he was better off allowing the crowd
its assumption in this inhospitable environment. He reasoned
that the truth, that he intended to enlist in the Navy the moment
the tournament was over, was potentially worse. In all matters
Army and Navy, better to remain neutral.

Dudley sympathized with Snead, even attempting to quell a
crowd rabidly rooting against him, to the extent that one wayward shot from Turnesa magically reappeared on the fairway, a
propitious Army boot from a well-meaning soldier.

"I'm sorry, Sam," Dudley said. "But there's nothing we can do
about it."

"I know it, Ed," Snead replied. "Did I say anything? I ain't
complaining."

Snead understood that his best course of action was silence,
that by feigning indifference he would discourage the unruly
doughboys from escalating their animus. He was seething inside,

but outwardly he gave no indication that the crowd was unnerving him.

Each time Snead stood over a putt, "those Fort Dix boys would start jabbering and caterwauling," he said. Dudley's efforts to restore decorum were considerable failures.

"Just let them rant and rave, Ed," Snead said. "I'd rather have steady noise than to have it stop for a while and then start again."

Snead's reasoning was that had Dudley succeeded in quieting them down, they'd likely erupt again when he was in midstroke, the death knell for a golfer attempting to concentrate.

In fact, what was unnerving Snead was not the noise, but the play of Turnesa, who through twenty-three holes was three up on Snead. He nonetheless clawed his way back to even, which aroused the ire of the soldiers. The way the soldiers were behaving, Snead reckoned, "you'd have thought I was a German or a Jap."

Snead took pride in his ability to read an opponent, and on the twenty-eighth tee he read fright in Turnesa. He noted that Turnesa doubled the number of waggles he ordinarily took while addressing the ball, from two to four, and that the forward press he used to start his swing had lost its rhythm, each an indication that his nerves were betraying him. Snead knew that he had gained an advantage.

The notion that he might disappoint the crowd, his Army buddies, had invaded Turnesa's psyche, and he pulled his next drive into the woods. The match began to slip away from the corporal, who finally lost when Snead holed a fifty-foot chip shot on the thirty-fifth hole. The victory was Snead's first in a major championship, elevating him to another level in professional golf.

"In a way," Snead said, "I felt like I'd done my part for the war effort. I knew that once those Army boys got themselves some guns, God help any enemy that got in their way."

The next day, Snead joined the Navy and left for Norfolk, Virginia, for training.

"I'm kind of curious," Snead said to the naval recruiting officer. "If I'd signed the enlistment papers last week, would you have let me off for the tournament?"

"Negative, Snead," the officer said.

4

A MEDAL FOR HOGAN

The Hale America Open

The name of the event was long enough to accommodate a par five—the Hale America National Open Golf Tournament. It was short only on clarity. Was it indeed the National Open, as the press usually referred to the U.S. Open? Or was it something less, as the United States Golf Association intended? The USGA's grandiose vision for the Hale America National Open Golf Tournament was that it was to be a celebration of the American spirit, a giant lawn party for a worthwhile cause. Buried somewhere within was a golf event of indeterminate importance.

Little more than a month before the event was scheduled to begin, the Hale America was suffering from an identity crisis that contributed to its inability to gain traction among American golfers. By the first week in May, only two hundred entries had been received, half of them from amateurs. The U.S. Open, which the Hale America was scheduled in lieu of, typically received upwards of a thousand entries, and tournament organizers had been predicting they would receive more than fifteen hundred entries for the Hale America.

The Hale America was cosponsored by the USGA, the PGA of America, and the Chicago District Golf Association, and was dedicated to raising money for the United Service Organizations and the Navy Relief Society. Its identity crisis grew from the fact that the associations carefully chose some words in the title but carelessly picked others. For instance, it was called a tournament rather than a championship, an attempt to prevent the perception that something of high import was at stake. Paradoxically, *National Open* indicated an event of paramount importance, an equivalent of the now-dormant U.S. Open.

Further confusing the substance of the event, Bob Hope and Bing Crosby were among the twenty-five golfers who were invited to play and excluded from having to qualify. They were both reasonably good players; Crosby had even reached U.S. Open sectional qualifying the year before (though rounds of 83 and 77 at Winged Foot in Mamaroneck, New York, left him five shots shy of earning an Open berth). Hope and Crosby guaranteed a crowd, certainly; the PGA of America recognized their marquee value and had been employing them in a series of golf exhibitions for war-related charities. Extending them invitations to play in the Hale America, however, was a transparent attempt by tournament sponsors to sell tickets to what was being billed as a bona fide golf competition. The invitations to Crosby and Hope raised a legitimate question: Was it a vaudeville show or a golf tournament?

George S. May, an ambitious, aggressive promoter who saw an opening created by the USGA's cancellation of the U.S. Open, added further confusion by calling his own July tournament at Tam O'Shanter Country Club in Chicago the National Open and offering a record purse, $15,000, that was more indicative of a national championship than the USGA's annual prize offering, $6,000 every year since 1929. Finally, a measure of ignorance was added to the clutter. The host club, Ridgemoor Country Club in Chicago, had a prominent member with the last name of Hale, causing the uninformed in the local media to conclude that Hale had conceived of the tournament and as a reward had had his name included in the title.

The message that the confusion relayed to golfers around the country was that the tournament was not as important as the U.S. Open and they could afford to pass on it. Reinforcing their apathy was the fact that other than twenty-one selected professionals and four amateurs, everyone else was required to play in qualifiers, most of them in a thirty-six-hole local qualifier followed by a fifty-four-hole sectional qualifier. At a time when traveling was a trial, arranging to travel to two qualifiers in advance of the actual event seemed too much of an inconvenience for a tournament that even for its eventual winner would not likely add luster to a resume.

In early May of 1942, PGA president Ed Dudley was so alarmed by the lack of interest that he considered canceling the event. The USGA quickly answered Dudley's pessimism with some welcome news, announcing that Ben Hogan and Bobby Jones had entered, the latter name almost singularly providing the gravity heretofore missing from the tournament.

Jones emerging from retirement to play in a USGA event was headline news. Nearly twelve years earlier, in 1930, he had walked away from competitive golf, endowing the game with the Grand Slam on his way out, winning all four major championships (the U.S. Open, U.S. Amateur, British Open, and British Amateur) in the same year. Since then, he had limited his tournament golf to only a single event, his own, the Masters, which was originally designed not as a hypercompetitive tournament, but as a gathering of friends.

"Just today we received entries from Bobby Jones and Ben Hogan," said Francis Ouimet, a former Open champion and a member of the USGA Executive Committee, who had been selected by the organizations to chair the event. "We already had the entries of Craig Wood, the Open champion, Byron Nelson, winner of the Augusta Masters, Gene Sarazen, Paul Runyan, Horton Smith, Lloyd Mangrum, Herman Barron, and other stars exempt from the qualifying play. They will all be on hand at Chicago.

"Of course, we have been concerned with the number of entries. But, as a rule, half the total entries for the Open do not reach us until the last two days before closing time. Such is human nature. For the Hale America Open all entries have to be in the USGA office in New York by Wednesday, May 13."

Ouimet reiterated the expectation that at least 1,500 entries would be received by the deadline less than two weeks away.

Dudley's fears that the tournament would be canceled on account of an apathetic reception were unfounded. Jones's commitment, along with that of Walter Hagen, another semiretired star returning from the pages of golf history, spurred others to submit entries, eventually boosting the number of interested players to 1,528, the largest number of entries for a golf open in American history.

Excitement began to build among the public as well. Revenue from advance ticket sales eventually reached $15,000, a record for a golf tournament. Inasmuch as servicemen were admitted free, a substantial crowd was guaranteed.

Jones further heightened anticipation by playing remarkably well in the fifty-four-hole sectional qualifier ten days before the tournament, at his home course, East Lake Country Club in

Atlanta. Jones was exempt from qualifying but chose to play anyway to test the condition of his skills and to chip away whatever rust he could. He had rounds of 67, 71, and 67 to lead his qualifier by five shots. The Associated Press called his swing "as smooth as Dixie molasses."

The field was eventually set at 107, "beyond doubt the most brilliant ever to take part in a golf tournament," *The New York Times* said, injecting the event with a dose of hyperbole about which the sponsors were not going to complain. Fifty major championships had been won by the players in the field, including the thirteen won by Jones and the eleven won by Hagen. Other than Sam Snead, who had joined the Navy and was in training and unable to secure leave, every active player of note was entered. The quality of the field deflated one of the USGA's principal arguments for canceling the Open, that war service would thin the quality of the field to the extent that it would not be representative enough to justify crowning a national champion.

The defections of Hope and Crosby helped elevate the tournament's credibility by eliminating the carnival atmosphere and enhancing the integrity of the competition. Hope had declined his invitation, though he was on hand to play an exhibition before the start of tournament play. Crosby had accepted his invitation, but withdrew before the start, reportedly as a result of the unreliability of train travel and his fear of flying.

The tournament began to take on the aura of a national championship even before it started. Officials of the USGA became alarmed that Sam Byrd's irons might have grooves that did not adhere to specifications outlined in the Rules of Golf. The USGA decided that it had to inspect them. The association was responsible for writing the rules, but it typically was on hand to enforce them only at its national championships. The fact that it was concerned enough about a potential infraction that was inadvertent and minor in nature suggested that the Hale America was something greater than a glorified fund-raiser. USGA officials used a "micrometer microscope" to measure the grooves and concluded that they did not conform to the rules, requiring that Byrd replace them.

What often distinguishes major championships from lesser tournaments is the pedigree of their winners. On that count, the Hale America National Open Golf Tournament was setting itself up for disappointment. Thirty-six holes into the tournament, the leader was Mike Turnesa, who had a prominent last name (one of the golfing Turnesa brothers) but otherwise lacked star power.

At least Ben Hogan was lurking three strokes behind Turnesa and had appropriated the headlines from the leader. Hogan had opened with a 72 that did not sit well on his palate, and before teeing off for the second round, he put himself through an arduous two-hour session on the practice tee. The hard work paid a substantial dividend. In the second round, he missed only one fairway, missed only a single green. He had eight birdies, an eagle, and nine pars. He went out in six-under-par 30 and came in with a four-under-par 32, a score of 62, the finest ever shot in a national competition.

"It was the nearest thing possible to a perfect round," his playing partner, Tommy Armour, said.

Even the often dour Hogan was giddy afterward. "Think I could get in the money if I get two more sixty-twos?" he asked rhetorically.

Turnesa's lead evaporated in the third round, when rainstorms saturated the course in the morning. Teeing off early, he shot a 72, while Hogan went off after the rain had subsided, in the afternoon, and the course was more favorable to quality scoring. Hogan actually opened a two-stroke lead on Turnesa, before giving back two strokes on the back nine en route to a round of 69 and a share of the lead heading into the final round.

For the final round, Hogan was paired with Bobby Jones, despite the fact that Jones trailed the leaders by fourteen strokes. The pairing was designed to increase the gate, and it delivered; one estimate had the crowd exceeding twelve thousand, harkening back to the days when Jones was a transcendent star, the sporting equivalent of Charles Lindbergh. This time, the crowd's adulation was split; it was nostalgically rooting for Jones, while cheering on a candidate to succeed him in the pantheon of dominant golfers.

Hogan obliged them, shooting a final round of 68, three strokes better than Turnesa, to win the tournament by three strokes. The Hale America National Open Golf Tournament had proved its mettle by delivering a worthy champion, an emerging star on the threshold of greatness. As for Bobby Jones, his assignment, to resurrect his glory days, was simply unrealistic. He played admirably, for a forty-year-old who had not played competitively for nearly twelve years. He had rounds of 70, 75, 72, and 73, for a total of two-over-par 290, nineteen shots more than Hogan's winning score of 271, which tied him for thirty-fifth. "What can you do, when you go out and shoot par [sic] golf and still find yourself eight strokes behind?" he asked. "They were just too good for me at Chicago."

THE HALE AMERICA NATIONAL OPEN GOLF Tournament delivered on its promise to raise a veritable windfall on behalf of the war agencies. The year before, the U.S. Open returned a net profit of $12,567 to the USGA. The Hale America netted in excess of $25,000, all of it handed over to the USO and Navy Relief. Moreover, Hogan gladly agreed to auction the putter and ball he used in winning. The least valuable club in Hogan's bag fetched $1,000, and the ball raised another $650. The money was added to the receipts the tournament handed over.

For winning, Hogan received $1,000, paid in war bonds, as well as the gold medal traditionally awarded the winner of the U.S. Open. The USGA had already purchased the medal for the U.S. Open champion. Only the engraving was different— *Hale America National Open Golf Tournament* instead of *United States Open Championship* on the back of the medal. More telling was the perpetual trophy that Hogan did not receive, which traditionally went to the winner of the U.S. Open. It remained with the reigning champion, Craig Wood, which reiterated the USGA's position that Hogan had not won its national championship.

The New York Times, meanwhile, alternately referred to it as "the war time substitute for the national open" and "a synthetic reproduction" of the U.S. Open. Fred Corcoran, the PGA tournament manager, wrote in *The Professional Golfer of America* magazine, "It had all the color and pageantry of the Open [but] it was only a substitute . . . a title test in everything but the name."

Others saw the victory not as anything synthetic, but as an authentic national championship, the opening argument in a debate that was certain to endure. Among them was Charles Bartlett, the golf writer for *The Chicago Tribune,* who not only conceded Hogan the Open, but argued that his winning score of 271 would go down as an Open record by ten shots. Bartlett wrote: "He scored his first victory in a tournament officially designated as national, for the Hale America was golf's No. 1 event of the year. His feat will be duly recorded in the annual yearbook of the United States Golf Association, which, its own conducted events canceled for the duration, lists Ralph Guldahl's 281 at Detroit as the National Open record."

Bartlett might have added that Hogan would also have established Open records for low score (62) and the low fifty-four-hole total (203), all of which could suggest that the course was beneath usual USGA standards on the difficulty front, notwithstanding Hogan's paramount skill. The course yielded fifty rounds in the 60s, or two more sub-70 rounds than had been shot in the previous eight Opens combined.

The tournament was conducted without a thirty-six-hole cut, which weakened the argument that the Hale America National Open Golf Tournament was the equivalent of the U.S. Open. So did the circuslike atmosphere under which it was played. There were long drive and accuracy contests, a clinic, even a trick-shot exhibition.

It was evident throughout that it was only superficially a major championship, that although it was a remarkable week that produced a memorable tournament and a worthy champion, it was at the core a momentary diversion from a war that was more responsible than the competition itself for bringing the players together in Chicago. The players weren't there to identify a national champion, but to raise money for war relief. Ironically, there was no relief from war, and it was evident the moment the last putt fell. Bobby Jones said his farewells and left for New York, where a day later he was scheduled to report for active duty in the Army Air Corps.

IS INTEGRITY A CHARACTER FLAW when it compels a man to pursue a perilous path on behalf of his nation, though he has children at home who need a father? What is a wife to do when her husband is dangerously incapable of countermanding the gravitational pull of decency and honor?

Bobby Jones's inherent selflessness prohibited him from treating the war as a sport that required his service only from tee to green. He could have opted to play golf in the service of his country, of course; he turned forty on March 17, 1942, he was married and the father of three, and his service classification was 4-F as a result of varicose veins in his legs. More than eleven years after retiring from competitive golf, he remained the reigning marquee player of a game that had lost some of its sheen since he walked away. He could have honorably served by playing a series of Red Cross exhibitions that would have raised tens of thousands of dollars, for which the nation would have been grateful and asked nothing more of him.

A dozen years earlier, Jones was given the key to the city of Atlanta, but it was Mayor Isaac N. Ragsdale's proclamation that came with it that underscored the qualities inherent in Jones's inability to put self above selflessness by taking the easy way out and engaging the enemy from a distance, one hole at a time. Ragsdale's proclamation read:

> When purpose masters impulse, when patience rules hot blood and tingling nerves, when courage crowns itself with wisdom, when triumph clothes itself with modesty, and good sense is mated to good will, there is established the fairest of kingdoms and the happiest pages in human history.
>
> And thence this scroll, symbolizing the love, esteem, and appreciation of your fellow townsmen, not alone because you have accomplished a record in the greatest of sports that will endure while the world stands, but because you have achieved a character so that all the world, while marveling at your skill, pays highest tribute to your soul.

Jones was an athletic anomaly; he was once the best player in a sport without teammates, a feat ordinarily achieved only by those intrinsically self-centered, or the antithesis of Jones. Genuine humility tended to be an obstacle to realizing greatness in an individual endeavor. Still, Jones invariably put others' interests ahead of his own. He was only twenty-eight when he retired from competitive golf, after winning the Grand Slam in 1930. He no longer cared to endure the escalating pressure he placed on himself not to disappoint his friends by losing a tournament they expected him to win. His retirement was not so much about him as it was about those to whom he was closest.

The easy way out in a time of war was anathema to his personality. There was the matter, too, of his having missed the First World War. He was only sixteen when it ended in 1918, precluding him from assisting in the victory over Germany, other than by playing golf exhibitions to raise money on behalf of the war effort. He later joined the ROTC while attending Georgia Tech, and he became a captain in the Army Reserves, a post he held until his commission expired in 1941.

World War II presented an opportunity for Jones to serve his country in something more meaningful than a Walker Cup Match. In May of 1942, Jones submitted his application to rejoin the service, though his age and 4-F classification cast doubt as to whether the military would accommodate his request.

One newspaper, the *News,* of Wilmington, North Carolina, cast its editorial vote in favor of a Jones commission anyway. The *News* wrote:

> Bobby Jones of imperishable golf fame wants a commission in the Army Air Force. And it is reported his application will be acted upon favorably.
>
> As he is too old to become a flying cadet, what post he will be given is not known. But because the diminutive wielder of the niblick is an energetic gentleman with undisputed mental attributes, we may be sure it will be an important one.
>
> Bobby Jones was too young to enlist in the last war. He was

only 16 when it ended. Now, at 40, he is beyond the active service age for recruits. But he studied mechanical engineering at Georgia Tech before he got his law degree from Emory University. The War Department will have no difficulty finding a place for a man of his abilities.

Anyone who can win the four major championships in a year, which he did in 1930, and which has not since been equaled, would be an asset to any man's army.

Jones went so far as to lobby the commanding officer of his Army Reserve unit. He made it clear that a ceremonial commission was unacceptable, that he had no intention of returning to the Army to play golf with generals. "I don't want to be a hoopty-da officer of some camp," Jones told the commanding officer. This was a debate that was won before the first objection was raised. Few men in America were more persuasive than Jones, who had the studied speech of the attorney he was, backed by an aura of celebrity that transcended his chosen field to a degree exceeded, perhaps, only by Charles Lindbergh and Babe Ruth. He was, to boot, fundamentally a gentleman.

Eventually the Army agreed with Jones's request. On June 8, 1942, the War Department announced that Jones had been commissioned a captain in the Army Air Corps, and he was ordered to report to active duty at Mitchel Field on Long Island, N.Y.

"I'm very happy over this opportunity to serve," Jones said. "I had been looking around to see what I could do. I am very glad that it has come through and I am anxious to get going."

A few days later, Jones went to Fort McPherson to get fitted for a uniform, after which he was required to sit for the obligatory photo shoot that came when a celebrity joined the armed forces. Wire service photographers were dispatched to the offices of Jones, Powers, Williams & Dorsey, an Atlanta law firm. Jones's friend and biographer, O. B. Keeler, was there, and asked him whether he'd had difficulty finding an Army cap that fit his fat head. This was not a reference to a swelled head, as conceit was never a Jones failing. He simply had a head that was physically larger than most. Grantland Rice took note of this early in the golfer's career. "The head served as a perfect anchor for those shots that later would flow so flawlessly from his clubhead," Rice once wrote.

Jones accepted Keeler's barb in the humor in which it was intended. "They must have some large heads in the Army," Jones said. "Or else mine has shrunk lately. This cap's only seven and three eighths. First time in my life I ever wore one under seven and a half."

On June 23, 1942, he reported to Brigadier General John K. Cannon, commander of the First Fighter Command, who assigned him to the Aircraft Warning Service. The AWS was a group of citizens who had volunteered to staff observation posts along the Atlantic seaboard. Jones was ordered to take a class in aircraft warning before assuming a position overseeing large groups of volunteers.

It was not the front, but neither was it the first tee. It was a reasonable compromise for Jones, who was committed to helping his country win a war. It was also an exemplary gesture for others to follow, its message clear: Whatever your stature, a world at war binds people from every walk of life.

5

———•———

THE GRASS IS NOT GREENER

Golf Clubs and the War

The project was top secret, known only to high-ranking government and military officials and every cabdriver in the Washington, D.C., area. Cabbies' suspicions had been aroused and later confirmed by the number of young men without golf clubs seeking rides to a posh country club. Among them was Army officer Aaron Bank.

"Congressional Country Club, please," Bank told his cabdriver one morning.

"Oh, you're one of those guerrillas," the cabbie replied.

Word was out that something other than golf was going on at Congressional Country Club, which heretofore had been a playground for Washington's power brokers. The club had been founded in 1921 by congressmen who wanted a place to play golf and to conduct government and personal business. The cornerstone of the clubhouse was even dedicated by President Her-

71

bert Hoover in 1923. It had become among the most influential clubs in and around the District of Columbia.

Congressional, however, had not fully recovered from the Depression, and with the onset of war, its financial situation was not going to brighten anytime soon. Club officials decided that soliciting a government benefactor would help on two fronts: It would alleviate the financial burden on the club, and it would provide an assist to the Allied war effort. Congressional Country Club officials began trolling for a government lease. Almost immediately, a new government agency, the Office of Strategic Services, expressed interest and agreed to lease the club for $4,000 a month, for purposes initially unknown. By April 1943, Congressional had become the training ground for the government's new Office of Strategic Services, a centralized intelligence agency that had been proposed by General William Donovan, better known far and wide as Wild Bill Donovan.

The training ground was code-named Area F. Congressional's clubhouse served as headquarters. Quonset huts sprang up around the clubhouse and on the club's tennis courts. The golf course became an obstacle course. Hundreds of men trained in a variety of disciplines, among them skydiving, espionage, sabotage, and demolition. They learned the art of "silent killing," a useful skill for raids conducted behind enemy lines.

Thus one of the more prestigious addresses in golf began to assume an important role in the Allied war effort. It was part of a pattern that was developing across the nation's links landscape, a movement that began, literally, at the grass roots. When the Army Corps of Engineers came asking in 1942, the membership at the Philadelphia Country Club willfully surrendered its Spring Mill Course. The Corps used its fairways (while generously sparing the greens) to test a chemical it was developing that would discolor grass as a means of camouflaging it. Only the inconvenience was minor. The message it sent was major, that no sacrifice was too great to make on behalf of winning the war, even if it meant turning your pristine green fairways to brown. The Spring Mill Course was no cow pasture on which eighteen flagpoles had been stuck either. It had architectural bloodlines of a bluish hue—it was originally designed by William Flynn, who had also built the renowned Country Club in Brookline, Massachusetts, and had been remodeled by Perry Maxwell, whose portfolio included Southern Hills Country Club in Tulsa, Oklahoma.

The Spring Mill Course had also hosted the 1939 U.S. Open less than three years earlier. The '39 Open was memorable for the toll it exacted on Sam Snead, who needed only a par on the seventy-second hole to win the tournament. There were no scoreboards to apprise him of his standing, however, and he concluded that he needed a birdie to win. So he needlessly ratcheted up his aggressiveness, which off the tee got him into trouble from which he never recovered. He made a triple-bogey 8 on the hole, one of history's most ignominious implosions, and finished two strokes behind the winner, Byron Nelson. "That night," Snead said, "I was ready to go out with a gun and pay somebody to shoot me."

No doubt Snead was among those in favor of dumping a load of chemicals on the Spring Mill Course.

The Philadelphia Country Club's magnanimity in risking its prestigious track provided literal evidence that golf's determination to mobilize on behalf of the war effort would begin at the grass roots level, at municipal courses and country clubs from Long Island to Long Beach. It would have to begin there, on the coastal courses, east and west. The war was largely being waged on foreign soil, but it threatened to spread to the home front as well. In the week before Christmas 1941, nine Japanese submarines had attacked eight American merchant ships, sinking two of them off the West Coast of the U.S. In February, golfers playing Cypress Point and the Monterey Peninsula Country Club noticed an American tanker offshore with clouds of smoke billowing from its funnel and moving in an erratic manner. They kept playing, oblivious to the fact that a Japanese submarine was in pursuit and that the captain of the tanker was maneuvering in a zigzag fashion to reduce the size of the target it was presenting. German U-boats, meanwhile, were operating off the East Coast and shooting torpedoes at American ships.

Philadelphia Country Club's response to the war was not atypical of clubs around the country. The members there formed a War Activities Committee, the purpose of which was to create ways of assisting the war effort. Among its ideas was to invite wounded servicemen to enjoy its myriad activities, including golf, swimming, bowling on the green, croquet, badminton, and tennis—activities, the committee assumed with a degree of certainty, that would cause them to work up not just an appetite, but an insatiable thirst. The soldiers were invited to dine and dance, as well, but to ensure that they not participate in the latter with an inappropriate degree of gusto, the committee issued the following directives to its members:

> Please do not boost your morale with a hard drink while waiting for the boys to arrive. The aroma may linger.

> If, during the evening, you see any group of boys overindulging in beer and they ask you to take and refill their pitcher, take it, but do not return.

Apparently the committee had concluded that the injured soldiers and sailors had suffered enough; no need to add a morning-after headache to their maladies.

THE GOLF CONSTITUENCY generally understood its obligation, that country came before country club. It co-opted as its own mantra (replacing *baseball* with *golf*) the words of a former golf official, George Trautman, who was president of the American Association of Baseball Clubs. "The question isn't what the war will do to baseball," he said poignantly, "it's what baseball can do to help win the war."

Noted golf writer Herb Graffis beat this drum on a monthly basis, consistently and emphatically reminding readers that they ought to continue to play, but for the right reasons. He wrote in *Golfing* magazine:

> Let golf not kid itself! Not another thing matters now but winning the war. Not even life itself. . . . We know what the Nazi and Jap record is. We'd be a miserable nation of dopes were we to let ourselves be misled by hope, blind selfishness, and inertia to the extent of allowing anything to take precedence over winning this war.
>
> So, if we have the sense we need for self-preservation, we won't think of golf as an essential in wartime.
>
> It absolutely isn't. . . .
>
> Golf these days can justify itself only if it does help the fight. . . .
>
> Your golf this year is not one of those luxuries to be enjoyed in your leisure in a free, secure nation. It's a privilege given you so you can do a better job in wartime.

The war inevitably took its toll on golf. Lido Golf Club on Long Island was a masterpiece, a course suitable for framing and displaying in a museum. Cornelius Vanderbilt III, heir to the Vanderbilt railroad and shipping fortune, was among those who had commissioned the architectural legend C. B. Macdonald to build Lido Golf Club. Macdonald in turn employed another architectural star, Seth Raynor, to assist him on the seaside links, which had been built on one hundred fifteen acres of reclaimed swampland.

"Lido will stand as Seth Raynor's monumental piece of construction, a Herculean task, requiring a course to be practically raised from the sea," Macdonald wrote.

He was wrong. The war precluded it from standing as anything but a victim of a world that had lost its bearings. When the war began, the Navy saw the seaside holes as a strategically situated site on which to conduct drills, and it appropriated the land. Lido's superintendent, Charles Mayo, sensing the deformation of a renowned golf course, photographed the seaside holes from every conceivable angle to assist in postwar reconstruction, were it necessary. Lido was nevertheless effectively and indelibly altered beyond repair.

It was a steep but necessary price to pay, with freedom at stake. The war effort obviously superseded golf, which was prepared for the sacrifices that might have to be made on behalf of winning the war. Indeed, the Germans weren't likely to be repelled by a barrage of birdies.

The War Department in fact viewed golf not as a frivolous pastime but as a potential ally. It began by ordering a feasibility study of New York City area golf courses to see whether any of them had fairways that might easily be converted into landing strips for U.S. warplanes as part of a large-scale contingency plan in the event of emergencies.

The idea was fostered by Albert W. Lewis, a member of a firm that had built a variety of courses in eastern cities. The plan was to locate courses with long, flat parallel holes that could be converted to landing strips simply by cutting down the trees separating the fairways and leveling elevated greens. An inherent problem was that warplanes of the era landed at speeds in excess of eighty miles per hour and required runways of up to six hundred yards, or an exceptionally long par 5, of which there were few.

On the West Coast, the Army closed several municipal courses in the Los Angeles area, some of them representing possible landing strips for enemy aircraft. Seattle represented a viable target as well. It was home to Boeing, an aircraft manufacturer that was important to the Allied war effort. A few blocks south of downtown Seattle is a public golf complex, Jefferson Park. On one of its nines, at Columbus Way South and South Snoqualmie Street, antiaircraft battalions were installed.

The War Department also hired Franklin L. Miller as an expert consultant to devise ways that golf clubs might assist in civilian defense. A year earlier, a full ten months before the Japanese attack on Pearl Harbor, Miller, a World War I veteran who was active in golf circles in the Cleveland area, had presented the War Department with an outline of ways that golf clubs could assist in the nation's defense, earning the department's trust and gratitude.

Miller mailed questionnaires to clubs around the country, asking them about their availability to convert their structures to emergency hospitals or temporary convalescent centers, even evacuation posts. The war was only months old and already there was a dearth of convalescent hospital space for soldiers. Miller was looking ahead. The questionnaire asked:

    I. Will the club permit the use of its buildings for:
        Convalescent Hospitalization?
        Emergency Hospitalization?
    II. Will the club endeavor to organize:
        1. An American Red Cross Volunteer Nurses' Aid Class
        2. An American Red Cross Home Nursing Class

      3. An America Red Cross First Aid Class

      4. An Entertainment Unit

III. How many and at what cost per man will the club make available the present sleeping rooms or provide sleeping quarters to be used for periods as "rest and relaxation" locations for combat forces after arduous active duty? (i.e., Aircraft Pilots, Submarine & Destroyer Crews). Would your club be willing to cooperate with nearest Naval station in providing moderate use of course playing privileges at times–number of men agreeable to you?

The question regarding the possibility of allowing servicemen to play their courses was strategically placed at the end of the questionnaire, after its audience had been softened with requests to care for the injured. Had Miller opened the questionnaire by asking club representatives to make their courses available to servicemen, they might have read no farther. Either way, Miller knew that he was asking a lot of private clubs whose members in peacetime surely would disapprove of the suggestion that they mingle with the unwashed.

Miller's intention to enlist the help of golf clubs was inspired by the Russians' successful air defense of Moscow in November and December of 1941, which was in part the result of employing defense stations in outlying regions encircling the city. Most U.S. golf clubs were built beyond the city limits, by necessity, of course; the outlying areas had the only available land. They tended to encircle population centers, making them strategically situated to contribute to defense. They featured terrain suitable for fortifications and even camouflage, since many were built in wooded areas. Their fairways and buildings could be deployed as places of assembly. Clubs also had motorized traction equipment and their own water supplies.

Miller also considered the strength-in-numbers proposition. The math revealed that there was literally an army of golfers. The United States Golf Association counted eight hundred twenty clubs on its membership rolls. There were an additional twenty-four hundred private clubs that likely would volunteer to participate. The average membership of these clubs was two hundred, excluding family members. Nearly two thousand public, semiprivate, and daily-fee courses serviced hundreds of thousands of golfers. The sum was more than two million citizens, a large percentage of whom were too old to join the armed forces. Those not otherwise engaged in the war effort would be available to help in the event that they were needed.

Many clubs took proactive measures to support the war effort. Carlisle Country Club in Carlisle, Pennsylvania, developed a program that began with a dance to which officers from the Carlisle Barracks were invited. Its plans included transforming the clubhouse into an emergency hospital in the event of air raids; planting wheat on a forty-acre tract of land adjacent to the course; conducting tournaments and exhibitions and donating the proceeds to the Red Cross and Army and Navy Relief; waiving the clubhouse rental fee for organizations holding dances at the clubhouse and donating proceeds to the war effort; and having its women's committee offering its services to the Red Cross.

Those in leadership positions in golf underscored the suggestion that golfers continue to flail away as often as possible. Morton G. Bogue, a vice president of the United States Golf Association, issued a slogan for clubs to use: "Keep 'em Swinging." There were important reasons to keep the populace on course; golfers had money that the nation needed in its costly defense of freedom. In other words, the government was just another match-play opponent, attempting to pick a pocket, though for a worthy cause. Glenn Morris, the director of the National

Golf Foundation, estimated that golfers would pay $30 million in taxes on their golf in 1942.

No one was suggesting that golfers abolish the friendly wager, of course. The incentive for playing might have changed, but the incentive for playing well was indelibly the same. Gambling was an inherent part of the game, an important part, too, so long as it wasn't the raison d'être for playing. In fact, golfers had already started to pay off golf gambling debts with defense stamps in lieu of cash as a means of helping the war effort. It was an idea that was advanced by Morris, who suggested that $5 million in defense stamps might be sold should the practice of paying gambling debts with them be embraced on a large scale.

There was a movement afoot for golfers to help the United Services Organization achieve its goal of raising $32 million between May 11 and July 4 of 1942. A golfer, Prescott Bush, was at the helm of the USO, its national campaign chairman. The Bush family tree, in fact, seemed to have been planted on a golf course. Prescott Bush's father, Samuel Prescott Bush, was among the founders of the Scioto Country Club in Columbus, Ohio, site of the 1926 U.S. Open that was won by Bobby Jones. Young Prescott Bush was on the work crew that built Scioto, for which he was paid a dollar a day. Prescott married Dorothy Walker, whose father was George Herbert Walker, the president of the United States Golf Association in 1920 and the man for whom the Walker Cup was named. Prescott Bush became a fine player, whose handicap was 2. He frequently won the club championship at Cape Arundel Golf Club near the family's Kennebunkport, Maine, compound. Prescott was also a former USGA president and had passed on the family golf gene to his son, George Herbert Walker Bush, who was preparing to join the Navy.

In February of 1942, Prescott Bush had been named the national campaign chairman of the new USO, a position he gleefully accepted. Pres Bush believed that a man's obligations to public service increased in direct proportion to the advantages he had in life. Toward that end, he was also the chairman of the National War Fund, which oversaw six hundred war relief groups.

Pres Bush's golf lineage was an asset; golfers were urged to help one of their own raise vast sums of money on behalf of the war, particularly those with whom Bush had an acquaintance, a number that easily topped ten thousand, according to one estimate.

The golfers at Poland Country Club in Youngstown, Ohio, agreed that their game represented an opportunity to help. They increased entry fees to club tournaments by a quarter, earmarking the additional fee for the Red Cross. Macomb Country Club in Macomb, Illinois, a nine-holer with 190 players, began fining players a nickel for hitting a ball out of bounds on the five outside holes. A crab apple grove between the fourth and fifth fairways also became a source of income; anyone hitting into it was penalized a dime.

"If some such plan could be installed at each club throughout the country I believe the golfers would get behind it one hundred percent," said Macomb club president E. J. Swanson. "We have a lot of fun with the jar and at the same time are helping a worthy cause."

There were other ways to help. A club pro, Spencer Murphy of Glen Oaks on Long Island, donated more than two hundred clubheads to a scrap drive. "We can't make any more clubs, so why hold these heads when they can be used on the Nazis and Japs?" he said. Another New York club, Wykagyl Country Club, donated its tee markers, which weighed several pounds each, to a scrap drive, replacing them with wooden markers.

Courses public and private, in large cities and small, began offering free golf to men in the armed services. Many courses surrendered their properties on behalf of the Allied war effort. The Navy, for instance, appropriated Pickwick Golf Course in Glenview, Illinois, near Chicago, to expand its Naval Aviation Training Base. The Army Air Force Technical Training Command took over Pine Needles Country Club in Southern Pines, North Carolina, though the course was kept open for play by soldiers and a smattering of civilians.

The most notable appropriation of a golf establishment was that of the Greenbrier in White Sulphur Springs, West Virginia, a landmark hotel with golf courses and Sam Snead as its host professional. The Greenbrier already had a history of assisting in a war effort; as battles waged nearby during the Civil War, the Greenbrier alternately served as Union and Confederate hospitals.

The Greenbrier was renowned for its mineral water and the curative powers it was said to possess. Guests frequently traveled there to "take the cure." It opened its first inn in 1780 and nearly from the outset had become the destination of choice for the Eastern elite. Confederate general Robert E. Lee often summered there. Joseph Kennedy and his new bride, Rose, honeymooned there. A host of presidents visited regularly, as did a variety of Carnegies, Rockefellers, and Vanderbilts.

President Roosevelt's secretary of state, Cordell Hull, had also been a visitor there. When the U.S. declared war on Japan and Germany, the secretary requested that the hotel allow diplomats and foreign news correspondents from enemy countries to be detained there. The Greenbrier's isolation would simplify the matter of guarding those who might be interned there. The hotel agreed. On December 19, 1941, Dr. Hans Thomsen, chargé d'affaires of the German Embassy, and his wife, left by limousine for the Greenbrier. Another party of 157—the rest of the German Embassy staff, German newspaper correspondents, as well as a dozen members of the Hungarian Legation staff—left for the resort via bus. The news put the Greenbrier on the front page of *The New York Times,* beneath the headline:

NAZI DIPLOMATS ARE SENT
TO WEST VIRGINIA RESORT

Suffice it to say, the Greenbrier was the finest, most comfortable, upscale POW camp in history, though it wasn't referred to as a POW camp. Those interned, the *Times* wrote, "will have full range of the hotel grounds, golf course, and recreation facilities while here for an indefinite stay, pending departure from the United States." Four days after they arrived, the fifteen German children in the group enjoyed a Christmas visit from Kris Kringle.

The news that the enemy was being quartered at the legendary hotel was not favorably received in the area. Angry residents held a meeting in Lewisburg nearby, but their fears were allayed when they were informed that American diplomats had been detained at Bad Nauheim, a German mineral spa. How the German diplomats were treated at the Greenbrier would be reflected in how the Americans would be treated at Bad Nauheim.

A prisoner exchange was completed by July 15, 1942, at which point the Greenbrier became a resort again, however temporarily. Six weeks later, the Army took it over under the War Powers Act and paid the owners, C & O Railroad, $3.3 million for a resort estimated to be worth $5.4 million. The Army wanted it as a hospital, one eventually dubbed "the Shangri-La for wounded soldiers."

Golf understood that business as usual was no longer possible, or even preferable, in one instance. The Chevy Chase Club in

Chevy Chase, Maryland, had conducted an annual tournament, the Japanese Trophy, until the Japanese attacked Pearl Harbor and declared war against the United States. The tournament was immediately scrapped and the Japanese Trophy was put in storage. "Guarantee to fill it with TNT and drop it on Hirohito and Chevy Chase probably will give you the prize," *Golfdom* magazine wrote.

THE CONTINENTAL UNITED STATES at least was safely removed from the war zone. Great Britain's proximity to the European continent made it a frequent target of Hitler's warplanes and dramatically altered its golf landscape.

Sandy Herd was a saddened eyewitness. A living treasure in Great Britain, a relic whose presence offered a temporary respite from the mayhem that Hitler had unleashed on the world, Herd was a reminder of better days, when the overriding concern in the auld country was not a Luftwaffe bomb landing in the living room, but perhaps a pot bunker guarding a green. He was British golf personified, equal parts royal and ancient, the latter by virtue of his seventy-four years. His crowning achievement was winning the British Open Championship in 1902, which along with his age gave him elder statesmanship in the British golf community. He had much to say and not much time to say it.

From his suburban London home, the old man had seen his beloved country decimated by German ambition that also threatened to destroy the game that he loved. The future of British golf was largely engaged in the war, talented young men whose ranks were certain to be noticeably thinner at the end of the war than they were at the beginning.

Between the bombings and through the tears, Herd even

played golf occasionally, though in the interest of conserving the diminishing time he had left in this world he surely took fewer waggles over the ball. His swing was once flawless by turn-of-the-century standards, and it always began with a series of waggles, too many to count, or so it seemed to those patiently awaiting the poetry that the ensuing rhythmic motion resembled. "The number of his waggles," the British golf writer Bernard Darwin wrote, "is only exceeded by that of his friends."

His friendship was his enduring gift to the game and those with whom he played it, that and the fact that he singularly revolutionized the game. Coburn Haskell, an employee of the Goodrich Tire and Rubber Company in the United States, had developed a ball with a rubber core that was wrapped with elastic thread and covered. In the 1902 Open at Hoylake, Herd reluctantly agreed to use the Haskell ball and was the only player in the field so daring. He then beat Harry Vardon and James Braid by a shot, a victory that effectively spelled the demise of the gutta-percha ball, the previous standard.

Everyone loves a winner, but in his case the admiration was genuine, and it had more to do with his demeanor than his Open success. His temperament was so even that it could have been charted with a straight edge, at least until the Germans began the London Blitz in the summer of 1940.

On August 15, 1940, one thousand Luftwaffe aircraft made their way across the English Channel, determined to rain death and destruction on the British. From his home outside London, Sandy Herd, in his seventies and attempting to fend off the infirmities that accompany the passage of time, was close enough to see and hear the carnage, to feel its wrath, the explosions filling his heart with a hatred of which he had never known he was capable. Each day brought more of the same. Then on September 4, Adolf Hitler strode to a podium and conjured up a ration of his trademark rage while delivering a speech in which he threatened to flatten the whole of Great Britain.

It was not regarded as an idle threat. A week later, Winston Churchill, the prime minister of the United Kingdom, delivered his own speech, warning the British that the Germans were preparing to invade and were gathering the requisite ships and troops for the impending assault. For its part, Britain had amassed an auxiliary defense force of more than one million Brits, who patrolled the coast, armed with anything that might be used as a weapon to fend off an advancing German, even golf clubs.

In the coastal town of Sandwich, southeast of London, was Royal St. George's, an historic links course on which eight British Opens had been played, the first in 1894. Its roll call of winners included Vardon and Walter Hagen, the latter famously responsible for issuing the reminder to stop and smell the roses. It was a grand sentiment that in 1940 was eviscerated by the overpowering stench of burning buildings that had had the misfortune of standing in the path of German bombshells.

Ronnie Crittenden was a member at Royal St. George's, and he smelled only doom. His club was situated directly on the flight path between the European continent and London, and he was certain that catastrophe was homing in on the historic old course. Antiaircraft guns had been installed on the course, which was akin to painting a giant bull's-eye on it. As an unarmed golf course, it would have appeared as nothing more than a meadow from an altitude of ten thousand feet. As a source of hostile fire, it became a Luftwaffe target. So Crittenden decided to play a farewell round. He enlisted his butler to carry his bag, which was a few ounces heavier than usual as a result of the bottle of champagne he'd brought along, a quaff for auld lang syne.

The wide, generally flat fairways of a number of historic seaside courses made them vulnerable to a German invasion. They had the potential to work as rudimentary landing strips for German aircraft.

One such course was the Rye Golf Club on England's southeastern coast, which had had its clubhouse damaged and nearly destroyed by enemy shells. Rye's fairways were nearly flat and featureless; were the Germans inclined to launch a land assault, the Rye Golf Club was an enticing staging ground. British soldiers recognized the inherent danger and added new hazards to the fairways: mines and barbed-wire barriers.

Other courses, including the revered Old Course at St. Andrews, took preventative measures as well, installing stakes and digging large trenches in their fairways to discourage landings by enemy aircraft. At Hoylake, the oldest seaside course in England (built in 1869) and the site of Bobby Jones's victory in the 1930 British Open en route to his winning the Grand Slam, greens that bordered the Dee Estuary were surrounded by miles of barbed wire. Searchlights installed near its famous Royal green illuminated the sky, hunting enemy aircraft. Belts of gorse, ordinarily there to act as debilitating rough that collected wayward shots, provided cover for snipers' posts.

Inland courses were vulnerable to Hitler's wrath as well, given their proximity to population centers. Richmond Golf Club featured a parkland course above the historic Market Town that had opened in 1892 and had been nearing its golden anniversary when it became a target. The members played on, though not without temporary rules to govern play in a time of war. When gunfire erupted or bombs were falling, players were generously allowed to seek shelter without incurring a penalty. If a ball in play were to have the misfortune of meeting its demise by Luftwaffe weaponry, the player could replace it, no nearer the hole, without penalty.

Golf might have been a Scottish invention, but the Germans were redefining what the Brits called hazards. German planes were creating their own version of the bunker, craters their bombs left on golf courses. They targeted the shipyards in Clydebank, near Glasgow, Scotland, and generally missed, their misdirected bombs leveling houses and inflicting damage to the Clydebank Golf Course. They left gaping holes in the fairways from which golfers were later required to play.

Turnberry, destined to join the rotation of British Open courses, transformed its course into an airport by constructing hangars and turning its fairways into landing strips for RAF planes. But as a result it became a Luftwaffe target too. German bombs left craters of a size that with a little sand might have made serviceable bunkers. The Turnberry Hotel, meanwhile, temporarily became a military hospital.

The Germans were writing history, but they were also destroying it. A scant six miles from the Old Course at St. Andrews, in the East Neuk of Fife, was Kingsbarns, the twelfth oldest course in the world, with written records establishing its existence as early as 1793. Villagers loved the old nine-hole course and took pride in its history, which included matches between teams from Kingsbarns and Crail, dating at least to the early nineteenth century, according to Crail records. Kingsbarns golfers wore blue jackets, while Crail golfers wore red.

The Fife coastline, however, represented an inviting site for a German invasion, given the links land that would have simplified the landing of watercraft. Moreover, the coastline was virtually undefended. The decision was made to appropriate Kingsbarns for military purposes, initially for maneuvers, and later for bombing practice, which essentially spelled its demise.

Petroleum shortages resulted in a ban on pleasure driving, requiring those wishing to pursue the game to take a train to the depot nearest the course, then strap their bag on their back and walk the rest of the way. Where trains weren't available, bicycles were used. One man of fifty-three was so determined to continue his weekly golf outing that he pedaled a bicycle eighteen miles to the course, played eighteen holes, then pedaled eighteen miles home every Sunday.

Golf balls were rationed, though players were still able to buy two new balls each time they played. However, fairways after the war resembled the rough before the war, and the rough after the war resembled the underbrush that a jungle might produce. A single errant shot could result in the loss of half a player's new-ball allotment. There were no caddies to assist in the search either. Perhaps the only similarity to prewar golf was the popularity of the nineteenth hole, which was as good a reason as any to play on.

Many British courses addressed a labor shortage by leaving the maintenance of their fairways to herds of grazing sheep. It was not uncommon for golfers to have to play over or around them. To prevent sheep from ruining greens, they were surrounded by electrical wiring. This was the brainchild of the staff at Research Station in Bingley, England. It installed two strands of fourteen-gauge wire, fifteen and thirty inches from the ground, respectively, and attached to posts at ten-yard intervals. A third wire seven or eight inches from the ground was used in the event that the herd had lambs. What the staff discovered was that the sheep who wandered into the wire and received an electrical shock quickly learned to avoid it, never grazing closer than nine inches from it. These educated sheep allowed the staff to shut down the electrical current during the day, to allow golfers to play on without concern of inadvertently shocking themselves.

British ingenuity manifested itself in myriad ways. The Wentworth Club outside London opened in 1924 and two years later hosted what was the forerunner of the Ryder Cup. A complex bunker was built forty-five feet beneath the clubhouse as an emergency headquarters for those running the war. The bunker was accessed via the laundry room and a long sloping tunnel constructed with the same equipment used in building London's Tube. Concrete six feet thick and presumed to be strong enough to withstand bombs was used for the walls. An escape tunnel was built, which would have deposited those leaving in a hurry somewhere near the eighteenth green on the East course.

The Wentworth bunker was never used. The outmanned British responded admirably to the German assault and repelled the enemy, and in the process discouraged their launching an invasion. The threat of bombs falling in and around London had subsided, but Britons' rage continued unabated. Sandy Herd felt it as he sat down in May of 1942 to write a letter to his friend D. Scott Chisholm, a Scottish golf writer living in America. A thousand thoughts began competing for inclusion on the blank pages in front of Herd, but melancholy and nostalgia gave way to resentment and hate, all of it infused with the guilt that occasionally haunts those who take stock of their lives in a time of strife and discover that they've been unduly blessed.

The letter was from the heart, one that was by turns light and airy and vengeful. What emerged from the pen of this seventy-four-year-old man who was nearing the end of his life was an honest assessment of golf in the United Kingdom and his wish to take one last stab at an opponent, should the opportunity present itself. It read in part:

Dear Davie,

. . . We have quite a lot of golf played here. There are a great many folks over here who are glad of a break as most of them are

all OUT—to win the war. . . . It is exactly 12 months since we had the last hell upon earth here. London, from my club, looked like a great fireworks display. One would have thought that it was entirely gone. But it is still there and she's going to stay right there. . . .

I have three grand-daughters, a grandson, and others all in this job of war—two sons also—and if the Hun ever attempts to invade this country old man Herd wouldn't be idle as I have a debt to pay these swine back. They made one of my daughters and her four children homeless. They lost all and luckily they were all in a shelter at the time. There were many killed all around her so if I ever get a chance, I'll stick the first son of a German I come across no matter his size or age. I have a big long knife all ready for the slaughter hanging by my side.

I was 74 last April—just 40 years since I won the British Open—and I am feeling not so bad these days. . . . I am now playing a few rounds per week and can sometimes beat my age. I can't punch so hard these days but I'm never off the line and I can thank God for the short shotties. . . .

There is no professional golf over here except for Red Cross. I see there's to be some sort of an Open near Chicago in June so if you get there, look up my brother Jim and my nephew Bruce. Also give my best to old pals such as Hagen, Sarazen, Bobby Jones, Mac Smith, and all my other friends over in America.

That Hogan lad must be awful good. But you have in America today so many great ones. By their performances I feel the old country, by the time this war is over, will be very badly off for talent as all our young players are in some service and a great many getting killed in the air. Mrs. Herd sends her best—so do all the family. I hope we shall meet again some day but I have me doots aboot it.

All the best from your friend,
Sandy Herd

Herd's concern that the future of British golf was being eradicated by enemy fire was well founded. Dale Bourne, runner-up in the British Amateur in 1933, was killed in action. Another renowned amateur, Count John Bendern, known in America as John de Forest, the 1932 British Amateur champion and a member of the Great Britain–Ireland Walker Cup team in 1932, was taken prisoner in Libya. A faction of British golf history was in harm's way as well. Cyril Tolley, who had lost to Bobby Jones, one-up, in a memorable fourth-round match in the British Amateur in 1930, was a major with the British Army in this, his second war stint. Tolley had been an officer in the Tank Corps during the First World War. Richard Burton, the 1939 British Open champion, was commissioned a pilot-officer in the RAF.

But golfers were a stalwart group, determined as they were to continue playing their games around and through the bombing raids. A Royal Air Force pilot shot down over Kent, England, during the Battle of Britain parachuted to safety but was bloodied and required first aid. He was taken to a local golf club, where he overheard golfers on the eighteenth green complaining that the noise the Luftwaffe planes were making overhead was impairing their concentration.

6

AUTUMN LEAVES AND A SPALDING DOT

Shortages Hit Golf

A Spalding Dot had become the equivalent of a gold nugget by the autumn of 1942—rare and valuable. The ball famine had arrived as predicted, and the Spalding Dot, the finest ball made, had joined the endangered species list.

At the Algonquin Golf Club in the St. Louis suburb of Glendale, there were no Spalding Dots to be found other than those in the locker of R. C. Geekie, one of the better players in the club. Mr. Geekie was a polished player and demanded that his equipment reflect the quality of his golf. In addition to his collection of Spalding Dots, he also owned a set of custom-made Louisville woods and irons. The woods were works of art, polished persimmon, with white nylon inserts.

His equipment and the superiority of his game weren't alone in setting him apart. He was also identifiable by his hair, which had arrived at midlife ahead of the rest of him. It was prematurely gray, and he parted it fancifully *down the middle*—familiar terrain for a golfer whose handicap seldom ventured beyond two.

Mr. Geekie's regular caddie was Larry Etzkorn, a thirteen-year-old otherwise known as Skinhead in the caddie shack at Algonquin. The assignation of colorful nicknames has always been a rite of passage in the caddie shack. At Algonquin, there were Red Ryder Reilley, Wino Sullivan, Crow Nose Keller, Iron Eyes McDonnell, and Tattoo Keller. Etzkorn became Skinhead by virtue of his crew cut, one of the first haircuts of its kind among the neighborhood kids.

Skinhead Etzkorn had begun caddying for Mr. Geekie in the summer of 1941. They were a compatible pair; Etzkorn's appeal was his reliability, an important trait for an employer disinclined to stray from routine, while Mr. Geekie's appeal was that he paid well. For an eighteen-hole loop, Skinhead Etzkorn received the standard $1.25, augmented by a generous tip from Mr. Geekie.

Every caddie's job was tenuous by the fall of '42, however, even the reliable Skinhead Etzkorn's. By then, a caddie's chief responsibility was to keep his eye on the ball. The ball shortage brought about by the need to use available rubber for war-related purposes was becoming a real threat to the game, and a caddie allowing his man to lose a decent one was grounds for dismissal. This was not a considerable concern for Etzkorn, who had a man who did not miss many fairways. Mr. Geekie's marksmanship fit neatly into his predictable nature. So did the fact that at the turn of every round he would announce that he was heading into the clubhouse for "a little hair oil." Moreover, he always seemed to play better on the back nine than the front, which may or may not have had something to do with the hair oil, as well as the fact that it wasn't his hair that was getting oiled. Mr. Geekie also always played with the same set of characters. (They included J. R. Keraney Jr., whose principal objective was to win the club championship. Toward that end, Keraney went so far as to hire Henry Picard, the 1938 Masters champion, to give him a nine-hole playing lesson at Algonquin every Friday throughout the summer, an ambitious undertaking insofar as Picard was living in Cleveland at the time.)

One memorable Saturday afternoon in the fall of 1942, Mr. Geekie was playing one of his valuable Spalding Dots. After nine holes, he announced per his custom that he was repairing to the clubhouse for "a little hair oil." When he returned to the golf course a few minutes later, he was a new man, fortified for his assault on the back nine.

He strode to the tenth tee, where Skinhead Etzkorn handed him his prized persimmon driver. However, his was not the most formidable wood at the Algonquin Golf Club, which featured a short, narrow course thickly lined with wood, mostly post oak, red oak, and elm. The trees framed the course beautifully, but they stood sentry, capably defending the integrity of par by knocking down wayward shots. The trees were even more of a menace in the fall, when they shed their leaves. Invariably, a ball would vanish among the litter of leaves, ostensibly never to be seen again.

The tenth hole at Algonquin featured a ninety-degree dogleg left, the fairway bending around a pond. The skilled player generally attempted to drive his ball over the corner of the pond, substantially shortening the hole. On the near side of the pond was a swale, into which thousands of brilliantly colored leaves had gathered, at a depth of two feet in many places.

Mr. Geekie teed his Spalding Dot and took a careless swipe at it. As a quantity of "hair oil" is wont to do, it had thrown his tempo awry, and he duck-hooked his tee shot short of the pond. The ball rolled into the swale and disappeared beneath the pile of leaves. Uncertain of its whereabouts, he teed another ball and hit a provisional, this one landing safely in the fairway. When Mr. Geekie and Skinhead Etzkorn arrived at the swale, an exhaustive search followed. Still unable to locate the dimpled gemstone, an angry Mr. Geekie gave up and instructed Skinhead Etzkorn to go wait for him by his provisional ball. Etzkorn retrieved his man's golf bag, and as he began walking away, he glanced back at Mr. Geekie, who, to his horror, was stooping, matches in hand, and setting the leaves ablaze.

"If I can't find it, neither will anyone else," Mr. Geekie muttered to himself.

The dried leaves did not need encouragement to form a raging bonfire. It took only a matter of seconds.

"Oh, my God," Skinhead Etzkorn thought. "We're burning the whole neighborhood down."

Beyond the trees were houses, whose inhabitants did not immediately take notice of the blaze that was not all that far from their backyards. It was not until Mr. Geekie and his playing partners reached the eleventh green that they heard sirens. Only the foursome and their caddies ever knew who started the fire.

By the end of the round, Mr. Geekie was no longer angry. He'd won money, notwithstanding the errant tee shot at ten. Skinhead Etzkorn kept his mouth shut, as any good caddie would, and retained his job. As for the miscreant Spalding Dot, it was never found.

THE BALL CRISIS was proving more than an inconvenience in a game that for some resembled an addiction. There is no fix without golf balls, and the prospect of running out of them deprived otherwise ordinary men of their moral equilibrium. One driving range in the vicinity of New York City estimated that in a single Sunday afternoon as many as six hundred fifty of its practice balls disappeared. The count was too high to attribute to wayward shots that the range's netting was incapable of stopping. Their disappearance was clearly an act of thievery.

There were those who accepted the vanishing supply of golf balls in good humor. A magazine cartoon, for instance, showed an armored car parked in front of a house. Three armed guards watched the perimeter, while a fourth, clutching a pistol in one hand and a small bag in the other, asked the man of the house, "Where do you want this golf ball?"

A column by Larry Smith, written in the form of an open letter in an issue of *Golfing*, facetiously suggested several new local rules designed to prevent the loss of even a single valuable golf ball. Among them:

- There is an assertion on the card that children under 10 are not permitted on the course. Change this. Encourage their attendance. They might find a ball.
- The local rules frown on fivesomes. This must also be stricken. Fivesomes, tensomes—the more the better. Let the whole membership tee off together. Somebody is certain to see any ball that leaves the tee.
- Anyone who even attempted to drive across a lake would be penalized two strokes.

Golfers jokingly discussed buying life insurance for their golf balls, in the event that one of them drowned or was bludgeoned to death by a bellied iron. Others wryly suggested putting locks on the ball compartments of their golf bags, a hedge against the pickpocket looking to shore up his own dwindling supply. This was as close to the truth as it was to a joke. Gulph Mills Golf Club, a Philadelphia-area course, actually stored its supply of balls in a bank vault.

Many players began hoarding balls, further contributing to the shortage. George Pulver, the pro at McGregor Links in

Saratoga, New York, was concerned that without rationing, clubs might be forced to buy back balls from members who had stockpiled them, no doubt at a substantial profit to the sellers. "Either buy the balls back at a premium to keep peace in the club and fulfill their function," he said, "or be out of luck."

An anonymous author writing for *Golfing* magazine penned this searing poetic epitaph to a fictional character who selfishly hoarded golf balls:

> *The rotting bones of Gruntwald*
> *Puttermoss lie here;*
> *He grabbed six dozen golf balls*
> *To play five times a year.*
> *He tried to sell his surplus*
> *For more than we could pay.*
> *And now the worms are welcome*
> *To Gruntwald's mortal clay.*

Some saw the ball shortage as an opportunity to cash in. Among them was John Clancy, the professional at Mosholu Golf Course in Van Cortlandt Park in the Bronx in New York City. Clancy took a box and cut a small round hole in the top. He placed the box in the center of the golf shop at Mosholu and encouraged customers to drop a used ball through the hole. In exchange, they would get a draw on a punchboard and a chance at winning a new ball. A punchboard was a gambling device popular in saloons; it featured a board with several small holes, each containing a slip of paper that told the gambler whether he had won. Clancy's board featured slips that told them whether they'd won a new golf ball. If they lost, no harm done; they had merely rid themselves of a ball they no longer wanted anyway.

Clancy in turn would take the old balls and return them to

the factory at which they had been made. He had them resurfaced for three dollars a dozen, then resold them at a healthy profit, at least until the authorities learned of his gaming operation. A plainclothes patrolman witnessed the operation, then moved in and arrested Clancy. He was escorted to Bronx Magistrate's Court, where he was charged with operating a gambling device.

Ball manufacturers quickly recognized that their survival required alternatives, including the refurbishing of used balls, increasingly few of which were ever discarded. For instance, the entry fee for a Blind Bogey at White Lakes Country Club in Topeka, Kansas, was five used balls.

On the practice tee at the Masters earlier in the year, Sam Snead and Gene Sarazen each tested a passel of Wilson balls that had been refurbished using the "potato peeler" method. This was a technique that required balls with cuts that were only superficial, no deeper than the cover. They were placed onto a machine that employed an abrasive action to peel the cover until the cut had been eliminated. The ball was then re-covered with the same kind of balata used for a new ball. "They rolled out of the box lopsided," Snead said.

But when Snead and Sarazen each hit a variety of wood and iron shots with these kinds of refurbished balls, they found to their surprise that they performed as well as new balls, even inexplicably proving more stable on shots hit into the wind. Sarazen was so encouraged that he even played the second round of the Masters using a refurbished ball. He shot 74 with it and declared it a suitable replacement. Sarazen later warned the golfing public against discarding used balls. He urged golfers to have their used golf balls reprocessed, lest "next year you'll be swinging at potatoes," he said.

The ball shortage was so acute and the forecast so bleak that professionals squeezed as much use from a single ball as they could. Snead claimed he used the same ball once for fifty-four straight holes, after which, he said, it was so soft that he could pinch it between his fingers. Hyperbole was his calling card, of course, but a balata-covered golf ball was incapable of withstanding the recurring impact imparted by a top professional. Snead wore it out quickly but continued to use it nonetheless.

One company, Hercules Powder, made an unsuccessful attempt at innovation. It constructed an all-plastic golf ball that was said to be ninety percent as long as regular balls. However, it was rock hard, and the golfer who hit one felt the reverberations all the way up the arms.

The ball famine rendered losing them an unacceptable outcome. For instance, an advertisement in the *Pinehurst Outlook* in Pinehurst, North Carolina, carried the headline SAVE GOLF BALLS. It was an ad offering instruction geared toward hitting the ball on the sweet spot to reduce ball wear and the prospect of losing balls. Golfers still lost them at the same rate as before, but now it had become imperative that they be found. Toward that end, the prestigious Westchester Country Club in Rye, New York, hired professional divers to retrieve balls from its murky ponds, oystermen, in a sense, diving for pearls. The Black Rock Club in Atlanta eschewed the diver in favor of pulling the plug. It drained its ponds, then simply scooped up the bounty—an estimated sixteen thousand balls. From the "Off the Fairway" column in the *San Francisco Examiner:* "One of the richest caches of old golf balls is in the water of the cove between the tee and green at Cypress Point's two-hundred-twenty-yard sixteenth." One of the best par 3's in the world, the sixteenth at Cypress required a carry over a chasm of sea that had an insatiable appetite for golf balls struck with anything less than a perfect swing.

Winter rules, officially known as preferred lies, became more rule than exception the year round, as a means of minimizing wear and tear on balls that were increasingly in short supply. Better to award lesser-skilled players with perfect lies than to have them slay a good ball with an ungainly hack ill-suited to remove it from the divot in which it had come to rest.

The Japanese curiously had no such ball issues, or so they would have the Americans believe. The Japanese Welfare Ministry declared on a radio broadcast monitored by an American news agency that its citizens continued to participate in sports, the war notwithstanding, and that to assist those who called themselves golfers, it announced that it had arranged to distribute more than ninety thousand dozen new rubber golf balls throughout the country by the middle of the month. The cynical media, noting the date of the missive (April 1, 1942), wondered whether it was some kind of April Fool's propaganda.

The hard truth is that a war effort siphons substantial quantities of products and materials from the general populace, often creating shortages and requiring rationing. Rubber and gasoline were among the products that were rationed, creating a logistical nightmare: A man who needed a new tire first went to the rationing board, which checked its records to ensure that he had not used his allotment of new tires. Once assured, the board gave the man a form that required signatures from two separate garages, vouching for the fact that the damaged tire could not be repaired. Once the signatures were obtained, the man had to return to the rationing board, which then issued him a coupon that entitled him to purchase a new tire, assuming he could find one in the proper size and without expending extra gas in searching for one.

Transportation, obviously, became an immediate concern for the golf industry, which depended as much on gasoline (and working tires) as on golf balls to sustain itself. Golf courses were not typically built near city squares and population centers, where they'd have been readily accessible via public transportation. Courses were built where open land allowed them to be built, on the outskirts of towns, usually beyond the reach of bus lines or train stops. Their subsistence depended largely on automobiles powered by gasoline that was now in short supply.

Gas rationing began to spell the demise of outlying courses. Shelburne Farms Golf Links was among them. It had opened on the shore of Vermont's Lake Champlain in 1895, the first North American design of Scottish architect Willie Park Jr. The course was so remote that it failed to generate enough business to keep it operating and it passed into history, reverting to pastureland shortly after the outset of the war in 1942.

At the prestigious Merion Golf Club in Ardmore, Pennsylvania, members began to see their gas mileage diminish dramatically, until they figured out why: A thief was siphoning gas from their cars at night, requiring that the club install floodlights as a deterrent.

The restrictions on pleasure driving forced clubs and public courses to develop creative ways to bring golfers to the first tee. A pair of Detroit clubs, Hilltop and Plymouth, offered a dollar credit toward pro shop purchases to those driving to the club with three or more golfers in tow. One course moved the first tee to the players. The closest the bus stopped to the clubhouse at Meridian Municipal Golf Course in Meridian, Connecticut, was by the fifteenth hole. Course management decided to allow golfers arriving via bus to begin their rounds on the fifteenth hole and dispatched a starter there to collect their green fees.

The renowned Pinehurst resort in Pinehurst, North Carolina, advertised its "dry, invigorating pine air" and its ability to "relax tight nerves and build up your reserve of energy." Its ads noted that no automobile was necessary; the resort could be accessed "overnight from New York via Seaboard R.R."

The gasoline shortage made horsepower popular again. Canoe Brook Country Club in Summit, New Jersey, purchased a team of horses and a tallyho, a carriage that required four horses to pull it. Golfers paid a fare of twenty-five cents for a roundtrip from the Summit railroad station to the course and back. Glen Oaks in Lakeville, on Long Island, had enough horsepower to ferry fifty golfers simultaneously from the train station to the club. Baltusrol Golf Club in Springfield, New Jersey, responded swiftly when gas rationing was instituted, by buying a pair of horse-drawn carriages, securing the use of horses to pull them, and constructing stalls to house them.

Even the bicycle attempted a comeback. There was a time that it was among the principal modes of golf transport, as *The New York Times* noted on May 30, 1897. It wrote then, "The bicycle costume answers equally well for the links and one of the notable sights is the large number of bicycles always seen in the racks at the Morristown [N.J.] Club."

A golfer arrived at Bethpage Park in Farmingdale, Long Island, one day in June 1942, on a bicycle, his clubs in tow. However, he never came back; presumably the awkwardness of pedaling a bicycle with golf clubs strapped to his back was a burden he was unwilling to endure more than once.

POTENTIALLY THE MOST disturbing shortage was revealed at the annual meeting of the Club Managers Association of America, at the Drake Hotel in Chicago in March of '42. Among the speakers was Laurens W. Cook Jr., president of the Illinois Hotel Foundation, who in the midst of his otherwise wearisome speech delivered the kind of news that will jolt a slumbering audience to rapt attention: Cook warned that the country's liquor supply was in jeopardy as a result of the war. An audible gasp went up from the audience, whose clientele largely viewed the game as one played not over eighteen holes, but over nineteen holes, the nineteenth hole largely a raison d'être for the first eighteen. In wine is truth, the old proverb says, and the truth is that golfers collectively would have preferred a ball shortage to a liquor shortage.

Cook guessed that the supply of bourbon would run out in two and a half years at the normal rate of consumption. Scotch, he said, was even more scarce, a year's supply at most still available. As for gin, "I think if we have any more for the duration of the war we are just going to be lucky," he said. He also reported that the government was exploring the possibility of taking over four varieties of California grapes, to use them for raisins rather than wine. To this crowd, which was responsible for the services provided at clubs, including food and beverage, Cook was talking grapes of wrath.

The Merion Golf Club went so far as to dispatch employees to liquor stores near and far, asking them to buy up whatever supplies were available, often only a bottle at a time. One such store was found with a substantial supply of scotch, however; its customers simply did not ask for it much. So Merion traded a case of rye for a case of scotch.

A more immediate concern proved to be the evaporating availability of caddies. A preponderance of older boys from the caddie ranks had gone off to war. The younger caddies began to fulfill other, more important jobs vacated by older boys. Even the government identified the caddie shack as a potential source of labor for more important endeavors, according to a letter written on U.S. Department of Agriculture letterhead, dated March 13, 1942, and addressed to the Associated Golfers of America:

Gentlemen:

There appears to be a great shortage of labor in the vicinity of Chicago on the vegetable producing farms. The type of labor required on these farms could easily be handled by boys of grade school age. This is the same age group which acts as caddies on golf courses.

    I would like to suggest that if your organization feels that they could make some contributions to the labor shortage around Chicago that you get in touch with Mr. Carl M. Bormet, Chairman of the County USGA War Board, 2412 W. Grove St., Blue Island, and arrange for a conference.

    I am sure that every patriotic American is willing to do his part in this war effort.

Very truly yours,
Lee M. Gentry, Chairman
Illinois USDA War Board

Golf's hierarchy recognized the necessity of putting aside selfish inclinations, though initially not to the extent that they would consider toting their own bags as a viable option. Thought was given to employing female caddies, though there were some who concluded that the "fairer sex" was not up to the task of lugging a weighty golf bag up and down hills for four hours. A story in *Golfdom* magazine bluntly addressed the issue of employing girls:

Yes, it makes good publicity, but let's be sensible about it. Even if we could get some Amazons to tote our bags and even if we cut them down to three clubs and a Sunday bag, do the officials want to run the danger of injury and physical strain to the girls?

    Then there is the question that they are girls, after all. Pictures show them in shorts. Why? Can the boys keep their minds on the game that way? The shorts mean attraction, don't they? Who dressed them that way? And how about taking them back to town? No, I think the careful club will avoid the employment of girl caddies.

The caddie shack remained largely a male bastion—no need to distract the golfing brotherhood unnecessarily when it's facing an important birdie putt—although not all the male caddies were happy with their treatment. The pro at Monroe Golf and Country Club in Monroe, Michigan, decided that on behalf of the war effort the caddies should be tipped in war stamps, an idea that the younger loopers embraced enthusiastically. The older caddies, meanwhile, still preferred cash, a commodity that worked better in procuring a pint or a place at the poker table.

More than caddies were scarce; the entire workforce at private clubs had thinned as a result of the help going to war. For well-heeled club members who were accustomed to leaving the manual labor to others, this represented a crisis. The exclusive Los Angeles Country Club, for instance, was a bastion of local power and wealth. Imagine the members' horror when the supply of help dwindled to the point that their world-class golf course threatened to go to seed. The solution was only moderately more appealing; the members might dirty a manicured nail by lending a hand. As an enticement, the club offered free beer and lunch (in that order) to members willing to help weed the fairways.

The war routinely interfered with the quality of life for which the wealthy were willing to pay handsomely. Among the unwelcome restraints on them was the fact that their servants were summoned to help out in more important endeavors, notably defeating the Germans and Japanese. The increasing scarcity of domestic help, however, proved a boon to country-club dining-room traffic.

Even there, shortages prevailed. Sugar was among the products in short supply and it, too, required rationing. The membership at Westmoreland Country Club reminded diners of the diminishing supply there by placing on each table a small card—patriotically printed in red, white, and blue—on which was written:

LESS SWEET

FOR THE YAP

MEANS

FINIS FOR THE JAP

WESTMORELAND COOPERATES

Though members and guests, poetry aficionados surely, routinely filched the cards, sugar consumption at Westmoreland declined to less than one teaspoonful per meal per member, guest, or employee—a harbinger, surely, of what was in store for the Japanese.

In the meantime, the Japanese had more pressing concerns: Bob Hope and Bing Crosby were on the warpath. Improbable as it sounded, they were ready to join the Navy (or so they said), volunteering their services, Hope and Crosby, *On the Road to Norfolk*, for basic training. On December 7, 1941, Hope and Crosby were guests of Elliott Roosevelt, at his home in Colorado Springs, Colorado. When news of the Japanese attack on Pearl Harbor reached them, they declared themselves ready to enlist. Elliott began making calls on their behalf, one to Frank Knox, the secretary of the Navy, another to Elliott's father, President Franklin Delano Roosevelt, at the White House.

Hope and Crosby were already on the road to show business immortality, each of them having become a film star in complement to the skills that launched his career—Hope and his comic riffs and Crosby and his crooning. Moreover, Crosby had just recorded Irving Berlin's new song "White Christmas" for the film *Holiday Inn*, and it was already a hit. They were entertainment icons who believed passionately that success without benevolence was empty, that giving back was their civic duty. They were ready to serve their country in its hour of need. Where, they asked, do they sign?

Their intentions were noble, if misguided. What did they intend to do, pummel the enemy with a soft-shoe? They were entertainers, not ensigns, and both were approaching their fortieth birthdays. Roosevelt recognized that their value to the war effort was not in a torpedo room, but on a stage, or a golf course. He asked that they continue to do what they had been doing, essentially ordering them to play golf, then perform a little vaudeville for the folks. For much of the year preceding America's entry into the war, Hope and Crosby had played exhibition matches to raise money for the War Relief Fund. Roosevelt's request was the impetus behind the two of them forming their Victory Caravan, which they did later in the year. Each week they intended to travel to a different military base and perform a show that doubled as a radio broadcast. Often, the two of them would schedule golf exhibitions in conjunction with the broadcast.

Then in February 1942, at Crosby's annual clambake, the Bing Crosby Pro-Am, at Rancho Santa Fe Country Club in north San Diego County, PGA president Ed Dudley and tournament bureau manager Fred Corcoran enlisted the help of Crosby and Hope over lunch. Dudley asked whether they'd be amenable to playing a series of exhibition golf matches under the auspices of the PGA during its Texas swing, each of them pairing with a tour star, to raise money for defense bonds and war relief. Tour stars could draw a crowd consisting only of those with an interest in golf. Bringing Hope and Crosby into the mix would enable the exhibitions to transcend golf, inviting thousands of those who had never before set foot on a golf course to traipse onto one simply in hopes of catching a glimpse of a couple of entertainment icons. In turn, a veritable mob scene was certain to turn out, exponentially expanding the bottom line. The two of them quickly agreed.

Hope and Crosby made their PGA exhibition debut on February 11, 1942, at Brook Hollow Golf Club in Dallas, Texas, an event *The Dallas Morning News* was calling "Dallas's most glamorous golf show of all time." Joining them were golf stars Ben Hogan and Byron Nelson, each of them a native of nearby Fort Worth, and Lawson Little and Jimmy Demaret of Houston. Actor and former Olympic swimming star Johnny Weismuller also agreed to play.

A crowd of four thousand was anticipated, "the largest gallery in Dallas links history," the *Morning News* wrote. Instead, seven thousand turned out and began lining the first fairway even before the stars were finished with their lunch in the Brook Hollow clubhouse. They finished lunch prematurely, all but Hope; a fire broke out in the Brook Hollow kitchen, sounding a fire alarm that emptied the place. Only Hope, who had just launched into a tongue sandwich, remained behind. "I'm staying," he said. "This meat needs to be cooked a little more."

Hope and Crosby also played a fund-raiser the following day at Brae Burn Country Club in Houston. Hope paired with Nelson and Crosby with Demaret, while Weismuller essentially played along for kicks, spending most of his time in the trees, where he belonged, he said, as the star of the film *Tarzan*. This time the crowd reached an estimated ten thousand, the largest gallery in the history of Texas golf, exceeding even that of the U.S. Open played the year before at Colonial Country Club in Fort Worth. The match wound up halved. Individually, Nelson shot 70, Demaret 71, Crosby 78, and Hope 80. The number that mattered, however, was $30,000, the sum donated to the war effort.

More than two thirds of that, $22,500, was raised afterward, when Hope auctioned off several of Crosby's albums. One buyer bid $1,500 for a set of five Crosby albums, valued at thirty-five cents apiece were he to have bought them in a store. Several thousand dollars more were collected the following day, when Hope, Crosby, and Weismuller participated in the pro-am prior to the start of the Texas Open in San Antonio.

Three days of exhibition golf produced a net of nearly $50,000 in defense bond sales and war relief contributions. The exhibitions were eye-opening demonstrations of how a game whose popularity mystifies those who don't play it can shed its arrogance and elevate its stature with an economic boost to the Allied war effort.

The key was an attractive mix of tour stars and celebrities from other fields. In the run-up to the Hale America National Open Golf Tournament, Hope teamed with reigning U.S. Open champion Craig Wood and defeated former PGA Championship winner Vic Ghezzi, now an Army corporal, and former baseball star Babe Ruth, 4 and 2, at the Forest Hill Field Club in Bloomfield, New Jersey. The exhibition attracted more than two thousand fans who contributed in excess of $2,000 for Army and Navy Relief.

The Victory Caravan, meanwhile, was scheduled to encompass sixty-five cities. Crosby joined it on May 5, 1942, in Chicago, and a day later played his first exhibition match as part of the caravan. The Edgewater Golf Club was the host and the funds were earmarked for the Fort Sheridan Athletics and Recreation Fund. The Edgewater was a private club whose bylaws need not have included a dress code requiring that only deep pockets were allowed among the membership, for it was generally understood that Edgewater was not for the economically disadvantaged. It was the kind of club that in peacetime never would have considered hosting an event to which the public would be invited to storm its gates and soil its turf. The fact that soldiers would be the beneficiary of the exhibition rendered it palatable to the members.

Hope and Crosby were to play with Tommy Armour and Chick Evans. Armour was a World War I veteran, while Evans, a former U.S. Open and U.S. Amateur champion, had played a series of fund-raisers during World War I, helping generate more than $300,000 for the war effort.

The day was a gloomy, uninviting one—rainy, cold, and windy. Crosby already had a cold and was advised by his doctor to forgo the golf and remain indoors to rest for the Victory Caravan performance scheduled for that night. Hope, meanwhile, had a mild case of laryngitis; he, too, was told by his doctor to stay out of the cold. Old show-biz hands know intuitively that the show must go on, and both neglected their doctors' orders.

Afterward, one of the club's well-heeled members lamented the inclement weather that prevented a crowd of more than twenty thousand from turning out. A reporter, attempting to pander to the membership, wondered aloud what that many people trampling the course would have done to it. The member, who in peacetime would have scoffed at allowing a foursome from the public sector to play his country club, became indignant at the preposterous nature of the suggestion.

"Well, they'd pay twenty thousand dollars so the boys at Fort Sheridan could have some fun while they've still got a chance," the member said, "and who'd give a damn about a little damage to grass after seeing today's papers?"

Crosby and Chick Evans defeated Hope and Tommy Armour,

2-up, over nine holes, while Crosby bettered Hope, 1-up, in his personal match on which a fistful of cash changed hands. This was a match that set the tone for the entire exhibition tour. The crowd was so unruly that the final nine holes had to be canceled. Any appearance by Hope and Crosby transcended golf once the gates opened and the public was ushered in. Golf decorum was generally a foreign concept to the crowds.

Another match was scheduled for the following day at Meadowbrook Country Club in St. Louis. This time Crosby teamed with trick-shot artist Bob Morse and defeated Hope and host pro Johnny Manion, 1-up, over twelve holes. Again the match was abbreviated as a result of the crowd of two thousand paying no heed to golf etiquette.

This was the way it was going to be whenever the two of them teed it up for public consumption. For one such match, at Tam O'Shanter Club in Chicago, thousands ringed the tee box and fairway at the fourth hole, few of them versed in the etiquette of golf. It wasn't golf they were there to see, of course. They were there to see a soft-shoe, perhaps, or vaudeville on a meticulously manicured stage of grass.

"Hey, Hope," a self-anointed comedian yelled from the crowd as Hope was addressing his ball. "Your slip is showing."

Hope gracefully stepped away from his ball, wheeled, and, with the pinpoint timing of an authentic comedian, replied, "Your father's slip is showing."

The crowd erupted in a chorus of laughter. Crosby laughed so hard that he had tears in his eyes. Each of them took their golf seriously, but were less inclined to take themselves seriously. They relished beating each other, yet even in the course of a spirited match, they were unable to suppress the showmanship that had made them stars of stage and screen. They both had twin passions—an audience and golf. A course then became a perfect stage on which to perform in the interest of raising money on behalf of war relief. They knew how to entertain, a skill for which most golfers were found lacking. Hope, for instance, arrived late for one particular fund-raiser. When he finally walked onto the first tee, he dropped his bag at Crosby's feet and said, "Take this bag, son," evoking raucous laughter.

At the first hole, Crosby took an inordinate amount of time lining up his birdie putt. Finally, he asked a caddie, "Have the greens been cut today?" The caddie nodded yes. When it was Hope's turn to putt, he mimicked Crosby's preputt routine, including the final act of crouching behind the ball for a final peek at the line, at which point he looked toward the same caddie, and asked, "What time?"

The success of the Hope and Crosby exhibitions piqued the interest of a host of entertainers, who volunteered to participate on behalf of the war effort. Among them were Randolph Scott, Fred Astaire, Mickey Rooney, Jack Benny, Ronald Reagan, Humphrey Bogart, Harpo Marx, and the ventriloquist Edgar Bergen and his dummy, Charlie McCarthy. Rooney, Bergen, and McCarthy, along with former U.S. Amateur champion George Von Elm, planned a fund-raising golf tour that included stops in Salt Lake City, Denver, and San Francisco. Jack Benny and Fred Allen agreed to take their faux stage feud onto the golf course, teaming with Gene Sarazen and Walter Hagen. The Marx Brothers and the Ritz Brothers agreed to play, as did a foursome of Randolph Scott, Fred Astaire, Humphrey Bogart, and the Singing Cowboy, Gene Autry. Even the women of stage and screen were volunteering to put their golf skills on display for this worthy cause, including Katharine Hepburn, Jane Wyman, and Ruby Keeler.

Golf pros, meanwhile, continued to work before lesser crowds, but their contributions were no less important, particularly for the beneficiaries. When Wiffy Cox and Joe Turnesa teamed against Willie Klein and Jack Mallon in an exhibition at Rockville Country Club in Rockville Center, Long Island, they raised enough money to send one million cigarettes to servicemen overseas—proof beyond the ball crisis that the game, indeed, was going up in smoke.

7

HUNKERING DOWN

An Elite Sport Comes Under Attack

A dozen years earlier, Bobby Jones had stood atop a hill in the quiet town of Augusta, Georgia, and pensively and covetously gazed down at the land that would become the Augusta National Golf Club. He pictured in his mind an exquisite golf course unfolding beneath him, and never for a moment had he envisioned an odorous cow pasture there. Ruefully, he would get both.

By October 1, 1942, it had become evident that the war was destined to endure. Only a few days earlier, German troops had reached the center of Stalingrad. Hitler was fighting a multifront war, though his army had yet to exhibit vulnerability on any front. The Pacific Theater promised a long and deadly conflict.

Augusta was a national club by design, its members largely living elsewhere. In peacetime, traveling there was logistically complex. In wartime, with gasoline rationing, it was virtually impossible for members to make the trek, even for those living in Atlanta ninety miles away. Moreover, many of the club's 128 members, Jones among them, were in uniform and in all likelihood would have neither the time nor the inclination to make the trip to play the course. The town's hotels, meanwhile, were in the process of being appropriated by the Army.

Jones and Clifford Roberts, the club's cofounders, recognized that their options had dwindled to one: Close the club for the duration of the war. Actually, there was a second option, but one that neither wished to consider at that point, that of closing the club for good, writing it off as a good idea gone bad. It had never been solvent, anyway, despite the affluence of the membership. One influential member even informed Roberts of his regrets over the demise of the club.

On October 1, 1942, Roberts mailed letters to the members, announcing that the club was closing for the duration of the war. "Some months ago we cut down our staff to just a skeleton maintenance crew," Roberts wrote, "but the golf course and the plants are being properly cared for and we can prepare to open just as soon as the war's end is definitely in sight." The letter also announced that the 1943 Masters was canceled and that the tournament would not resume until the war was over. It was an easy decision, if a bitter one. In the spring, Byron Nelson and Ben Hogan had given the Masters the sheen it required to join the major championship pantheon. The Masters in turn could have created the momentum the club needed to move into the black in perpetuity.

Roberts and Jones were determined to keep it solvent during the war, preserving a club they expected to flourish eventually. Roberts quickly cobbled together a budget that would cover the cost of the superintendent and various caretaking expenses, as well as taxes. The number at which he arrived was $12,000 a year. The members were informed that their dues were being suspended—the club could not rightfully continue to collect fees for which they would provide no services—but that they were encouraged to make a suggested donation of $100 annually for maintenance purposes. Were they all to agree, the club would generate $12,800 a year, slightly more than enough to fend off irreparable dilapidation.

Jones might have been preoccupied with his work in serving his country, but he still gave considerable thought to his beloved Augusta National. He pondered its future and ways that might help prevent it from slipping irreversibly from dim to dark. He came up with a solution: cows. The purchase of a herd of steer that would graze on Augusta National's grass would serve a dual purpose: The cattle would keep the grass in check, allowing the club to save on maintenance costs, and it would help alleviate a meat shortage brought on by the onset of war. The idea was ratified by club hierarchy after it consulted with a cattle expert and was told that the club had sufficient property to support two hundred steers.

Indefinitely out of the golf business, Augusta National Golf Club went into the cattle business. "The course wasn't doing anyone a bit of good," Jones said. "It was just idle ground. So we thought we would add it to grazing lands available for the war effort."

Winston Churchill surely would have found delightful irony in the transformation. He once said, "Playing golf is like chasing a quinine pill around a cow pasture." The pasture, in fact, was a sound idea in theory, but in practice it proved to be a costly mistake. The fact that the course would not be open for play until the end of the war eliminated the need to overseed the Bermuda grass with a winter grass. Bermuda grass, of course, goes dormant in the winter, as it did at Augusta. The cows, then, had no more food of the grass variety and in their hunger turned to the club's prized (and valuable) azaleas, as well as other flora. It became immediately evident to club officials as well that for the months that the Bermuda was dormant they'd now have to buy feed for the steers, which promised to erase the savings the club had expected to realize from not having to pay a maintenance crew.

Mooing or mowing, it was a wash.

The simple fact that the Augusta National Golf Club had become a cow pasture was symbolic of the uncertainty that permeated the game. It was also an indication that golf was destined to experience setbacks during the war. Augusta was not alone in turning to farming; some clubs were raising pigs by feeding them the clubhouse garbage; others pondered the possibility of taking a page from British golf and using sheep to keep the fairways manicured. Historic Baltusrol Golf Club in Springfield, New Jersey, site of the U.S. Open in 1903, 1915, and 1936, was among the clubs that went into the farming business. It had thirty steers, a hundred forty sheep, four milk cows, eight calves, eight horses, and ten heifers roaming its property. The club's goal was to help alleviate the meat shortage, though it did so with more success than its friends at Augusta National. Its animals eventually paid for themselves once the club began selling them off.

The PGA of America, meanwhile, had become concerned that golf was the victim of an unfair stigma that was harming the game, that playing a round in a time of war was either unpatriotic or apathetic. It was not an original issue; during World War I, some were afraid to venture onto a golf course for fear that their indulgence would be considered anathema to the war effort, wasted energy that would be more useful elsewhere. P. C. Pulver, the old editor of *Professional Golfer* magazine, countered by reminding his readers that Walter Camp, known as the father of American football and the man who had created the position of quarterback, once said, "Men who pursue the golf ball do not have to chase the doctor."

GOLF HAD CAREFULLY TAKEN STEPS to combat its reputation as a game only for the affluent. Augusta National's contribution of a practice facility at Camp Gordon was an important step, one of many taken by golf on behalf of the war effort.

The game's hierarchy, in fact, could look back on a year that it could rightfully be proud of. On the professional front, Nelson (the Masters) and Snead (the PGA Championship) won major championships and Hogan (Hale America) won the de facto national championship—the three best players in the world dutifully providing the sport a decent send-off in the event that it would be forced into hibernation. The PGA played a relatively full schedule, twenty-four events, of which Hogan won six. Lloyd Mangrum and Byron Nelson won three tournaments apiece, while Snead won a pair of events.

The sport had begun to distinguish itself in other ways too. When it added its charitable receipts, it became evident that golf, a game that was more accustomed to bringing out the worst in people, was now coaxing the best from them. More than 500 clubs, public courses, and associations had arranged to hold 2,964 tournaments of various sorts to benefit the American Red Cross.

Fred Corcoran, the PGA's Tournament Bureau manager, noted that by the end of 1942, golf was expected to have raised more than one million dollars for war relief agencies. The PGA alone expected to donate more than a quarter million dollars. Its two-day Ryder Cup substitute not only netted more than $20,000, but those two days were billed as PGA War Relief days.

The PGA asked each of its more than 2,100 members to play in some kind of exhibition match or tournament and donate the proceeds to war relief.

The actual Ryder Cup, a biennial event matching teams from the U.S. and Great Britain, had not been played since 1937. England's involvement in the war resulted in the cancellation of both the '39 and '41 events. The PGA chose to honor the U.S. Ryder Cup team anyway, by pitting it against another team of American tour pros in a match in 1940 at Oakland Hills Country Club in Bloomfield Hills, Michigan. Its intention was to raise money for the Red Cross, but it raised hackles, too, by opening old wounds. Captain Walter Hagen's Ryder Cup team consisted of Vic Ghezzi, Ralph Guldahl, Jimmy Hines, Jug McSpaden, Dick Metz, Byron Nelson, Henry Picard, Paul Runyan, Horton Smith, and Sam Snead. Conspicuous by his absence was Gene Sarazen, who was miffed. Never one to forfeit an opportunity to concoct a controversy, the jilted Squire boldly announced that he could pick ten players who would defeat the U.S. team. When the exhibition match was suggested, Sarazen was a logical choice to captain the second team, even giving local sportswriters a hook on which to hype the event. Sarazen chose Tommy Armour, Billy Burke, Harry Cooper, Jimmy Demaret, Ben Hogan, Lawson Little, Porky Oliver, Jimmy Thompson, Al Watrous, and Craig Wood. His team may have lacked the depth of the Ryder Cup team, but it was not lacking a star. Ben Hogan hadn't won his first PGA Tournament until 1940, so he was not a part of the '39 Ryder Cup team. In 1940, his ascent toward the apex of the golf world had begun in earnest. Hagen's squad prevailed, 7–5, notwithstanding the fact that Hogan was anchoring the opposition. More importantly $10,000 was raised on behalf of the Red Cross.

The idea proved so successful that it was copied in 1941 and again in 1942 at Oakland Hills, the latter event turning a profit nearly equal to the two preceding events. A. J. Ditman, head-quarters representative of the American Red Cross, called it "one of the greatest golf matches for charity of all time. . . . In my esti-mation, the match did more to stimulate interest in America's grandest game than any other match I have seen."

Those in the game relentlessly looked for creative ways to mine the pockets of golfers and golf fans. They began by learn-ing a history lesson. Golf had come to the financial aid of the United States by holding fund-raising exhibitions during the First World War. In one of them, Walter Travis, a three-time U.S. Amateur champion and a former British Amateur champion, squared off in a match with Finlay Douglas in Garden City, New Jersey. Afterward, the putter that Travis had used to win the British Amateur was auctioned off. The winning bid was $1,700, while the match itself netted nearly $5,000 for the United War Work Fund. Chick Evans, the reigning U.S. Open and U.S. Ama-teur champion, estimated that he traveled more than twenty-six thousand miles and played in more than fifty exhibitions in six months. The Western Golf Association estimated that Evans alone helped raise $250,000 on behalf of winning the war.

Another suggestion borrowed from World War I was putting up for bid the services of celebrity caddies, including Bobby Jones, Evans, Walter Hagen, and Francis Ouimet. Imagine the bidding wars for the caddie services of Byron Nelson or Ben Hogan, either of whom might be worth the investment by virtue of swing suggestions or course management advice in the midst of a high-stakes match.

Those from the golf world, circa 1942, were equally prepared to serve. By the end of 1942, more than two hundred club pro-fessionals were serving the U.S. in the armed forces. "As a re-membrance from the National Association, a carton of cigarettes has been mailed to you, under separate cover, at the same location this letter is being sent as this was your latest address we were able to obtain," wrote PGA president Ed Dudley in a letter to them. "We sincerely hope these cigarettes reach you in good condition."

The exhibition tour that included Bob Hope and Bing Crosby helped raise funds sufficient for the PGA hierarchy to purchase a pair of ambulances for the Red Cross, each of them bearing the inscription of the association.

Golf clubs were encouraged to turn a portion of their properties into Victory gardens, for growing fruits and vegetables, which were in short supply. Even the Los Angeles Country Club developed a Victory garden, which supplied the club dining rooms with homegrown vegetables. Clubs that agreed to do so often put their gardens in proximity to fairways or greens. In other words, they were in play for golfers hitting wayward shots. Some suspect that Victory gardens were the genesis of the common phrase that a shot hit into any overgrown area had been hit into the cabbage.

Victory gardens also proved fertile for sarcasm. "This year, a ball may be moved two club lengths from broccoli, tomatoes, and lettuce, without penalty," a wag from *Golfing* magazine wrote. "If you're lying close to a cabbage and have played five or more strokes, the new rules allow you to play the cabbage from that point on."

Many golf course operators realized they had ample ground on the periphery of the course on which to plant Victory gardens. It was seen as well as a way for clubs to ease the antagonism that some inexplicably had toward them, by demonstrating a concerted effort toward helping their fellow Americans. W. W. Crenshaw, the owner of Oakmont Country Club in Glendale, California, tended his club's Victory garden himself. The property had a history as a fertile growing ground, having been the site of a vineyard before golf intervened. Crenshaw plowed up forty acres of rough for his garden. He raised tomatoes, potatoes, corn, lettuce, carrots, and eggplants on Oakmont property. When the tomatoes began to ripen, an average of five hundred pounds a day were harvested. Members passing through the grill room were encouraged to buy boxes of tomatoes, for which they would receive the bonus of a dozen fruit jars with each purchase.

One hundred fifty tons of tomatoes grown on the grounds of Briergate Golf Club in Deerfield, Illinois, were supplied to the government, which in turn canned them for use by the Army and the Navy. Eleven locations around the course were used for tomato plants, only marginally interfering with play. A free drop was accorded those hitting into the tomatoes, denoted by signs dotting the course: *LIFT WITHOUT PENALTY FROM TOMATO PLANTINGS.*

Gardens were also attempted in England, though with uneven success. The Ministry of Agriculture and Fisheries called for every golf course with land conducive to growing crops to contribute food to the war effort. The ministry concluded that fifteen to twenty acres on an eighteen-hole course should be given over to crops, though not in a way that would require decimating greens, fairways, or bunkers. It was not a suggestion that was accepted in good humor; golfers wondered why idle grassland, which abounded in the U.K., could not be used instead.

As 1943 approached, it was clear that the golf landscape was rapidly shifting, façades notwithstanding. *Golf,* a magazine published by the Netherlands Golf Committee, attempted and failed to convince its readers that nothing had changed there. The country was under Nazi occupation, and the publication of *Golf* was thought to have been allowed as a propaganda tool. One issue featured only twenty pages with less than one full page of advertising—one eighth of a page devoted to beer, gin, and wine ads, one-half page to a hotel ad. It contained a single photo-graph, of a group of golfers at a Dutch pro-am tournament. The contestants all appeared as though they'd just played the worst rounds of their lives.

The Nazis, meanwhile, had seized one of Czechoslovakia's newest and finest layouts, Praha Golf Course, which was now played almost exclusively by German officers. Germany, in fact, had declared that all of Czechoslovakia's golf courses had be-come part of the German Golf Union.

Back in the States, Clifford Roberts, Jones's friend and part-ner at Augusta National, somberly assessed the war and its effect on the club that he loved. He was unable to provide any answers to his own questions.

"The Lord only knows when we will again operate as a golf club," Roberts wrote in a letter, his melancholy staining the page.

GLUTTONY SUPERSEDED MELANCHOLY at the Washington, D.C., home of financier Bernard Baruch one December evening in 1942. Nearby Georgetown University offered fewer courses than Baruch was serving (and none as appetizing). The occasion was a fete in honor of newlyweds Harry Hopkins and the latest Mrs. Hopkins, wife number three for FDR's New Deal enforcer, reaf-firming his 1930s commitment to social outreach.

Hopkins was Roosevelt's assistant, his closest adviser, even living at the White House. The corridors of power were just outside his bedroom door. He was a man for whom a lavish fete was a worth-while investment, whatever the occasion. The dinner began with caviar, setting the appropriate tone for the orgiastic epicurean feast that would follow. The menu included foie gras, cheese croquettes, baked oysters *bonne femme, tortue clair (en terrine), crème au champignon frais, profiterole, truite en gelée, homard en aspic,* terrapin (Baltimore style), chicken à la king, mousse of chicken, galatine of capon, cold tongue, beef à la mode, corned beef in jelly, crisp lettuce with sliced tomatoes and calves'-head vinaigrette, iced black cherries, socle of raspberry ice, petit fours, and demitasse.

The war required sacrifice, as Hopkins had reminded his audience in an article he wrote for the December 1942 issue of *American Magazine,* only a few days before the Baruch affair, where sacrifice was asked only of an assortment of farm animals and game birds that were baked, broiled, sautéed, or cured on behalf of the happy couple. Hopkins had negotiated to write a series of stories for *American Magazine,* which paid him $5,000 apiece, a princely sum that precisely (and conveniently) covered the annual alimony payment he was required to make to his first wife (his second wife had died). Hopkins in turn employed a ghostwriter to produce the stories on his behalf.

The article in question suggested that in wartime the masses ought to forgo luxuries and even what otherwise might be considered necessities, in the interest of helping the Allies defeat the Axis. Hopkins wrote that, "under total war, our over-all standard of living will be as low as it was at the bottom of the Depression in 1932. . . . Generally there will be nobody living in luxury, nobody living in poverty. We shall be forced to do without almost everything but the necessities of life. Children will have plenty to eat, but most adults will not be fed quite as well as are the men in our fighting forces, which is as it should be. No family should object to meat rationing when they realize that the beef and bacon they don't get is being served to their sons and brothers in the Army." He wrote that "golf as usual" should be curtailed, even implying that those who failed to comply were guilty of malfeasance. He decried citizens who weren't actively engaged in the war effort and whiled away their free time playing eighteen holes before repairing to the nineteenth hole.

The theme of Hopkins's story—that sacrifice was required in these dire times—was not an issue with his critics, notwithstanding his illogical conclusion that forgoing golf would help bring down the Hun. The issue was Hopkins's gluttonous hypocrisy—a collision between his plea for sacrifice and his profligacy that left him bloodied and bowed once news of the party leaked and the media's own voracious appetite for scandal was aroused.

"Throughout the function," one Washington columnist wrote, "the face of Hopkins, who warned his countrymen in a recent magazine article that they will have to forgo milk and tea and predicted drastic curtailment of all civilian industries except coffinmaking, was wreathed in smiles."

Westbrook Pegler, the acerbic syndicated columnist ("I claim authority to speak for the rabble because I am a member of the rabble in good standing," he once wrote), placed Hopkins on a tee and took his best shot. "People who used to golf were months ahead of him in recognizing that golf must be from now on only a weekend relaxation, if not just a memory," he wrote. "Who is this Hopkins to be warning and threatening the Americans and lecturing them as though all those not in the services of the government were a lot of drunks?"

The golf media were similarly enraged by Hopkins for pandering to the proletariat at the expense of its game. "Hopkins is a man who lies around the White House half sick because he didn't take sensible care of himself physically," *Golfdom* wrote, "but is able to get up and be a guest of honor at an extravagant cocktail party given by Barney Baruch—the sort of a party that the Hopkins magazine piece said was a flagrant disservice to this nation." In another critical piece, the magazine wrote, "Harry Hopkins fakes a magazine article, per a literary ghost, in which he condemns 'golf as usual' during wartime, although golf was the first sport to declare that it was not going to be 'as usual' during the war but would completely adjust itself to war aid."

Herb Graffis was the most outspoken writer regarding golfers' responsibility to the war effort. "Golf, to deserve its right to boast of itself as being a gentleman's game, isn't to be played these days unless it's played for somebody else," he wrote in *Golfing,* "the soldiers, sailors and marines that we who are not in uniform must back up in our fullest, fittest way."

The golf industry viewed Hopkins's *American Magazine* story as piling on. The game had already been taking a beating. Its aggressive, proactive strategy in ensuring that it was above reproach in its conduct vis-à-vis the war was nullified by the fact that few were aware that the game was behaving responsibly and that it even had the government's blessing. It was generally unknown that golf had been the first sport to respond to the crisis, when the USGA canceled its national championships without taking a cue from President Roosevelt, as baseball did a few days later in January of 1942. Golf moreover was committed to continuing only in the interest of assisting the war effort in any manner possible, as evidenced by the millions of dollars it was raising to that end.

Yet ignorance drove the prevailing perception that playing a round of golf while your countrymen were engaged on the battlefield was inappropriate behavior, as though a war abroad precluded the pursuit of recreational fun at home. The damage the perception was doing was documented in a letter a golf course owner wrote to the USGA in response to its request to host a war relief tournament: "We are trying hard to stay in business," the course owner wrote. "Better promote something for the relief of golf courses."

Golf writers became defensive. One wrote that an American spent less time on the golf course than German citizens and residents in countries occupied by Germany were required to spend listening to speeches by Adolf Hitler, Joseph Goebbels, and Hermann Goering each week.

Herb Graffis wrote:

> The truth is that golf has failed so badly to tell its story as an exceedingly valuable aid to war effort that some people who don't at all mind going to the movies, to football, basketball, and baseball games, or to go bowling, are shy about being seen with a bag of golf clubs. This is notwithstanding the fact that golf as a physical and mental conditioner has a wartime case for adults, sounder than that of the previously mentioned recreations.

The *elitist* tag was permanently affixed to golf, and in the first year of the war it was augmented by the fact that the War Manpower Commission had classified golf course–related labor among nonessential jobs. A presidential executive order had given Paul V. McNutt, the chairman of the WMC, authority over both labor and the draft, potentially a devastating left-right combination for golf courses, whose business depends largely on maintenance crews. The executive order said that "no employer shall retain in his employ any worker whose services are more urgently needed in any establishment, plant, facility, occupation, or area designated as more essential." The nonessential classification made course workers susceptible to the draft (even those up to forty-five years old) and made them available for work in war-related industries at the behest of the WMC.

A column in *The Long Island Press* took the WMC to task for its shortsightedness on the part of golf, suggesting that golf's tireless efforts on behalf of service organizations warranted a review of WMC policies. It read:

All that is required to keep a course on fairly good condition is four or five men, but the average laborer between 38 and 45 lives in fear of being tapped on the shoulder by his local draft board and won't work on the course. It doesn't seem logical for Paul V. McNutt to endorse golf as a morale builder and have a sport that ranks second in the nation for donations to the Red Cross, USO, and similar agencies. What was done down at the Texas Open last weekend when $2,300,000 in war bonds were sold to spectators can be done in every section of the country. Why discriminate against golf?

Ed Dudley, the president of the PGA, wanted an audience with McNutt. "During the past year," Dudley wrote, "golf has been seriously handicapped by an adverse psychological influence, due to the fact that many who wanted to play the game and get beneficial exercise were afraid that they would appear unpatriotic by doing so. This was a stigma that for some reason did not appear to attach to any other game."

Early in 1942, the PGA had even informed its membership that "your Association wishes to request that at any time you, as a member of our Association, can be of assistance to the United States Government in any of its activities, we implore you to do so. Your cooperation in civilian defense is necessary, the purchase of Defense Stamps and Bonds is urgently needed. The support of the American Red Cross is vital and we ask you to be ready to act in any emergency."

Golf was not shirking its duty, a message that Dudley intended to impart to McNutt. When the two of them finally met, McNutt told Dudley that he was surprised to learn of the perception of the game and how it was suffering as a result. McNutt indirectly came to the game's defense, by emphasizing the importance of physical fitness for those involved in assisting the war effort at home.

"The importance of physical fitness in this great emergency cannot be overemphasized," McNutt wrote in a statement. "The objective of our program cannot be realized unless every individual in each community is made conscious of the value of physical well-being."

Dudley employed McNutt's words in defense of his sport. "Mr. McNutt . . . pointed out the emphasis which the armed services place upon physical fitness through recreation and exercise," Dudley wrote. "While certainly professional sports can never expect any kind of favored treatment either in draft deferment or in competition with essential or wartime industries, recreational sports as such, he felt, would be a good thing. . . . The war effort comes first, but don't be afraid to get out and exercise and relax on the golf course at the right time. Our enemies are great believers in physical fitness. And we have always been the most physically fit of nations, as witness our Olympic Games record. Let us remain so, but never forget that our prime aim in life is to win this war—and win it as soon as possible. Don't feel that it is unpatriotic to play golf."

Golf began to spread its message. The reigning USGA president, George Blossom Jr., weighed in on behalf of the game in a speech he delivered to its constituents on January 9, 1943, at the Waldorf-Astoria Hotel in New York.

"There is a natural feeling among most of us at home," Blossom said, "that we should all do something for the war effort. One way in which we have been able to cooperate in this emergency is by denying ourselves certain things. However, when it comes to denying ourselves various forms of recreation, whereby we benefit physically and mentally, careful consideration should be given before the type of program is sacrificed. Health and morale are certainly not luxuries. It is common knowledge that the young men who first went into the service were, on the whole, found wanting when it came to physical fitness. As an example of what the Air Force considers a part of their training I quote the following statement: 'Golf may contribute to the physical fitness program in a number of ways. While its value to direct conditioning may not be as high as many other activities, it has a place in this program for several reasons. The soldier or officer working long hours under great tension may do much toward regaining his balance and restoring his energy with a short round of golf. The game is of value in that it affords relaxing for body and mind, and is a factor in developing coordination, self-control, balance, timing, and accuracy of movement.'

"Golf plays a dual role for those who make it their form of relaxation. It is a participating sport (as distinguished from a sport at which a few play and thousands look on) where one has the benefits of physical exertion outdoors, coupled with the pleasant companionship of friends.

"The USGA would like to make it very clear that it is our firm conviction that golf is a patriotic and proper form of exercise for the men and women of this country, and that one should not have the feeling that it is in poor taste to play a game of golf in serious times like these, provided, of course, that it doesn't interfere with the war effort. It is my considered opinion that all who can afford it should continue, financially and otherwise, to sponsor their clubs, private, semiprivate, and public, thereby making them available for the men in armed services as well as for themselves.

"We are going to need all the enthusiasm, vitality, and stamina we can muster to get through the trying period, and I can't help but feel that we will all be better able to carry on if we plan a few hours each week for recreation and exercise. And it is surprising how morale is benefited and troubles are dissipated on the golf course."

Blossom also wrote an article for the Associated Press that

appeared in newspapers across the country, including *The New York Times*. He reiterated the theme that fitness was important and that golf was a means of achieving it. "If it is patriotic to be in shape physically, mentally, and spiritually," he wrote, "then it is patriotic to play golf. Of course, we won't win the war with a mashie. Further, we shouldn't use the mashie when that would interfere with the war effort. But golf can further the well-being of some 2,351,000 Americans—just as it has been doing all these years—and that is valuable. . . . There is no wartime newness about golf's benefits—such things as man's most natural exercise, walking, and four to five miles of it. . . . Golf, then, can be particularly useful in our present situation—just by being its own natural self. I call upon golfers to reevaluate their game. I call upon them to realize it is a patriotic duty to keep in shape and that it is their patriotic duty to play golf, within proper limits."

THE GAME ALSO received a boost from a speech that Wisconsin congressman LaVern R. Dilweg delivered before the U.S. House of Representatives, urging those who play golf to play more golf. Dilweg, who had starred in football for Marquette University and the Green Bay Packers, was speaking on behalf of sports and their role in the war effort. But as an aging athlete who was by necessity moving away from contact sports and toward the more passive pursuit of knocking a golf ball around, he generously sprinkled golf references throughout his address.

"It is my purpose today to call your attention to the part sports are playing in our American victory drive—to bring you up to date, perhaps, on how sports must serve all of us as we prosecute the most heroic task ever assigned to the American people," Dilweg said on the floor of the House. "The point I will make is that sports on the American scene—instead of being curtailed for the duration—should be encouraged on a wider scale, with all of us engaging in some kind of physical activity.... Those of us, for example, who have played golf in the past should play more golf today. We should play harder at golf to utilize the game for its contributions to physical fitness. If we do not play golf, we should find some other physical hobby—some sport, some game—that we will play for enjoyment and from which we will derive physical work.... All of us must take up some physical sports, whether it is golfing, swimming, bowling, handball, wrestling, walking, tennis, softball, horseshoe pitching, or any of scores of games, determining beforehand the condition of our heart and other organs, and choosing a physical hobby, a sport that befits our age. We must play hard at that sport every day to reap the full benefits of physical fitness."

Dilweg even made a case for providing draft deferments to professional athletes from spectator sports. "I contend that five hundred men playing major league baseball—and with draft deferments—can do more good for this country in time of war than the same five hundred men could if the national pastime were abandoned and these baseball artists were given menial jobs in some other essential industries. What does baseball do for America? Well, first of all, it provides an opportunity for hundreds of thousands of war workers to relax in the fresh air and sunshine—and to continue to enjoy something that has been a significant part of American life for almost one hundred years.... Baseball news is a refreshing balance against the worrisome news that we are fighting a war.... What holds true for baseball, holds true for all other spectator sports.... Sports are the American way for achieving that physical fitness through exercise, which is a must requirement of every one of us on the home front today.... Spectator sports are a national tonic, a change of pace, a relief from the more serious aspects of total war. The sports way is the American way. Let us keep our sports on the American scene for their contributions to American victory. And let all of us remember that it is patriotic to be fit, patriotic to play and play hard for the physical strength and endurance that will allow us to take our daily physical tasks in stride, with enough in reserve to accept additional physical burdens, when and if necessary."

Play away, America, and leave your guilt at home, the congressman was saying to all who would listen. Hopkins was not among them. He was tone deaf to the plight of the ordinary Americans to whom he professed to be committed. Perhaps had golf been a game bird instead of a game, it might have been held in better stead by Hopkins. Indeed, it might even have had a place of honor at the Baruch dinner on that memorable December night, a place next to the mousse of chicken, perhaps.

8

EISENHOWER AND JONES

Kindred Spirits and Warriors

Dwight Eisenhower might have given the impression that in a previous life he would have preferred doing a turn as Old Tom Morris (or even Young Tom Morris) to one as Ulysses S. Grant, but the truth was that he preferred the order that his life had followed. He was a soldier first and a golfer (a distant) second, though he was concerned that he might be required to fight the war from behind a Washington desk. A taxi driver in Washington, D.C., said, "I've never seen so many uniforms as there are here now . . . and so few soldiers." Ike would have concurred.

Destiny quickly concluded that he was better suited to fight the war on the European front than on the political front, however. Six months after his arrival in Washington in December of 1941, he had a new rank and a new assignment; Major General Eisenhower was tapped as the commander of the European Theater of Operations. He would finally be going off to war.

Eisenhower, naturally, took his golf clubs with him. He was going first to London, where a proliferation of historic golf courses was within driving distance, and Eisenhower intended to partake of a few of them should the opportunity present itself. Home for Eisenhower in London was initially Claridge's, an upscale, trendy hotel at which he shared a suite of rooms with his friend and naval aide, Lieutenant Commander Harry C. Butcher. Claridge's was not Eisenhower's style; it was too ornate, too highbrow, even for a Military Academy graduate who moved comfortably in any tony country-club setting in which he ever found himself.

"I feel like I'm living in sin," he told Butcher.

Claridge's was also a potential hazard, an unstable building that could easily have been reduced to rubble by a single Luftwaffe bomb. So he moved into the Dorchester, a more modern concrete-and-steel structure across from Hyde Park and a short walk to his headquarters.

Eisenhower immersed himself in his work, which was relentlessly stressful; he was in a foreign country, attempting to balance the desires of two governments, while every decision he made was of the life-and-death sort for those under his command. He found living and working in London to be stifling. He considered moving his headquarters well outside London, but logistically it was impractical; he needed easy access to England's Ministry of Defense and its Air Ministry, and to Downing Street. He pondered a compromise, a retreat in the country. His counterparts in the British military, as well as ranking politicians, all seemed to have weekend retreats outside London. Eisenhower decided that he wanted one, too, and sent Butcher looking for a suitable home. Butcher found a two-story, five-bedroom, mock-Tudor home called Telegraph Cottage, situated near Kingston, a forty-minute drive from his headquarters. It was set back a secure distance from the street, and, incidentally (and perhaps not coincidentally), backed up to a golf course.

A stressful job requires a diversion, which for Eisenhower meant time on a golf course. The back gate of his Telegraph Cottage property opened to the thirteenth hole at Coombe Hill Golf Club, providing him easy access to one of the best golf courses built in proximity to London. It had been designed by J. F. Abercromby, who at one time was among the most respected course architects in the United Kingdom. Coombe Hill provided a modicum of serenity in dangerous times; it featured a small stream that meandered through parts of the course, and fairways that were elegantly flanked by silver birch trees, conifers, and oaks. For a man attempting to direct the course of history, Coombe Hill Golf Club was an appropriate venue, given its own gilded history. Its first professional had been Sandy Herd, the 1902 British Open champion and the Open runner-up in the year in which he was hired, 1910. Winston Churchill was among its first members. King Edward VIII and the duke of York played there often. Another former Coombe Hill pro, Archie Compton, once defeated American legend Walter Hagen, 18 and 17, in a thirty-six-hole challenge match that was still recalled in these parts.

Eisenhower spent many weekends at Telegraph Cottage, affording him an opportunity to catch his breath, even to play a few holes. For safety reasons—not wishing to venture too far from home and wishing to remain close enough to a car to rush back to the office in the event of an emergency—Eisenhower played only five of Coombe Hill's eighteen holes. His proximity to the thirteenth green enabled him to start his abbreviated rounds on the fourteenth tee, on a three-hundred-forty-yard par-4 hole that Bobby Jones called among the finest of its length he had ever played. Ike would also play fifteen, after which he would swing over and play eleven, twelve, and thirteen, his home hole.

It was golf in abbreviated form, but at least it helped sate his worsening habit. The few holes he played were a few more than he would have attempted had he remained in London full-time. He usually played with Butcher, and to inject purpose into their abbreviated match, they wagered a shilling a hole. It was never about the money, of course; the shillings that changed hands were simply symbolic of the de facto stakes for which they played, also known as pride.

Eisenhower seldom had time for more golf; he was in the process of planning the invasion of North Africa, which he might have described as a long, narrow par 4, with a small green protected by water. He assessed the strength of his forces and it ruefully resembled his golf skill. Simply put, he wasn't sure that he had enough game to accomplish the task.

ON NOVEMBER 8, 1942, Eisenhower and the Allies began the invasion of North Africa. His headquarters were in Algiers, on the Mediterranean coast. The game never strayed from his mind, even when more urgent matters jostled their way to the fore. It is the bane of the afflicted golfer, who won't let a day (or even an hour) pass without devoting at least some thought to his golf swing. So it was for General Eisenhower. His extraordinary responsibility did not preclude him from sneaking occasional thoughts about his golf throughout the day.

Ike's swing required tending to; his clubhead seldom took the same route to the ball, except in his mind's eye, a myopic view of reality as it were. Nonetheless, he played flawlessly (albeit contemplatively) between the incessant meetings and phone calls, the latter including one he received one morning early in 1943, informing him that Bob Hope and his troupe had arrived, as part of a USO tour.

Hope and friends were staying at the Aletti Hotel, where the night before the writer Quentin Reynolds (as writers were wont to do) had turned up a generous supply of hooch that he shared with Hope, actor Bruce Cabot, and another newsman, H. R. Knickerbocker. Their makeshift party had gone well past midnight.

A bleary-eyed Hope was in the midst of rehearsals at the Red Cross building the next morning when he was informed by an aide to Eisenhower that the general wanted to see him. Hope, now wishing that he had gotten more sleep, nervously accompanied the aide to Eisenhower's office. When they arrived, the general was sitting behind his desk, studying a map of North Africa. Ike stood, walked around the desk, extended his hand, and before he even said hello, he asked Hope, "How's your golf?"

Of course. The question is a strategic one for the golfer, who uses it as a springboard to delivering a dissertation on the state of his own game. For the next several minutes, the general and the comedian, a pair of strangers, one there to lead the troops, the other there to entertain them, talked animatedly about the game that bound them and formed the foundation on which an enduring friendship was built.

Work eventually beckoned Eisenhower back to reality and their visit came to a close. Eisenhower inquired about recent bombings that Hope had had to endure on his travels. Hope replied that that indeed was the case and that given his druthers he'd rather not experience them again. "They affect my backswing," he said.

Eisenhower attempted to alleviate Hope's concerns, informing his new friend that he was safe in Algiers, that the area had not been bombed in weeks. "You'll get a nice rest tonight," Ike said.

Early the next morning, German planes began attacking the city. Hope and his entourage, scared witless (at least until the bombing stopped), quickly ran to the basement, a wine cellar in peacetime, an air raid shelter in wartime. Just before he left the next day, Hope sent a note to Eisenhower. "Thanks for the rest," it read.

As for the assignment in North Africa, Eisenhower's troops indeed had enough game. On May 13, 1943, the war in North Africa ended with the surrender of more than a quarter of a million German and Italian troops.

ONE OF GENERAL EISENHOWER'S IDOLS was Bobby Jones, with whom he would have concluded he had nothing in common. He would have been wrong. Jones shared Eisenhower's concern that the war was going to pass him by. He was certain that a stateside appointment was his destination, that he'd be lost behind sheafs of paperwork, largely forgotten.

The Army Air Corps was not about to forget a man of his stature, an icon everywhere he went, one to whom the citizens would listen more attentively. Jones's prominence was the only megaphone necessary for him to be heard wherever he spoke, particularly in Georgia, where one newspaper, *The Atlanta Journal,* compared him with "the Cyclorama, Stone Mountain, and Margaret Mitchell as a top Atlanta attraction." The Army wanted him to talk. It asked that he warn the citizens of Atlanta and surrounding areas that they had a target on them, and that the German Luftwaffe was likely to have Atlanta in its crosshairs at some point in the near future. For a time, it appeared as though the Germans would take Dakar, on the westernmost point of the African continent, a strategic site from which to begin an Atlantic crossing and launch a U.S. invasion. The Army was legitimately concerned and expected the warning to be taken seriously, which required that it be issued by someone with a voice that commanded rapt attention. Who better to issue it than Robert Tyre Jones, Jr., Georgia native and American legend and now an Army major, courtesy of a promotion early in 1943?

It was a bittersweet assignment for Jones, who was dispatched to Atlanta in May of 1943 to deliver the message to the citizenry there. This was bad news, not the kind of news anyone wanted to convey, much less to friends and family. Conversely, it had to be delivered so that they might somehow be better prepared. Jones ensured a receptive audience.

He also got a trip home from it. This might have been the highlight of the ten months he had spent on active duty. Jones was frustrated in his bid to serve his country in something other than an innocuous (albeit important) job. His assignment was to direct civilian personnel enlisted to operate filter centers and information centers in the First Fighter Command, which was responsible for covering the entire eastern seaboard, from Maine's northern border to the southern tip of Florida.

Jones wanted to do more than oversee the work of civilian volunteers. If others were putting their lives on the line, why should he be entitled to remain comfortably ensconced behind a desk at Mitchel Field on Long Island, thousands of miles removed from the front? He wanted to see combat, though the likelihood of his doing so was remote. He was forty-one, a father, a husband, an American idol. What would it do for the country's morale were a man of Jones's stature, a national treasure, killed in action? Such was his celebrity that even those he had never met were certain they knew him intimately. Were he to take a bullet for his country, he'd be something other than another faceless casualty, and the Army was reluctant to take the risk. Thus Jones was assigned to fight the Germans from the relative safety of America's East Coast.

So it was that Jones found himself working largely with

women in his role with the Aircraft Warning Service. Ground observers, consisting of civilians from every profession, from farmers to bankers, were employed to look out for enemy aircraft. Upon a sighting, they were required to report what they saw to the closest filter center, established to coordinate these civilian reports and relay them to tactical operations in Charleston, South Carolina.

Four hundred women contributed eight to ten hours a week to the local filter center somewhere near Atlanta and were on call twenty-four hours a day. "Women in the Filter Center take their jobs seriously," Major Jones told the volunteers' director, Mrs. Robert F. Adamson. "They seem to feel their responsibility, and they don't talk about matters which are military secrets. These women and the spotters make up the largest volunteer army in the world."

Jones later addressed the volunteers and informed them that enemy bombs almost certainly would be unloosed on the city. He cited an article in the April issue of *American Mercury* that pointed out that the Army expected the country to come under attack and that some of the enemy planes would manage to get past U.S. defenses. The story bluntly echoed the Army's conviction that the Germans were determined to launch a blitzkrieg on the U.S. The enemy's goal, he said, was not necessarily to level America's cities in the manner of Germany's failed attempt to erase London from the map, but to strike terror among the citizens, to demoralize them.

Major Jones was accompanied by Lieutenant Colonel Keene N. Brundage, commanding officer of the Charleston Air Defense Region, which included Atlanta. "I tell you officially that certain areas in the Charleston Air Defense Region probably have just as much possibility of being bombed as any locality in the country," Brundage said.

Jones's presence was a soothing influence that helped prevent the two of them from scaring the masses to death. He was asking simply that the people be on the alert, that by spotting an enemy plane early on, they might allow the U.S. to respond quickly enough to repel the attack.

"In modern warfare," Major Jones said, "a country's first line of defense is its Aircraft Warning Service. Fighter planes afford the best defense against enemy bombers. Yet the best fighter is at a disadvantage if the surprise of the raid is complete. The advance warning must come in time to allow the defending planes to gain altitude for an advantageous attack. The complete job of assembling this valuable intelligence is performed by volunteer civilians, working under direct Army supervision. Volunteer ground observers report flights of aircraft and volunteers in the filter centers plot these flights. The result is a complete picture of flying over the area over which the Army is keeping watch. It is the largest organization of volunteers working for any army in the world. The men and women in our filter and information centers have been earnest and faithful to a remarkable degree. Their loyalty and trustworthiness have been inspiring. They are doing a jam-up military job without any hope of reward or glory, and even with far less public recognition than they deserve. They can be repaid only by the realization that without them we could have no Aircraft Warning Service."

Dakar did not fall into German hands and Jones was reassigned to Mitchel Field. He was given the charge of the filter and information centers in the First Fighter Command, covering an area from Maine to Florida. Jones described his job as overseeing thirty thousand women and "keeping them happy and interested when the need for their services was becoming more and more remote every day." He often referred to his job as "fighting the battle of the Fighter Command up and down the eastern seaboard."

Yet Jones wasn't the sort to pout. He did his job diligently, meanwhile hoping for a better assignment, preferably one that would enable him to engage the enemy up close. After several months of directing his female army of volunteers, he asked his commanding general for a transfer to Leavenworth for command and general staff school. The commanding general considered his age and his status as a reserve officer and denied his request.

EVEN GOLF FAILED to assuage his guilt at not playing a more meaningful role in the war effort. Never in his life had Jones been so far removed from the game that defined him. He played only rarely, though he retained the ability to break 70 on a good day. His second career, as a lawyer, was on hold.

Suddenly, his third career, as a U.S. Army Air Corps officer, took a turn for the better, at least from Jones's skewed perspective, that of an aging would-be warrior who wished to take up arms and enter the fray. He was assigned to attend the Army Air Corps Intelligence School in Harrisburg, Pennsylvania. Intelligence School was not assigned to those to whom the Army anticipated giving desk jobs. They were sent there to train for a role in a war zone.

The officers there were divided into groups of four—one was trained as a prisoner interrogator, another as a photographic interpreter, the third as an operations man, and the fourth as a supply person. Jones's background as an attorney made him a logical choice for prisoner interrogator in his group. He facetiously suggested that he was assigned the task of interrogating German prisoners because he had once confided to a superior officer that he had read German playwright Johann Wolfgang von Goethe's poetic drama *Faust*, meanwhile failing to tell him that he had read an English translation. The photographic interpreter in the group was Burt Etherington, a graduate of Princeton and an avid golfer, who worshipped the man with whom he was now working side by side.

The students studied long hours at a stretch at the Intelligence School, invariably leaving them mentally fatigued. Each of them sought their own venues at which to unwind, a local saloon for some. Jones one day opted for the golf course. He turned to Etherington and suggested that they play a round of golf together at Harrisburg Country Club, which had invited soldiers to use its facilities. Of course, Jones required no such invitation; he had access in perpetuity to any course in the country by virtue of his standing in the golf community.

"I don't think so," Etherington said, declining Jones's offer. "I'm not a very good player. I'd hold you up."

The prospect of playing a round with a man regarded as the best in history mortified Etherington, who also considered the crowd that Jones might attract. A crowd would amplify the intimidation factor and the chance that he might embarrass himself.

"Nonsense," Jones said. "I don't play against the player anyway. I always play the course."

Jones was referring to his eternal opponent, the one he called Old Man Par. It was a perfect mind-set for golf, a sport unlike any other; a player could control only his own score and had no bearing—physically, at least—on an opponent's score. In other words, a golfer can't play defense. Jones's philosophy was also a useful diplomatic device, a way for him to give assurance to a playing partner that disproportionate skill levels had no bearing on whether they would have a good time. If Jones were to have avoided playing golf with those of inferior skills, he would have usually played alone.

Etherington considered the offer again. Jones's graciousness and the opportunity for Etherington to say that he had played golf with the immortal Bobby Jones was too much incentive to resist.

"All right," Etherington said. "Let's go."

Etherington's concern that Jones might attract a crowd was not unfounded. Anytime Jones ventured onto a course was an occasion for those in the vicinity to drop what they were doing to have a look. When Jones and Etherington arrived at the first tee, a throng of three thousand was there waiting. Jones politely awarded Etherington the honor to hit first. A shaking Etherington declined and insisted that Jones go first, which allowed him a few more moments to see whether he could rein in his nervousness. After Jones hit his drive down the first fairway, Etherington nervously stuck a tee in the ground with shaking hands that made the simple task of teeing a ball a difficult one. He then addressed his ball and swung so hard that he had no control of the club. He missed the ball entirely, to his horror. The crowd groaned. His second effort was only moderately better; he hooked it wickedly, the ball screaming past the out-of-bounds stakes left of the fairway. More groans. He overcompensated with his third swing and sliced the ball so far right that it, too, went out of bounds.

The crowd at that point was laughing at the spectacle of this man, an Army officer, Jones's military equal, unable to control either his nerves or his golf ball. Jones finally sidled up to Etherington, threw an arm around him, and suggested that the ball would have a better chance at finding the fairway were he to slow down his swing, thus allowing his clubhead a greater chance at squaring itself at impact. Etherington gratefully accepted Jones's impromptu lesson, and his sixth stroke from the first tee sent the ball in an impressive arc down the fairway. The crowd erupted in cheers. Etherington relaxed and played reasonably well the rest of the day, alongside "one of the finest persons I have ever met."

It was an eventful day that Etherington was certain to remember, a blessed distraction from the grim realities that soldiers faced in a time of war. For Jones, it was a welcome respite from the daily grind of preparing for battle. The fact that his work was more important than his golf reintroduced him to the joy that the game had once routinely provided him. Jones, on this day, was a happy man, happier still that the war might have an important role for him after all.

After completing his Intelligence School courses, he was assigned to the 84th Fighter Wing of the Ninth Tactical Air Command of the Ninth Air Force, destination London and beyond. Bobby Jones's concerns were ultimately as unfounded as Eisenhower's. Jones, too, was finally going to war.

9

A CALL TO SERVE

Golfers Go to War

Clearly the stars were aligned in 1912. One by one they emerged from their mothers' wombs—Byron Nelson on February 4; Sam Snead on May 27; Ben Hogan on August 13. Thirty years later, they were the three best players in golf, collectively promising to make theirs the greatest era in golf history. Of course, thirty years later, America was at war and the three of them were of an age that required that they answer their nation's call to service. The era of Nelson, Snead, and Hogan was on hold.

The golf world continued to monitor them, nonetheless; it was waiting to see what form their service to the war effort took. The first to enter the service was Snead, who had enlisted in the Navy only a day after winning the PGA Championship in 1942. Late in 1942, Hogan decided to pursue flight school, ultimately intent on taking the teaching skills he had acquired helping others with their golf and applying them to teaching student pilots to fly. Nelson soon learned that he would never wear a uniform; he was a "free-bleeder," a condition that was considered a mild form of hemophilia, and was classified 4-F. He would have to find an alternative way of contributing.

None was likely to venture too far from a golf course during the war. Men of their skill and stature were attractive to stateside Army and Navy officers, who to a large degree were keenly interested in improving their golf games. Only at the outset of his naval career, for instance, was Seaman Sam Snead an ordinary swab in training, subject to the same indoctrination as anyone else. His duties included learning the words to the Navy song, though they failed to resonate in any meaningful way for him:

> *Anchors Aweigh, my boys, Anchors Aweigh.*
> *Farewell to college joys, we sail at break of day-ay-*
>   *ay-ay.*
> *Through our last night on shore, drink to the foam,*
> *Until we meet once more. Here's wishing you a happy*
>   *voyage home.*

Snead was destined to sail, though not in the traditional sense. He was going to sail through his Navy years largely on a golf course. The only opponents he was likely to encounter would be on the first tee.

Athletes did not always receive special treatment in the service. The exceptions were those in possession of a skill that a superior officer found appealing, and even useful. Among the exceptions was Snead, whose distinctive talent was a golf swing that was smoother than naval dress whites at inspection. It was evident shortly after the conclusion of his training at the Norfolk Naval Station that Snead was destined to play out his service on a golf course.

He was ordered to report to gunnery school in Pensacola, Florida, following indoctrination. He excelled in marksmanship—in a shooting contest, Seaman Snead hit four hundred out of four hundred targets. He was a celebrated sharpshooter, as those Army boys from Fort Dix had learned by watching him dismantle their own Private Jimmy Turnesa in the PGA Championship final earlier in the year.

Snead never made it to gunnery school, however. When word of his golf prowess—including his PGA victory—began to spread, the Navy brass changed his orders; he was to remain in Norfolk. The official reason given was that officers there wanted him to teach golf to pilots, for the purpose of improving their focus. Flying warplanes required unwavering concentration for hours on end, as did competitive golf. Of course, these disparate activities were not remotely similar. A mental lapse on the golf course might result in a bogey. A similar lapse in a dogfight might result in a bogey shooting you out of the sky. It was far more likely that the reason Snead was ordered to remain in Norfolk was to teach golf to and play golf with his superior officers.

Either way, Snead was not complaining to any significant degree. In 1942, the U.S. Navy had acquired a wonderful course in Norfolk, Sewell's Point Golf Club, by condemnation. It had opened in 1926 and was designed by the esteemed architect Donald Ross, a native of Dornoch, Scotland. Among the courses Ross built in America were the Number Two Course at Pinehurst, Scioto Country Club, Oakland Hills Country Club, Interlachen, Inverness Golf Club, and Oak Hill, a pantheon of architectural genius. The Navy appropriating a Donald Ross design was akin to an art gallery confiscating an original Monet. Sewell's Point was designed in a circle of holes that went clockwise, similar to the renowned Muirfield links in Scotland, with which Ross was so familiar.

Teaching golf and playing with officers failed to satisfy his competitive desires. Snead wanted action, and he discovered that he could find it at a club near the Navy base. When time permitted, Snead changed into his civvies and went over to the club to find a game with a potential reward attached to it. He began to pick pockets with such frequency there that the club pro reported him to his commanding officer.

"Have you been playing over there?" the captain asked him.

"Yes, sir. But I go in civilian clothes."

"You don't play in uniform?"

"No, sir. That'd be hard to do, sir. You couldn't swing very well in uniform."

"Well, cut it out, sailor," the captain said.

"Yes, sir."

Snead concluded that the club pro had probably been angry at him for stealing his action.

The Navy proved little more than an extension of home for Snead. A golfer by trade (and one who had been born and raised in Virginia), he had a Donald Ross course at his disposal and was ordered by a nation at war to play it with pilots and officers in tow. His battle station was the first tee.

THE INEVITABILITY THAT Ben Hogan would be asked to join the military fray got him thinking about how he might best serve his country. The Army was out, a wise decision, perhaps, in that it prevented the diminutive man (five feet eight inches tall) that the press habitually called Little Ben from being portrayed as a toy soldier. Little Ben, meanwhile, had grown accustomed to towering over the world of which he was a part, which in the early days of the war was golf. In 1942, he won six tournaments, including the Hale America National Open Golf Tournament. His career was soaring. Maybe he should soar too. He decided to learn how to fly. It was a curious choice for a man who was not entirely comfortable traveling by air, but inasmuch as he was already too old to qualify as a combat pilot, at least he could perform a service with which he was comfortable. His objective was to teach flying.

"I've been instructing golf for years," he said, "and I feel I should be able to convert whatever teaching ability I have to instructing fliers. I feel like I can do my part a little better this way."

So in November of 1942, with the tour virtually grounded because of the exodus of its marquee stars to various branches of the military, Hogan left his home in Fort Worth and traveled north to Tulsa, Oklahoma, where he enrolled in the Spartan School of Aeronautics, a civilian flight-training school. "I'm all through with golf until we get this war job done," Hogan said. "My job now is learning to fly."

Golf was not going to release its grip on Hogan so blithely, of course. Tulsa was home to one of the finest courses in the country, Southern Hills Country Club, and Hogan intended to become a regular there, keeping his game honed in the event that tournament golf would return sooner than expected. And the moment he arrived in Tulsa, he found himself in the company of another golfer; tour pro Ky Laffoon drove eighty miles from his home in Miami, Oklahoma, in the northeast corner of the state, to greet Hogan upon his arrival in Tulsa. Laffoon was pondering whether to join Hogan at the Spartan School, despite his own aversion to air travel. Laffoon eventually gave in to his apprehension, leaving Hogan to fly solo.

Hogan's reputation at the Spartan School preceded him, certainly; even before classroom instruction began, he was already a wanted man, with his choice of three flight-instructor jobs awaiting him once he completed flight school. He was not considering any of them; when he completed his training, he intended to remain at Spartan as an instructor, at least until his country beckoned him.

The nation's call came even before he concluded his training. On March 1, 1943, Hogan received his draft notice. The Tarrant County (Texas) Selective Service Board No. 2 was ordering him to report for a physical examination and induction into the armed services on March 25. He was joining the Army Air Corps.

THE ARMY ALSO WANTED Byron Nelson, whose sundry skills included an exceedingly useful one for a branch of the service with long-range armaments. He could judge distance. When Nelson wasn't on tour, he was the pro at Inverness Country Club in Toledo, Ohio. He frequently played there with a colonel from nearby Camp Perry, who marveled at Nelson's ability to eyeball a target and calculate the precise yardage to it. The colonel concluded that Nelson must be the best in the world at doing so. This skill's utility in golf stemmed from the fact that courses offered no yardage guidance, leaving it to the golfer's intuition to tell him which club to hit to a specific target. Only Gene Andrews, a skilled amateur from Missouri, had figured out that by pacing a course in advance of a round or a tournament, and recording the yardage, he could remove the guesswork from the equation. Andrews even went to the trouble of training himself on a football gridiron, walking from yard line to yard line, ten paces for ten yards, until the measurement was ingrained.

Even had Nelson thought to do so, he would have eschewed the practice as wholly unnecessary, as good as he was at calculating the distance strictly by feel. The colonel was indelibly impressed. He frequently queried Nelson on the yardage between his ball and the pin, chose his club accordingly, and routinely hit his ball the proper distance. Camp Perry was an artillery post. The ability to accurately gauge the distance to an enemy target was the secret to succeeding in the artillery game. The colonel saw an artillery all-star awaiting only induction.

"When your draft number comes up, tell me," the colonel said to Nelson one day. "I want you."

Nelson was certain that the artillery was his likely military calling, and like every able-bodied young American, he was eager to do his duty. The only obstacle was the able-bodied element of the equation. When Nelson was a boy, a simple nosebleed was a cause for alarm; once the bleeding started, it was disinclined to stop. He virtually thought nothing about this until his draft number was finally called. Yet even when he reported for his physical, he was only mildly concerned that his medical history would have a bearing on whether the Army would accept him. He was wrong. Typically, blood takes two and a half minutes to clot. His took nearly five minutes to clot. In other words, he was a leading candidate to bleed to death in the event that he began spilling quantities of blood on a battlefield. This was an unacceptable risk from the perspective of America's armed forces. Nelson was classified 4-F and politely told to go home.

This was a blow to any young American man, not that all of them were anxious to join a business that had others shooting at them. Shortly after the military deemed Nelson medically defective, it also rejected his friend and colleague Harold McSpaden, better known by his nickname, Jug. A Kansas City native, Jug McSpaden was ten when his interest in golf was piqued by Harry Vardon, who had played an exhibition in Kansas City where the youngster was in the crowd. When McSpaden turned professional in 1934, he began winning with regularity and considered himself a superior player to Nelson, to whom he even gave lessons. Each time Nelson suspected that his accuracy had gone awry—usually an illusion that had no basis in reality for the straightest hitter in golf—he would ask McSpaden for advice. A friendship quickly evolved, and eventually their careers became entwined when McSpaden was sidelined from war duty by his own medical condition, an irreparable sinus problem that earned him a 4-F classification as well.

One day, Nelson and McSpaden began discussing what they might do Stateside on behalf of the Allied war effort. A few days later, Fred Corcoran, manager of the PGA Tournament Bureau, called and suggested that they contribute by participating in a series of exhibitions designed to raise money for war-related causes. They readily and happily agreed to do so.

GOLF WAS A useful skill in the military; courses abounded at military bases around the country, each of them requiring a professional to give lessons and run tournaments, even in wartime. Officers typically were fanatical about golf and relished the opportunity to bring a famous touring pro aboard. Many of the pros gleefully accepted the opportunity to serve their country on a practice tee, where the only shrapnel was the divots launched by expertly struck shots.

Yet others enlisted with the intent of doing their part to defeat the Japanese or the Germans. Among them was Willie Turnesa, from the golfing Turnesas, a family of seven brothers, all of them skilled at golf. His brother Jimmy reached the final of the PGA Championship in 1942 only to lose to Snead. Another brother, Mike, was second to Hogan in the Hale America National Open Golf Tournament. Willie Turnesa won the U.S. Amateur in 1938 and was a career amateur who was widely regarded as second only to Bobby Jones among the greatest amateurs in American history. The esteemed British writer Bernard Darwin dubbed him "Willie the Wedge" after watching him get up and down in two shots from each of the thirteen bunkers he hit in the final.

"Crowns without coins" Willie called his amateur victories, for which he was given a trophy or a medallion but no money.

Willie enlisted in the Navy, a curious choice for a man who was terrified of the water and had never learned to swim. Turnesa's golf skills kept him landlocked at any rate, to his chagrin. He wanted to engage the enemy, but the Navy had other plans. Turnesa was sent to gunnery school at the Naval Air Station in Hollywood, Florida, where the shots he fired came entirely on the golf course, a plethora of them in the rounds of golf he played with superior officers. He was also assigned the task of teaching golf to sailors there.

Golf was high on officers' priority lists, even in a time of war. When Turnesa was there, Navy engineers who were supposed to be applying their training to the building of airstrips were ordered to construct an eighteen-hole golf course instead. When the course was completed, a sign was posted, noting the pecking order for those wishing to play: officers, officers' wives, noncommissioned officers, and enlisted men.

Rumors of the scam eventually reached Washington, D.C., and the office of United States senator Harry S. Truman, who was in charge of a Senate committee investigating fraud and waste at U.S. military bases. Truman, whose sporting interests failed to extend beyond horseshoes, was earning plaudits for the aggressive manner in which he pursued waste, and he wasn't going to pass on the possibility of unleashing his wrath on a game in which he had no interest. He decided to investigate the rumor further and made arrangements to travel to Florida.

When officers there heard that he was en route, they frantically attempted to devise a plan that might hoodwink the senator into concluding that the golf course was less a scam than a need. The best they could do in a panic was to create a new sign, reversing the pecking order of play, giving enlisted men the highest priority, followed by noncommissioned officers, officers' wives, and, finally, officers.

The idea proved to be ingenious, an act of inspired deception. When Truman arrived and saw the sign, he was delighted at the officers' collective thoughtfulness for putting the enlisted men's interests ahead of their own. Nothing was ever said about the expenditure again, and the original sign was put back in place.

Turnesa played there often, with a variety of officers, many of them looking for a free lesson. On one occasion, his commanding officer asked him to be his partner in a grudge match with officers at another course. On the day before the match, the CO ordered him to meet him at the base airfield. The CO was a pilot, who had secured a plane for the afternoon.

"Where are we going, sir?" Willie asked the CO.

"We're going to play a practice round," the CO replied.

"But we don't have any clubs," Willie said.

"We don't need any."

The CO intended to survey the course, which he had never before played. When the plane arrived over the course, the CO put it into a steep dive toward the first hole. He leveled off about one hundred feet above the ground and flew the length of the first hole, inspecting it for hidden hazards. This was his idea of playing a practice round, covering eighteen holes by plane, while putting the aircraft through a series of acrobatics to allow him to follow the terrain. A nervous flyer at the outset of the flight, Turnesa reaffirmed his commitment to travel on terra firma at the end of it.

Another amateur of renown also joined the Navy with the intention of serving a stint in the Pacific. Stanford University graduate Sandy Tatum was the reigning national collegiate champion when he enlisted in 1942. Golf was in his bloodstream; his father was a member at the exclusive Los Angeles Country Club, which had given young Sandy daily access to one of the finest golf courses in the world, the famed North Course there.

His was a life of privilege until duty called. The Navy ordered him to report to indoctrination school at the University of Arizona in Tucson. He was quartered in a gymnasium in which five hundred double bunks had been installed. A Stanford education was not necessary for Tatum to have determined that he now had nine hundred ninety-nine roommates. Among them was professional golfer Lawson Little, whom Tatum identified as an "extraordinary character, a raconteur who liked his grog." The troops would be dismissed every Saturday afternoon at one o'clock and would not be required to return until Sunday evening at five o'clock. Little would repair to a local bistro and hold court until the proprietor said that it was time to go home. Once the Navy brass learned that Little was a professional golfer and that Tatum was the national collegiate champion, their privileges expanded to include frequent golf outings. Eventually they were recruited to participate in a Red Cross exhibition at El Rio Country Club on behalf of the war effort, the two of them teaming against Bob Goldwater and Leo Diegel, the latter a prominent tour pro who was also the head pro at El Rio, the area's only private facility.

Goldwater was not enlisted to join the group simply to lend local celebrity to the ticket, although his name was a familiar one; he was part of the family that owned Goldwater's, a popular department store in Phoenix. Goldwater was recruited because he was an accomplished golfer, who had won the state championship at sixteen and might even have considered playing professionally had it paid better.

More than a thousand spectators were on hand at El Rio, and

they witnessed an even match, until Goldwater ducked into the clubhouse at the turn. He returned with a big cup of gin that helped untether his enormous talent and he birdied four straight holes to bury Tatum and Little.

Tatum, meanwhile, had begun to realize the benefits of bringing golf skill and a modicum of golf celebrity to the armed services, staffed largely by officers for whom golf was their principal diversion. Tatum was among the millions of angry Americans seeking to avenge Pearl Harbor, or, as he put it, "Like everybody else, I wanted to go out and get shot at." But he had a bad eye and an engineering degree, one precluding him from going to sea, the other an asset in the shipyard. He was sent to the naval shipyard at Mare Island, in San Pablo Bay north of San Francisco, where he worked on ship repair and refining his golf game.

A couple of admirals regularly invited him to play. Each of them also organized golf teams that engaged in spirited matches. Meanwhile, at the end of each working day, Tatum and three friends drove south to the Stanford University Golf Course, taking advantage of the extended daylight savings time. They often finished their rounds in pitch darkness, the flame from a cigarette lighter placed in the cup illuminating the target on the green.

Chick Harbert, perched ostensibly on the threshold of stardom, was another professional golfer who signed up, joining the Army Air Corps Reserve in 1942. He, too, intended to contribute to the war effort, but his age, twenty-seven, made him ineligible for combat flight training. Eventually the Army concluded that he could contribute best by raising money for the war effort through tournament and exhibition golf.

A host of others from the golf world joined the ranks of the uniformed. Porky Oliver was drafted and joined the Army;

Jimmy Thomson joined the Coast Guard. Snead was joined in the Navy by Jimmy Demaret, Lew Worsham, and Herman Keiser.

Not all of them would serve their country on the golf course either. Peter Page, the captain of the Princeton golf team in 1940 and 1941 and the president of the National Intercollegiate Golf Association, was a second lieutenant in the Marine Corps. He was with the torpedo plane forces in the South Pacific, when he was killed in action.

It was a sorrowful reminder of the indiscriminate nature of war and the price that even some of those from the sheltered world of golf were willing to pay on behalf of peace and freedom, those for whom there would be no *happy voyage home,* as the Navy song implored.

HOGAN EASILY PASSED his physical examination and weighed in at 138 pounds, a career high for Little Ben. On the prearranged day, he was sworn in to service in Dallas, then received the standard seven-day leave to get his affairs in order before reporting to the induction center at Camp Wolters in Mineral Wells, Texas, forty-five miles west of his home in Fort Worth. Once again, he declared that he was done playing competitive golf for the duration and hinted that even recreational golf was in jeopardy. "That's up to the government," he said. "Right now, I'm interested in making Uncle Sam a good soldier."

The fact was that Hogan and golf were inseparable, and even his service career was not likely to come between them. Once processing was completed at Camp Wolters, Hogan was ordered to report to Tarrant Field, site of the Army Air Corps combat crew school outside Fort Worth. He was required to live in the field's barracks for six weeks, after which he could begin commuting from home in Fort Worth. He was joined at Tarrant Field by another golfer of note, Earl Stewart, once a national collegiate champion. When the summer arrived, Hogan was sent to the Army Air Force Officer Candidates School in Miami, where he encountered another renowned golfer, Horton Smith. Moreover, drills at Officer Candidate School were conducted on the Bayshore Golf Course. Bayshore had opened in 1923, a part of the vision of developer Carl Fisher, whose goal was to entice wealthy golfers from northern climes to abandon the winter weather there and head south. The course was a popular one until the war came and the U.S. Army appropriated it as a training ground. Actually, the Army generously agreed to pay rent on the property—one dollar a year.

Hogan and Smith spent hours on the Bayshore Golf Course, without hitting a single shot. Their celebrity status did not excuse them from the minutiae of Army training, which included the requisite marching drills, perhaps reinforcing with Hogan the idea that repetition is the key to perfection and that it is found in the dirt—in this case in a left, left, left-right-left cadence.

In November of 1943, Hogan received his Army Air Corps commission and officially became Second Lieutenant Ben Hogan. He returned to Fort Worth, where he was allowed to live at home while working in the Civilian Pilot Training program. Yet again he declared that his "golf is over for the duration. But I'm planning to take up where I left off when the war is won." Eventually, Hogan was among those instructors given a leave of absence; pilots returning from war zones were better equipped to teach flying than Civilian Pilot Training instructors, leaving Hogan without a job other than returning the sheen to his golf game.

For three straight years—the two preceding the war and the first year of the war—Hogan had won the Vardon Trophy, presented to the player with the year's lowest scoring average. His reign was not necessarily over; his reputation ensured that golf was not over for the duration, his declarations notwithstanding, that there were too many colonels and generals who were determined to order him to report to the first tee to play a round of golf with them. Hogan was destined to spend much of his military career serving his country in eighteen-hole stretches, keeping his game finely honed.

Snead's Navy career could also be traced from golf course to golf course, usually in San Diego, where he had reported for duty on October 9, 1942, to the Naval Training Center there. For instance, on March 1, 1943, Snead shot a 58 on the Sail Ho Golf Course at the Naval Training Center, a remarkable score on which the press picked up, while failing to note the fact that the Sail Ho Course was exceedingly short and played to a par of 58. Another magazine account noted that "Sailor Sam Snead and Coastguardsman Jimmy Thomson played in an exhibition match against Lloyd Mangrum and Marvin Stahl on Mar. 21 at the San Diego naval training station golf course." The same year Snead won the San Diego County Open and shot a course-record 60 at Balboa Park Golf Course in San Diego. Snead also played regularly at the San Diego Country Club, which the Navy had commandeered. He often drew crowds too. One young San Diego boy, Gene Littler, an aspiring and promising golfer, often went out to San Diego Country Club and walked along with Snead, studying his graceful swing and his perfect tempo with the intention of incorporating both into his own developing swing.

So it was that two of golf's leading lights seemed destined to contribute little more than entertainment for military brass with the authority to bask in their reflected glory.

NELSON AND MCSPADEN BECAME entertainers too. In one year's time, they traveled back and forth across the country four times, staging fund-raisers and performing for soldiers. When Nelson's wife, Louise, was unable to make the trip—more often than not the case in 1943—Nelson and Jug often traveled together, crossing vast distances via train. (Commercial flying was not a viable option; when a plane was full, Nelson was required to pay for an extra ticket to account for his golf clubs.)

Nelson always kept a diary of sorts in a little black notebook he carried with him. To while away time on these monotonous, endless rail excursions, he enjoyed working with calculations. On one such trip, he began calculating how much money he would require to retire comfortably, eventually concluding that $100,000 should be enough. More than curiosity was behind his retirement ciphering; though he was only thirty-one, he had already decided he did not want to face any more important four-foot putts than were necessary to assure a reasonable standard of living for the rest of his life.

It was a pipe dream in 1943. Tournament golf was largely on hiatus, so most of the golf he was playing was on behalf of others. His efforts were tireless. He not only played with McSpaden, but with anyone else available in a particular time and place. An Associated Press story on February 28, 1943, recounted the thirty-fifth exhibition match that Nelson had played. He teamed with Bill Clark, a Texas club professional, and defeated Jimmy Demaret and another club pro, Don Murphy, 3 and 1, in a match in Texarkana, Texas, that raised $300 for the local Red Cross Canteen Fund.

The stage was small, the sum was smaller. But together they were symbolic of the sacrifice that Nelson intended to make due to his inability to don a uniform and march on Berlin. Nelson was willing to range far and wide, to big city or small, from the West Coast to the East, wherever his presence might help scrape together a few bucks on behalf of the war effort. Hundreds of dollars eventually added to thousands of dollars and eventually to tens of thousands of dollars. In the thirty-five exhibition dates he had played to that point, he had helped raise more than $60,000 for the Red Cross, Navy Relief, and the USO. And he was just getting started.

Nelson hooked up with Bob Hope and Bing Crosby for a series of exhibitions. The three of them often traveled via military plane, one of which bogeyed a landing on a rainy day in Memphis in 1943, sliding off a narrow runway and into a field of mud in which it became mired. A bulldozer was summoned to extricate the plane from the mud, at which point the three of them made a mad dash for the club, finally arriving ninety minutes late. The crowd gamely stayed put and was gleeful when they arrived.

On another occasion, Nelson and Crosby arrived via train in San Antonio. A car and driver were waiting to whisk them to Fort Sam Houston, where Crosby was scheduled to sing in addition to playing a golf exhibition with Nelson. Two armed soldiers stood sentry at the gate to the fort, yet the driver ignored them, never even bothering to slow down as he went through the gate. Two armed sentries at a second gate took notice of this breach, raised their rifles, pointed them at the car, and ordered the driver to stop. Nelson in the front seat and Crosby in the back both hit the floor, terrified that the guards were going to open fire. Fortunately for the future of the golf and entertainment industries, the driver braked and explained who his passengers were. The guards scolded the driver but allowed him to proceed.

For shorter treks on Nelson's itinerary, he traveled via automobile. Of those thirty-five matches to which he drove, he put fifteen thousand miles on his car at a time when gasoline was scarce and being rationed. To accommodate his automobile travel, those organizing the exhibitions provided the requisite gas stamps. He drove a 1939 Studebaker President, light-green, a four-door sedan with which he had been presented for winning the 1939 U.S. Open. Studebaker ads showed him posing with a Studebaker Champion, a two-door model that was insufficient for a traveling golfer loaded down with luggage and golf equipment, so he opted for the President.

The Texas license plates on his car, meanwhile, often betrayed the distances he had traveled, targeting him for derision. An apparently healthy young man in civilian clothes, driving a car with out-of-state plates, would strike observers as some sort of malingerer consuming more than his fair share of valuable fuel, a healthy wastrel failing to do his part to help defeat the enemy. On more than one occasion, he received menacing looks from those who did not recognize him. A man in Arizona shook his fist at him and Louise as they drove through the state en route to an exhibition. A man in Toledo once phoned the rationing board to complain about him. Nelson was summoned by the board to explain himself. He showed them his gas stamps, all of which were legal, and he was allowed to continue, to the greater good of the Allied war effort.

A kind, selfless man, Nelson may not have been able to fight the war, but he was still helping to win it.

OTHER THAN EXHIBITION and service golf, there was virtually no other kind to be played in 1943. Most tour professionals had service obligations, leaving a largely ragtag group behind to hold together what was left of the tour.

Among them was Lefty Stackhouse of Seguin, Texas, who traveled with only a modest supply of skill by professional standards, and at that it was largely kept under lock and key by too much hooch and not enough poise. He was a walking stick of dynamite at the end of a fuse that was no longer than a gimme and was detonated by a hooked tee shot that reliably surfaced at inopportune times.

Legend has it that Lefty once walked over to a thorny rosebush after hitting a nasty hook in a round with Ben Hogan. He stuck his right hand into the bush and began whipping it back and forth, the thorns tearing bloody gashes in his hand.

"That'll teach you to roll on me," he said to the offending hand. He then addressed his other hand.

"And don't think you're going to get away with it either," he said, as he began thrashing the rosebush with his left hand.

Lefty was known to punch his own chin in response to a wayward shot or a missed putt. Occasionally, he'd even bite himself, usually on the hand because it was the most accessible body part. When self-flagellation did not occur to him, his clubs bore the brunt of his anger. He frequently had to borrow a set, while his own were in the repair shop, having broken shafts replaced. One time, a sporting goods representative attempting to get his golf line some publicity convinced Lefty to try a set of his company's clubs in a practice round. When Stackhouse finished his round, he delivered a graphic assessment of the clubs. "I don't think they're quite right for me," he said to the company rep, as he turned the bag upside down, spilling pieces of broken clubs onto the ground.

Stackhouse once tossed his bag into a greenside pond, then for five dollars volunteered to jump in with it. When a curious onlooker ponied up the five dollars, in went Stackhouse. When he emerged from the murky pond, he grabbed the money and said, "At least I beat this sumbitch game for five dollars."

An insatiable thirst for alcohol elevated his volatility, at least until he passed out; on a bunker shot once, he was said to have fainted at the top of his backswing, collapsing face-first in the sand. He often brought the nineteenth hole onto the course with him, in a bottle he kept stashed in his bag.

At the height of the war, with a preponderance of his colleagues off in uniform somewhere, Stackhouse was one of eighteen professionals entered in a tournament that had committed to paying the top twenty finishers. This meant that every pro in the field would be remunerated, regardless of their performance, with one caveat: They had to complete the tournament.

On the night before the final round, Stackhouse began a party that ended only when he reported to the first tee the next morning. At the end of nine holes, Stackhouse was staggering as though he had been in a brawl, and on the losing side of one at that. In the gallery, as a guest of Tournament Bureau manager Fred Corcoran, was Alvin York, a decorated veteran of World War I, and a bona fide war hero, who had been accorded the Congressional Medal of Honor and the French Croix de Guerre. York had never played the game, never seen it played before, so when he saw Stackhouse sweating and stumbling as he made his way toward the ninth green, he was taken aback. "I had no idea golf was such a strenuous game," York said incredulously.

When Stackhouse holed out on the ninth green, he was feeling so poorly that he accepted Corcoran's suggestion that he repair to the clubhouse to take a nap before completing his round and collecting a check, an acceptable practice in those days. The quick nap inevitably became a deep sleep from which Stackhouse did not emerge until nightfall, when the clubhouse was closed and the course was empty. The fact that he failed to complete the tournament meant that he had no claim to the payday that was guaranteed before he nodded off.

Stackhouse's performance in the tournament was a metaphor for the state of wartime tournament golf; it was staggering and was struggling to regain its equilibrium. In 1943, the PGA sanctioned only three tournaments, not entirely from a sense that it was its duty to curtail the schedule out of deference to those off at war doing the nation's dirty work. The tour was abbreviated mostly because its stars, including Hogan and Snead, were otherwise occupied. Golf was never a particularly riveting sport; it depended on its marquee muscle to pull spectators to it. So tournament golf virtually vanished. The PGA announced in January that its tour would play only three events in 1943, with $17,000 in prize money. The U.S. Open had been postponed for the duration of the war, as had the Masters. The PGA Championship was canceled in 1943, and the British Open had been dormant since 1939. If the show must go on, who was going onstage?

Stand-ins were ready, for tournaments as well as players. Chicago became the hub of American golf. The Hale America National Open Golf Tournament in 1942 gave way to the Chicago Victory National Golf Championship, played at Beverly Country Club. The winner was Sam Byrd, the man who had replaced Babe Ruth in right field for the New York Yankees and had become a golf professional upon his retirement from baseball. No one argued that Byrd had won the national championship, as was done a year before when Hogan had won the Hale America. No one had either the energy or a strong enough argument to make a case on behalf of Byrd.

The Chicago Victory event wasn't even the most prestigious tournament in Chicago. The All-American Open at Tam O'Shanter Country Club was the year's marquee event. The product of promoter George May's ambition, the All-American Open was the offspring of the Tam O'Shanter National Open played the previous year. The dearth of events in 1943 enabled May to wrangle a commitment from the PGA to have the All-American become an official tour event. Jug McSpaden won the All-American by holing a twenty-five-foot birdie putt in a sudden-death play-off with Buck White, whose appearance near the top of a leader board was symbolic of the plight of the tour. White was an unknown professional who was able to contend only as a result of a notice-able lack of depth in a field that even included heavyweight boxer Joe Louis. On furlough from the Army, Louis missed the cut. The tournament nonetheless was an overwhelming success by virtue of its having sold $900,000 in war bonds.

The North and South Open Championship was also played, but it was not an official PGA event in '43, as it had been in previous years. Tournament officials recognized that it was useless to play the tournament as usual with most of the tour pros serving their country. Instead, they came up with the idea of restricting entry only to those who were older, eventually settling on a minimum age of thirty-eight. The winner was Bobby Cruickshank, a World War I veteran, who was forty-eight and a grandfather. Cruickshank's seventy-two-hole score was 291, twenty-one strokes more than Hogan had made in winning the event a year earlier.

The PGA finally concluded its anemic year with the Miami Open, played a few days before Christmas. An obscure pro, Steve Warga, won by three strokes. Warga was an airline radio operator by trade.

Neither Hogan nor Snead played in a single event. Nelson played in all three tour events, finishing no better than third. He won only a nontour event, the Kentucky Open, by three shots over Chick Harbert to earn a $1,000 war bond.

Even for those who earned their livings attempting to beat one another, 1943 was about beating only Hitler and Hirohito, the faces of the enemy, recognized as such even by golf. "Hirohito," one writer wrote of the Japanese emperor, "has to play golf alone, because nobody is worthy of playing with him; moreover, if you beat the head cheese, you'd be expected to commit hara-kiri."

As for Hitler, he had become a caricature, prominently featured by the Acushnet Company, manufacturer of the new Titleist golf ball, in a full-page advertisement that addressed the growing ball shortage. It was headlined, "Runner Up—1943." The ad copy read in part:

> There he is, boys—the competitor we have to beat this year. It may be a close match, it will be tough going most of the way, and it might run over to an extra hole or two in 1944. But he is the boy that's going to fork up for "caddies," "green fees," and "drinks" when the last putt is holed out.
>
> Yes, we're going to collect, but to do it we've got to play the game his way. That means more guns and less golf. . . . It means that the rubber we used to wind into the best golf balls we knew how to make has got to be sent out there in tires and gas masks and a thousand and one other pieces of essential equipment, to help keep Adolf pressing to stay up with the championship pace we're setting.

The ad could have been speaking for the game in its entirety. The war was America's only priority. Golf—and the promising era represented by Nelson, Snead, and Hogan—would have to wait.

10

———— • ————

GOOD ENOUGH TO
PLAY WITH
SNEAD AND NELSON

Service and Sacrifice

Eighteen holes one bright afternoon in the summer of 1931 were an awakening for Joe Burke, who for the better part of his fourteen years had valiantly attempted to engage his sibling in a rivalry. When the last putt had fallen that day, Joe finally surrendered to the reality that all men (or boys) are *not* created equal, not even twins.

Joe and John Burke were born minutes apart on St. Patrick's Day, 1917, in Newport, Rhode Island. They weren't two of a kind, nor even from the same deck, when the athletic genes were dealt. The Burkes were children of the Depression, though like other children of that time they weren't aware that they were poor. They even played the elitist game of golf, which was even less an egalitarian game in the worst of times, in the early thirties, when New York hotel clerks began asking guests at check-in whether they wanted a room for sleeping or for leaping. The Burkes' older brother Edmund was the professional at Wanumetonomy Golf and Country Club in Middletown, Rhode Island, giving the twins access to a rich man's game that might never have found room in the otherwise impenetrable troika of baseball, football, and basketball that occupied a boy's life.

Joe and John caddied at Wanumetonomy, each of them earning seventy-five cents a loop, plus a tip. On a busy day, they might have two loops apiece, giving them a bounty of around two dollars each. The Depression that had largely deprived fathers of honest work often required kids to contribute their earnings to the household income. The Burke twins always dutifully handed their two dollars to their mother. She in turn refunded twenty-five cents to each of the boys, who often spent it in the nefarious ways of youth, notably on gambling.

Mondays were caddie days at Wanumetonomy. The course was closed to the membership, which graciously allowed the caddies to play. One such Monday in the summer of their fourteenth year, Joe and John played a spirited match for their quarters. For Joe, his was a round that held the possibility of a breakthrough, a triumph over a brother who routinely reminded him that although they were twins they weren't identical. Pars came effortlessly for Joe, and even a couple of birdies turned up on his card to lessen the sting of the four bogeys that had ignominiously encroached on his fun. Still, the numbers added to a two-over-par 74, the best round of his young life and a triumphal occasion were it not for the fact that John countered with an even-par 72 to win Joe's hard-earned quarter.

Joe fished the quarter from his pocket and made his final payment to brother John. At that moment, he had decided to foreclose on mounting what might pass as a rivalry, choosing instead to surrender to the fact that if a ball were involved, his brother was simply better. He revealed his intention with a simple declaration:

"To heck with it," and from that point forward his role in Johnny's life was permanently altered. He was no longer going to offer himself up as a human sacrifice to Johnny's skill, no longer content with being his foil, and instead he joined the winning side, becoming his brother's biggest booster.

The size of the ball was immaterial to John's ability to excel with it. He was proficient enough at basketball that Georgetown University in Washington, D.C., awarded him a basketball scholarship. Emerging from the insolvency that the Depression wrought, the Burke family opened a combination bowling alley/pool hall, the Brunswick Bowling Alley, which afforded John a couple other stages on which to outperform the competition. He became an expert at duckpins, the type of bowling done at the Brunswick Bowling Alley. Duckpins was a derivative of regular bowling; everything was identical except the sizes of the ball and the pins, which were smaller. The game had been founded in Baltimore, in an alley owned by baseball icons Uncle Wilbert Robinson and John McGraw. When Robinson and McGraw first saw ten of the smaller pins scattered, one of the men observed, "It looks like a flock of flying ducks." A Baltimore sportswriter took note and gave the game its name.

Burke routinely scored in the 125 to 130 range, or the equivalent of scratch in golf. He was among the best players around the Newport area of Rhode Island. And when he wasn't bowling, he was on the billiards table there, where he could make the cue ball perform magic in a game of Three Cushion. He was as good at billiards as he was at duckpins.

Those games were winter diversions for Burke, who, once the weather warmed, returned to his calling. Golf was his game, not necessarily because he enjoyed it more than others, but because it had evolved into his forte. Other than the occasional tip from his brother Edmund, John had never been formally trained in the game. He had learned from watching the better players at Wanumetonomy, mentally absorbing their swings, building a visual library from which he was able to borrow in developing his own swing.

He was a natural, the kind of player for whom a seamless swing was innate. The best swings evoke the image of a door with hinges that have been oiled—a quiet, fluid movement void of strain. John Burke's swing was like that, an effortless motion that was repetitive, another hallmark of a quality player. He was also blessed with an even temperament that allowed him to dismiss mistakes rather than compound them by overheating from a bad shot or two.

Burke was only seventeen when he won the Rhode Island Amateur Championship for the first time, in 1934. He won it again the following year, defeating his opponent, Ray Lenahan, 9 and 8, in the thirty-six-hole final. In a five-year stretch, he won the state amateur four times; the only year he failed to win, 1937, he was late for a tee time and was disqualified. He won the Rhode Island Open in 1936 and 1938, an amateur beating professionals. In the latter victory, he established a tournament record, 284 for seventy-two holes, and his margin of victory was one over Jimmy Turnesa, one of seven brothers from the renowned Turnesa golfing family. Turnesa's brother, Willie, won the prestigious United States Amateur Championship that same year.

Burke was the most accomplished golfer in the history of Rhode Island, a small state, obviously, but not one without a golf heritage. Newport Country Club was among five founding clubs of the United States Golf Association and was the site of the first U.S. Open in 1895.

"That boy is going to be an internationally famous golfer one of these days," said George Gordon, the pro at nearby Wannamoisett Country Club, where Burke won the state amateur championship in 1936. "There never has been anything like him in Rhode Island. He may even become a second Bobby Jones."

Gordon was not simply exercising provincial pride. It was an opinion that was growing along with Burke's reputation. A golf club in his hands worked too efficiently for Burke to be blithely dismissed as a local phenomenon who would not hold up on a national stage.

At Georgetown, he was exposed to Wiffy Cox, the head professional at nearby Congressional Country Club and an accomplished player, who in 1934 had won the Texas Open by a stroke over Byron Nelson and Craig Wood. Congressional was Georgetown's home course, which provided Cox ample opportunity to assess young Burke's ability. Cox was convinced that Burke had a surfeit of skill and the additional benefit of an even temperament that allowed it to flourish. In Wiffy Cox's considered opinion, it was the composition of a star. "He can play on tour," Cox said. "He's good enough to play with Snead and Nelson and those guys."

The Washington press corps had also begun to take notice. "The red-haired Newport niblick nudger is remembered locally by his play in the Chevy Chase Invitation last May, when he curled a forty-foot putt on the final green to win medal honors with a 71," wrote Merrell Whittlesey in *The Washington Post* early in Burke's sophomore year at Georgetown.

The Newport niblick nudger was more than a local phenomenon. In 1938, Burke, a twenty-one-year-old sophomore, validated Cox's opinion by winning the National Intercollegiate Championship. Later in the summer he advanced to the semifinals of the prestigious Western Amateur, the first New Englander to advance that far in the tournament since Francis Ouimet won it in 1917, four years after winning the U.S. Open. Grantland Rice was even sufficiently moved by Burke's skill to commit him to verse. Rice counted Bobby Jones among his close friends and recognized a correlation in the way Burke and Jones comported themselves in public. The difference was that Jones's temperament on a golf course had to be learned; in his youth, a bad shot ignited a short fuse that set off a debilitating explosion. Jones often told the story on himself about his first-round match with another hothead, Eben Byers, in the U.S. Amateur in 1916, when Jones was fourteen. On one particular hole, an angered Byers flung his club over a hedge and would not allow his caddie to retrieve it. Jones eventually won the match, 3 and 1. "I won," Jones said later, "because Mr. Byers ran out of clubs first."

Burke was not in possession of a temper that needed taming. His demeanor enabled him to regard an errant shot as an aberration that required no further reaction or rejoinder. His manner on the course and pleasant disposition off it endeared him to anyone with whom he came in contact. It even provided him entrée into the world of privilege of which he was only peripherally aware, having grown up on the working-class side of town in Newport.

The same summer that he won the National Intercollegiate he was asked to play in the prestigious Newport Country Club Invitation, at a club that was a playground for the pedigreed socialites, many of whom called Newport home only in the summer. He was a pauper among princes, a former caddie and the son of a bowling-alley operator mingling with the bluebloods. *The Providence Journal* called him "the principal figure in a democratic turn of golfing events in Newport," a common man allowed onto the "golfing grounds of the social elite."

Burke was the best player in the field and predictably advanced easily through his bracket, until only he and Tommy Tailer remained, creating something of a rags-and-riches final. Tailer was at home among the Eastern elite, a favorite son of

Newport and a member of its revered and private country club, while Burke was a graduate of the caddie shack and represented the proletariat. Tailer could play too. The year before, Sam Snead had just won the St. Paul Open when he received a call from a friend, Bunny Bacon, who was enlisting his help for a game against Tailer and his partner, Dr. Walter Hochschield. Bacon had struck a bet with Tailer; he had wagered that he and a professional of his choosing could beat Tailer and Hochschield.

Snead was aware that Tailer was an accomplished amateur, though he was unaware how *accomplished* was defined in this instance. So he agreed to make the trip to Long Island to assist Bunny, who was absorbing the entire risk. That didn't prevent Snead from stammering when he stood on the first tee at the Meadowbrook Country Club and heard his partner suddenly suggest that they play for $7,000, a staggering sum of money by professional golf standards. The PGA's leading money winner the year before, in 1936, had been Horton Smith, who had earned only $7,600. Tailer quickly accepted the bet before Snead could lodge a protest. Snead began choking on his words, an unsavory portent of the golf to come. On the first tee, a quaking Snead topped his drive. He topped his second shot as well. Eventually Snead and Bacon prevailed by a single shot, only because Snead played the final ten holes in thirty-two strokes, which included an eagle on the seventeenth. Snead came away indelibly impressed with Tailer's skill.

Burke may have possessed a more developed public reputation, but Tailer was known to insiders, and theirs was a match that promised to be memorable. Accordingly, the Tailer-Burke pairing attracted a large and diverse crowd, some of them from downtown Newport, others from the Newport summer colony, from either side of the tracks, as it were. *The Providence Journal* noted that it may have been the greatest gathering ever of

Newport townfolk on the Newport Country Club grounds. As a result, the crowd was largely impartial, even as it represented a home game for Tailer. In one instance, an overzealous Burke fan even kicked his ball farther up the fairway. Burke politely had the ball returned to its original position.

The match was close, as expected, but Burke closed Tailer out on the seventeenth green to win, 2 and 1, a victory for the proletariat over the privileged in a match that in local golf circles was a topic for years to come. There was no animosity; Burke and Tailer became friends.

Destiny pointed him toward professional stardom, but that was not necessarily the direction that John Burke wanted his life to follow. The money in professional golf was largely inadequate, which explained why tour players routinely had club jobs to which they returned when they weren't on tour. Burke was initially more inclined to use his engineering degree from Georgetown. Anaconda Copper Mining Company recruited him while he was still a student, and once he graduated, he accepted the company's offer of a job.

Yet it seemed inevitable that Burke would eventually test his skills on the PGA Tour. The money might have been modest, but a club job and, perhaps, an equipment stipend could stretch a golfer's income to satisfactory levels, and the combination of playing and teaching a game that he enjoyed promised to eventually trump the prospect of working for a living for the rest of his life.

Golf understood this better than Burke; the game kept calling him, even after he joined Anaconda Copper. His national collegiate victory and assorted other successes would have earned him an invitation to represent his country in the Walker Cup Match, a biennial competition between teams from the U.S. and Great Britain, had the war in Europe not forced the cancellation of the match in 1940. Then on January 24, 1941, Burke received a letter with an Augusta, Georgia, postmark. It was a coveted invitation to compete in the Masters at the Augusta National Golf Club in April. His was one of thirteen invitations tendered by the club that day to heretofore unqualified players, who in the recent year or two had demonstrated a requisite quantity of skill.

Burke's job requirements with Anaconda Copper ruefully prevented him from playing in the Masters, where he would not have been out of his element. He was a bona fide star on the rise; his one-stroke victory over Jimmy Turnesa in the Rhode Island Open in 1938 indicated that he had not yet found his level of competition, that he had the skills to compete at a higher level. Turnesa was so talented that he went on to finish second to Sam Snead in the PGA Championship in 1942.

The clarion call of tournament golf promised to eventually wear Burke down, but any decision on a professional golf career was going to have to wait. In March of 1942, he received his draft notice, and he was ordered to report for Army duty in April '42.

His country needed him more than Anaconda Copper or golf did.

DALE BOURISSEAU WAS ONE-FOURTH Chippewa Indian, or a *half-breed,* as he was called by those employing the peculiar calculus of race. Bourisseau was neither Caucasian, nor was he a full-blooded Chippewa, and either way he turned during his childhood in Northport, Michigan, he found at least a measure of rejection. So he turned inward, his hedge against suffering the pain of exclusion.

Of course, this was not altogether unusual for a Bourisseau; isolation seemingly was inherent in the family. In 1885, Dale's grandfather, Lewis Bourisseau, became the acting first assistant to the lighthouse keeper on South Fox Island, a remote patch of land sprouting in Lake Michigan, seventeen miles off Cat's Head Point at the tip of Ledanau Peninsula north of Traverse City. By 1891, he was the keeper of the lighthouse, a position he held for twenty-four years. Lewis's son, Frank, became the second assistant keeper of the same lighthouse in 1928, a post in which he served for nearly nine years.

Obviously, keeping a lighthouse on a small island seventeen miles removed from the mainland requires an innate ability to pass long hours without interacting with others. A young Dale Bourisseau, heir to the lighthouse keepers, found his own metaphorical island, in the form of an abandoned basketball hoop, where he could while away hours on end working on skills that, ironically, would bring him the attention from which he otherwise shied away. Sports became his outlet, providing him an opportunity to establish an identity irrespective of race. Those with whom he was competing were generally blue-eyed and blond, which eventually became the least of the reasons he stood out in this crowd. Bourisseau became proficient at basketball, baseball, and boxing, or any other game to which he was introduced, including golf.

His skills, particularly those in basketball, diminished the importance of his mixed pedigree in the minds of those with whom and against whom he played. He was accomplished enough in basketball to earn a scholarship to play collegiately at Olivet College in Olivet, Michigan, southwest of Lansing.

Bourisseau also developed a golf habit. For a restless youth, spending summer months living on a tiny island quickly became too confining. He eventually chose not to accompany his father to South Fox Island, instead staying behind in Northport and taking a job as the caddie master at Northport Country Club, one of the two courses in town. Overseeing the caddie shack gave Bourisseau access to the golf course, which quickly became a summer sanctuary.

Ben Hogan *(left)* examines his scorecard with playing partner Bobby Jones during the Hale America National Open Golf Tournament in 1942, the "wartime substitute" for the U.S. Open. (COURTESY OF RIDGE-MOOR COUNTRY CLUB)

Caddie Bill Boston congratulates Ben Hogan upon his winning the Hale America National Open Golf Tournament. (COURTESY OF RIDGE-MOOR COUNTRY CLUB)

Ed Dudley, president of the PGA of America and head pro at Augusta National Golf Club, hits a shot in an exhibition for wounded sailors and soldiers at the Navy's Sail Ho Course in San Diego. Looking on from left to right are Sam Snead, Jimmy Thomson, Jimmy Demaret, and Byron Nelson. (COURTESY OF SAM SNEAD, JR.)

Cows graze in front of the clubhouse at the Augusta National Golf Club. The club was closed during the war and turned over to a herd of cows. (COURTESY OF HISTORIC GOLF PHOTOS)

Sam Snead
demonstrates his
form in an exhibition
for wounded troops.
(COURTESY OF SAM
SNEAD, JR.)

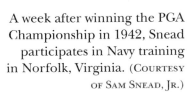

A week after winning the PGA
Championship in 1942, Snead
participates in Navy training
in Norfolk, Virginia. (COURTESY
OF SAM SNEAD, JR.)

Sam Snead, surrounded by sailors and soldiers, buys a war bond after winning the PGA Championship at Seaview Country Club in Atlantic City in 1942. (COURTESY OF THE PGA OF AMERICA)

Byron Nelson *(left)* receives the trophy for winning the Canadian Open in 1945, his eleventh straight victory and the last of his remarkable streak. (COURTESY OF THE ROYAL CANADIAN GOLF ASSOCIATION)

Lieutenant Colonel Bobby Jones in uniform (J. Hixon Kinsella)

Bobby Jones slashes a ball from the rough at Royal Lytham and St. Annes in 1944, shortly before returning to the United States. Jones won the British Open at Royal Lytham in 1926. (Courtesy of Royal Lytham and St. Annes)

Injured soldiers check out golf equipment at the Greenbrier in White Sulphur Springs, West Virginia, a landmark resort that the Army turned into a hospital, dubbed "the Shangri-La for wounded soldiers." (COURTESY OF THE GREENBRIER)

A soldier who lost part of his right leg plays golf at the Greenbrier as part of his rehabilitation. (COURTESY OF THE GREENBRIER)

Allied prisoners of war play on their course in the German camp
Stalag Luft III. (COURTESY OF THE USGA)

The ersatz golf balls used by the POWs, handmade from shoe leather.
(COURTESY OF THE USGA)

General Dwight Eisenhower in 1946 on the Old Course at St. Andrews, accompanied by St. Andrews captain Roger Weathered to his right. Eisenhower received an honorary life membership to the Royal and Ancient Golf Club of St. Andrews. (COURTESY OF THE UNIVERSITY OF ST. ANDREWS)

There is no better venue on which an athletic introvert can find welcome seclusion than a golf course, in pursuit of a game that is wholly individual, requiring no teammates or even playing partners. Virtually every summer afternoon, when his caddie duties were fulfilled for the day, Bourisseau played golf. His extraordinary hand-eye coordination had already evolved, and Bourisseau quickly became proficient at the game, methodically working his handicap toward scratch. Yet he eventually gravitated not toward a course, but toward a court, starring for Olivet in basketball, before taking a high school teaching and basketball coaching job in Grand Rapids, Michigan.

Then the war intervened. Bourisseau enlisted in the Army in 1942 and was sent to officer candidates school. In 1943, he was commissioned a second lieutenant. His wife was pregnant with their first child when he was sent to Italy as a platoon leader, in intelligence.

JOHN BURKE WAS UNFLAPPABLE and smart, and he had a roomful of trophies and a Georgetown University degree to prove it. He had an innate ability to keep a rein on the highs and lows of any endeavor. His composure allowed this son of poverty to move comfortably between the classes that divided Newport, Rhode Island. He was better suited to lead than to follow.

The Army thought so too. It sent him to officer candidates school in Miami, where he studied to become an intelligence officer. By the end of 1942, he was given his commission as a second lieutenant in the Army. Early the following year, he received his orders to deploy to the European Theater of Operations.

He had few regrets. He might have pursued professional golf, possibly allowing him to serve out the war as a pro at a military base, where the only hazards were those of the water variety. He was a pedigreed golfer, with a National Intercollegiate Championship to his credit, and accordingly could have invoked it to teach golf to captains and colonels, or to partner with generals in their grudge matches with admirals.

Burke never considered the easy way out. He was his own man, one who chose to enter the workforce against the advice of a golf world that had a starring role for him. At any rate, golf would still be waiting for him at war's end, should he eventually decide to pursue it.

He was going to North Africa, where the Desert Fox, Erwin Rommel, was operating with German forces that were inflicting substantial numbers of casualties. This wasn't an enemy armed with a deft putting touch that Burke would be facing. He was scared, surely, but he was undeterred. He had a job to do.

Burke said his farewells at home and set sail for North Africa. When he arrived, he began work as an intelligence officer for the Middle East Wing of the Air Transport Command in Tunisia. Even when he was not engaged in combat, the living quarters were spartan. He and another officer shared a tent. On May 7, 1943, John Burke was sitting on his cot, reading and rereading letters from home, as soldiers did in spare moments, clutching at their lifeline to a saner time and place. He thought of his brother David, an Army lieutenant, and his brother Edmund, the golf pro, now an Army corporal, and wondered how each of them was doing, whether they were staying out of harm's way. He thought of his twin brother, Joe, his friend, his biggest fan, who in yet another turn demonstrated that they weren't identical. Joe had the tremors, a term others used. "I call them jerks and twitches," he said. The tremors kept him out of the service, that and a wife and child at home. Joe was running the family's bowling alley. Just as well, John Burke thought, as he sat in his tent in a war zone, too close to the front line, too far from home.

His bunkmate was cleaning his rifle, a chore that soldiers were taught to do by rote. Though safety was an integral part of the training, war is wearisome, and his tired bunkmate carelessly began to break down the rifle without having done the most elemental safety check, that of looking first to see whether the rifle was loaded. There was a sharp crack as the rifle discharged.

Medics came and quickly concluded that the bullet was lodged in a precarious position against Burke's spine and required immediate attention. Burke was rushed to the operating room. A call was made to locate a Catholic chaplain. None had been assigned to the section, and an urgent order went out to find a priest. The search turned up Father John T. Coleman, a missionary in Liberia and a member of the Society of African Missions. Father Coleman had been doing mission work in Africa for more than twelve years. The Army had enlisted his help as an auxiliary chaplain during its crusade in North Africa. Father Coleman was summoned to the camp and arrived moments before surgery was to begin on Burke. The priest gave Burke communion on the operating table and administered last rites.

In surgery, doctors removed the slug, but John Burke never regained consciousness. He died the next morning, barely a year after joining the Army. Father Coleman officiated over his burial in the North Africa American Cemetery in Carthage, Tunisia. Burke's coffin was draped in an American flag. A group of soldiers from his unit stood stiffly by the gravesite, solemnly listening to Father Coleman read from the Bible, the Twenty-third Psalm:

Yea, though I walk through the valley of the shadow of death, I will fear no evil: for thou art with me; thy rod and thy staff, they comfort me.

Five days later, on May 13, 1943, an Army detail arrived at the Newport, Rhode Island, home of John Burke's parents and informed them of the death of their son in the service of his country. A family mourned. So did a town and a state. The headline over a page-one story in *The Providence Journal* read:

JOHNNY BURKE, GOLFING STAR,

KILLED IN AFRICAN CAMPAIGN

ABLEST PLAYER EVER DEVELOPED IN R.I.

War was indiscriminate and could not have considered that Burke was among the good ones, that he was kindly, soft-spoken, likable. No one will know whether golf history was indelibly altered on that fateful day in North Africa. The only certainty was that it no longer mattered.

ON A HILL overlooking the town of Cassino, Italy, northwest of Naples, is Monte Cassino, a Benedictine monastery founded in 529 A.D. On two occasions, it was destroyed by invaders, and on a third occasion by an earthquake. It was rebuilt each time better than before. It was for a time the leading monastery in Western Europe and was an esteemed center of learning, particularly in the field of medicine. In 1866, it became a national monument. By rights, this is the basis on which Monte Cassino should have assumed its place in history in perpetuity.

Instead, Monte Cassino became known for the battle in which the tide of World War II began to turn. When the Italian fascist regime collapsed in 1943, the Germans occupied Cassino and established a fortress at the monastery. The Allied forces, meanwhile, had established a beachhead in Anzio, on the western coast of Italy, only a short distance from Rome. The Fifth Army was determined to break German resistance at Monte Cassino and join the beachhead groups. In a grisly battle the Germans steadfastly held their ground, frustrating the Allied effort. The prolonged impasse allowed the Allies to plan a major offensive that eventually broke the Germans' grip on Monte Cassino, allowing the Allied forces to sweep into Rome, the first European capital they took.

It was into the five-month battle at Monte Cassino that Lieutenant Dale Bourisseau, with a pregnant wife at home, was sent. It was his job at night to spearhead a scouting patrol, its mission to determine the enemy's troop strength and movements. He was on patrol one night in January of 1944 when another soldier set off a trip wire, detonating a land mine near Bourisseau. The explosion tore off Bourisseau's right foot and damaged his right leg. A field amputation ensued, medics removing the remaining part of his leg below his knee.

Bourisseau was transported to a field hospital in North Africa. His war was over, and from his vantage point—lying on his back, beneath a sheet that was flat where his right shin and foot ought to have been—so was his life. Self-pity dominated every waking moment.

Once he'd recovered enough to travel, he returned home to the States, eventually settling in at a veterans hospital in Bricksville, Ohio. The only joy in his life was spelled *Joie,* the name of his baby daughter, who was born in April of 1944. He was otherwise despondent. He had been a gifted athlete, who had relied on his various skills for his identity, the means that had allowed him to emerge from his shell. No longer would he be able to run. For the moment, he couldn't even walk.

One day, a friend brought a golf club to his room at the veterans hospital in Bricksville. Bourisseau was eventually unable to resist the temptation for any golfer—to pick up a club, to waggle it, to swing it. He began to reach for the club more often, and as it grew more comfortable in his hands, his self-pity began to dissolve. Eventually, his outlook brightened. It occurred to him one day that he no longer wanted to be an invalid. He began speaking with other wounded veterans, each of them an amputee like himself, similarly anchored by self-pity. Bourisseau concluded that all of them could benefit from having an outlet for their plight, a way that would allow them to let it go so that they could get on with their lives, an activity, perhaps, that would provide them the camaraderie inherent in shared experiences.

He wondered whether his own return to a life worth living could begin on the first tee. Equipped with a prosthesis, he returned to the golf course and discovered that he could still play and that his dignity was intact. The game that had once been a refuge for a loner was still available for him to lean on for help. It became his therapy, reacquainting him with the world he had left behind when he answered the call to serve his country.

John Burke's death was a reminder that golf is only a game, and, when measured against the ravages of war, not an especially important one. Bourisseau's injury and the way he chose to deal with it was a reminder that it was not an unimportant game either.

11

STALAG GOLF

POWs Play Through

The quiet of a prisoner-of-war camp provided little respite from the chaos and cacophony of a war zone. It was still a dangerous place; only the weaponry was different. It left the body intact, more or less, depending on the consistency of the food supply. Instead, the mind was under perpetual assault by demons determined to erode a man's sanity. Hopelessness was a potent weapon. How do POWs mark time against an open-ended sentence, a moving target, as it were, the elusive end of the war? How do they repel dark thoughts in a threadbare camp encircled with barbed wire and manned by armed guards with orders to shoot to kill, in a region so remote that even a map won't readily give up its whereabouts?

Diversions were their only defense—the dog-eared pages of a book that long ago had shed its cover, or letters from home, some of them already committed to memory. A faction of them occupied time by hatching escape plans. Others sought solace at the bottom of a cup of intoxicating rotgut brewed from available food scraps—often dried fruit, potato skins, and sugar, a combination that, when allowed to ferment and then consumed in an ample quantity, enabled a POW to forget his troubles one night and to compound them the following morning when he regained consciousness.

Captured Royal Air Force pilot Sydney Smith discovered his own diversion in an oddly shaped Red Cross parcel that arrived for him one day early in 1943 in Stalag Luft III. Smith, a journalist with the *Daily Express* in London before the war, quickly unwrapped the parcel and learned that he had become the proud owner of an iron golf club. The used club contained a hickory shaft, and the clubhead bore the familiar horseshoe cleekmark above the *Welmade* inscription, the stamp of the skilled Scottish club maker Patrick of Leven. It was a woman's mashie—shorter and lighter than a man's 5-iron—but its size and weight failed to detract from its immeasurable value to a POW desperately concerned with keeping himself occupied.

Smith's dilemma was that he had nothing to hit with the club. He surveyed his surroundings and began to gather materials that he might cobble together to form a rudimentary golf ball. He took a piece of pine and carved it into an orb, roughly. He wound it with wool and cotton. Finally, he covered it with a piece of cloth that he stitched together in the manner of a baseball. The final result was no Spalding Dot, but it was a worthwhile replica for a man who otherwise had nothing to look forward to, other than abject monotony and hardship.

Smith took his mashie and his ball and went outside to play. He carefully propped the ball on a clump of dirt and took a hurried swing. Contact was clean and the ball sailed forty or fifty yards toward an imaginary green that might have been the eighteenth at St. Andrews, given the joy that it elicited.

This is how golf came to be played at Stalag Luft III.

IN THE SPRING OF 1942, one hundred miles southeast of Berlin, in the town of Sagan, the Germans had established a prisoner-of-war camp, Stalag Luft III, to house Allied Air Force officers, principally British and American. The treatment of POWs at Stalag Luft III was generally more humane than elsewhere. The camp fell under the control of the Luftwaffe and its chief, Hermann Goering, a flyer in the First World War. Goering, second-in-command to Hitler, was of the belief that there should be honor among aerial enemies—fraudulent nobility, as it were, from a man who had already issued the directive to a subordinate to prepare a "final solution" on the matter of Europe's Jews. As many as ten thousand Allied airmen were imprisoned at Stalag Luft III at any one time, if not happily, at least tolerably, compared with their previous stops on the POW itinerary.

BEFORE THE WAR, Pat Ward-Thomas was wandering happily and aimlessly into adulthood. On a whim, he took a "short-service commission" with the Royal Air Force in 1938, which freed him from a dead-end job with London Transport. A friend assured him that he'd still have ample time off to pursue his twin passions, cricket and golf. The Germans were still only a potentially troublesome lot at that point.

But once war was declared, short commissions were withdrawn, tying Ward-Thomas to the RAF indefinitely. The news failed to dampen his enthusiasm for life, even the prospect that his own now ran a heightened risk of ending prematurely. When his pilot training had concluded and he caught up to the war, the invincibility of youth became his copilot, accompanying him on his missions, even retaining its arrogance in the aftermath of a sea landing from which he and his crewmates were rescued from their dinghy after thirteen hours on the water.

Ward-Thomas immediately resumed flying. He usually returned from bombing runs to Germany at sunrise and often elected to forgo sleep to play a round of golf in Newmarket, only hours after eluding German antiaircraft fire. These brushes with death notwithstanding, he had never been happier than he was in those days, by night waging war with an enemy he couldn't see, by day playing golf, meanwhile blissfully ignorant of the perils he faced.

It was a counterfeit elation that failed to account for the dangerous nature of his existence; he was flying a slow-moving aircraft at twelve thousand feet, which gave the antiaircraft gunners on the ground the illusion that he was presenting a stationary target and the confidence that they could hit it. So it was that his blissful ignorance was shattered one November night, 1940, when antiaircraft fire staggered his plane. The engines sputtered, but the plane continued flying for a time. Then both its engines died over the Netherlands, north of Amsterdam, requiring that he and his crewmates bail out. Ward-Thomas landed safely in a canal. He climbed out of the water and sought refuge in a nearby farmhouse. Its occupants gave him dry clothes and a warm bed from which he was rousted by a German soldier a short time later, unceremoniously ending Ward-Thomas's war not long after it had begun. He and the other captured crewmen were transported to Dulag Luft, near Frankfurt, a processing center for Air Force prisoners of war. The first night there, in a barren room, he slept soundly, awoke refreshed, then began to ponder his plight. A life that had struck its high notes only a short time earlier plumbed the depths in this single moment, when it occurred to him that he wasn't going home that day, or any day soon.

Three years later and still imprisoned, Ward-Thomas was transferred to Stalag Luft III, where one afternoon he encountered Sydney Smith swinging his mashie and batting his rudimentary golf ball between the barracks. Only the promise of freedom, or a pretty woman, could have brightened his outlook more than discovering that golf had been introduced into his otherwise dreary existence.

IN 1938, Oliver Green was working in packing and dispatch for Winterthur Silks, Ltd., in London, earning ten shillings a week and playing cricket on weekends, when he was intrigued by a Royal Air Force offer of a "short-service commission": four years on active duty at full pay and a termination payment of 300 pounds.

The opportunity to fly appealed to him, but the severance represented found money to the pauper that he was, and it was of a sum that was so far beyond trifling that he considered that it might make him rich. Green quickly joined the RAF, then had to wait for three months before reporting for training. In the meantime, he was determined to keep himself physically fit, and he did so by running around the hills of Purley Downs, a golf course in Purley, outside London, where four years earlier he'd made a hole-in-one using one of his mother's clubs. In June of 1938, only eleven days after his eighteenth birthday, he finally reported for duty and was enrolled in the No. 13 Elementary and Reserve Flying Training School in White Waltham on the River Thames.

When he and his friends had a break in training and the price of a drink or two, they frequented the bar at the Skindles Hotel. The bar straddled the border between the towns of Berkshire and Surrey, which was significant inasmuch as Surrey required that its pubs close at 10:00 P.M., while Berkshire allowed its pubs to remain open a half hour later. The towns' border was marked with a large nail on the bar. When 10:00 P.M. arrived, those drinking on the Surrey side simply shifted to the Berkshire side and continued to imbibe.

In May of 1939, Green was assigned to a new fighter squadron that was headed to Egypt. He was to travel there on the HMS *Argus,* and as the ship began pulling away, Green saw that his trunk, kit, and golf clubs were still on the dock. Panicked, Green ran to the officer of the watch, who was not amused by the interruption, nor the cause of it. The officer nonetheless dispatched a seaman to quickly retrieve Green's possessions, much to his relief. The momentary prospect of going off to war without his golf clubs was a disturbing one for Green.

When Italy entered the war on the German side, on June 10, 1940, Green's squadron was prepped to join the fighting in Egypt. Thirteen months later, in July of 1941, Green's own war ended. He was flying his Curtis P-40 Tomahawk at ground level over the Egyptian desert and attempting to evade German aircraft when the oil tank on his plane was hit and exploded. His aircraft hit the ground at one hundred eighty miles per hour. When the plane finally skidded to a stop, Green scrambled to safety as German planes strafed the aircraft before departing the scene.

Suddenly, it was eerily quiet. Green was alone in a desert and basically lost. He knew only that if he were to walk east, he might avoid capture and eventually join up with Britain's forward outposts. So he began walking. Four days into his journey he was rescued by a group of Bedouin herding their camels. A few days later, weakening and unable to walk any longer, he was allowed to ride one of the camels. Eventually, the group came across a German soldier, who immediately made Green a prisoner of war.

Nearly two years later, in March of 1943, Green also wound up at Stalag Luft III, where he came across Smith and Ward-Thomas alternately hitting shots with the Patrick of Leven mashie that mystically connected them to the world they'd left behind.

AMERICAN AIRMAN ROBERT LAUBACH was born in Toledo, Ohio, in 1923, but his family moved to Frankfort, Michigan, prior to his starting high school. Frankfort was a waterfront town on Lake Michigan, southwest of Traverse City, and was home to one of the finest golf courses in America, Crystal Downs Country Club. The course was designed by Alister MacKenzie, the famed Scottish architect, whose roster of courses included Augusta National and Cypress Point. Its reputation held no special attraction for young Laubach, who was uninterested in golf beyond the money he earned for caddying at Crystal Downs.

When the war began, he enlisted in the Army Air Corps and eventually became the copilot of a B-17, the Flying Fortress, with the 388th Bomber Group, Eighth Air Force. On March 8, 1944, on a bombing run to Berlin, his plane was shot down east of the Zuider Zee in the Netherlands. He parachuted to safety but was captured by German soldiers, who made him a prisoner of war. He was taken to Frankfurt, Germany, where he was held in solitary confinement, awaiting transport to Stalag Luft III.

SMITH AND WARD-THOMAS SPENT hours a day knocking their golf ball around the grounds surrounding the barracks at Stalag Luft III, while other POWs looked on, incredulously at first, then enviously. Smith was willing to share his mashie, but not his golf ball. He invited anyone interested in joining them in their golf to fashion their own golf balls. Suddenly, the manufacturing of golf balls in Stalag Luft III took on the form of a contest, each participant determined to make a better ball than his colleague was able to produce. They typically began with a small, somewhat round, heavy core (such as the pine that Smith had used), about one centimeter in diameter. Then they wrapped it with rubber, usually crepe rubber from the sole of a shoe. Next, it was wound with thin pieces of rubber, often from rubber tobacco pouches that were cut into thin strips. Finally, pieces of leather from shoes were cut into figure eights that would wrap around the orb and were stitched together with homemade thread—strands of cotton spun together and covered with boot polish to make the thread waterproof and more durable.

Rubber was critical to the production of a quality ball. Accordingly, prisoners asked that the quarterly clothing parcels they received from home include rubber gym shoes. They also asked for air cushions and rubber tobacco pouches. When any of their requested items arrived, they were immediately shredded for the purpose of producing golf balls.

The ball maker had two objectives—to wrap the core with the proper tension, and to make the ball as close as possible to 1.62 ounces and 1.62 inches in diameter, which were the Royal and Ancient golf ball specifications at the time. A ball wound too tightly might cause the rubber to snap when struck, while a ball wound too loosely created a mushy effect, decreasing the distance it would carry.

Each ball took up to six hours to make, though the more skilled artisans among them could usually produce one in four. The best of them was an Australian bombardier, who was among

Green's regular playing partners. Green marveled at the man's slow, rhythmic swing, as well as the craftsmanship he brought to his ball manufacturing.

As the game gathered popularity inside Stalag Luft III, the need for additional clubs grew as well. These, too, were home-made, initially. The shafts were fashioned from strips of wood, of-ten from hockey sticks that were whittled down to the proper length and circumference. Cloth was used for the grip. The club-head represented a tricky challenge. The process began with a supply of foil collected from cigarette packs. To melt it, they de-vised a rudimentary blowtorch by twisting tin into the proper shape and using rendered margarine as fuel for the flame, which melted the foil into a previously created mold.

The finished clubs took on a variety of odd shapes and sizes, but generally they worked well enough to accommodate their purpose, which was to give the prisoners an activity that diverted their attention from their plight. Periodically, a club maker would rise to the challenge and produce a club that was appar-ently superior to the others. A Canadian POW, Don Elliott, de-veloped one such club that remarkably withstood the abuse of daily play. It was dubbed "Abort Annie."

Occasionally (and ruefully) a new ball was hit out of bounds on the first swing, sometimes over the barbed-wire fence, a dispiriting turn given how labor-intensive the making of a ball was. Attempt-ing to retrieve one would result in certain death by shooting. A passing guard, however, would occasionally recover a lost ball and toss it back over the fence. Tower guards periodically helped out by attempting to locate a lost ball with their binoculars.

Inside the fence was another hazard, a width of ground the prisoners were not permitted to enter. It was cordoned off with a small trip wire. However, when it became apparent that errant shots were going to routinely land in the forbidden zone, the

Germans graciously provided a couple of white jackets for the POWs to wear when they needed to retrieve a ball, a signal to the guards that they did not intend an escape attempt, but were merely recovering their wayward shots. The Germans viewed the prisoners' passion toward this peculiar game with ambivalence, but welcomed the fact that it kept them occupied doing something other than planning or attempting to execute an escape.

After a few weeks, so many POWs were playing golf that the group began calling itself the Sagan Golf Club. Many of them were skilled golfers, including Danny O'Brien, the best of the lot, a former Scottish schoolboy champion, and Ronnie Morgan, George Murray Frame (who before the war played to a low handicap at Troon), and Green.

The group quickly outgrew its reliance on homemade clubs. This was solved in part when Ward-Thomas asked a Danish girl, Doreen Wessel, with whom he had developed a pen-pal relationship, to round up some clubs and send them to Stalag Luft III. Eventually, Wessel sent a parcel containing ten hickory-shafted irons.

As for the course, the golfers' targets were initially trees, but eventually they came to include tall poles that frequently surrendered "holes-in-one" when a ball struck them eight, ten, or twelve feet off the ground. Tree stumps were also used as holes, as were an incinerator door and a young pine tree, eighteen inches tall.

The membership of the Sagan Golf Club continued to expand, to the point that its hierarchy decided that a tournament was in order. The players decided on a match-play event, the Sagan Open, for its first championship. Ward-Thomas and Hugh Falkus reached the final. Falkus was not a particularly skilled player, but his aim was fairly proficient when holing out entailed only hitting a protruding target. A controversy arose when Falkus attempted to claim that he had holed out by whistling his ball past the small pine and rustling a leaf in the process. Ward-Thomas and others argued that the trunk had to be struck. In the end, it didn't matter; Ward-Thomas won by a comfortable margin to become the first Open champion of the Sagan Golf Club.

The club then decided that it should build a regulation golf course, or at least a semblance of one. It constructed a nine-hole layout between the barracks and over the kitchen, employing hazards wherever possible in the limited space to increase the challenge. One green, for instance, was placed beyond the pool of filthy water that was there strictly in the event of a fire. Golfers often waded into the fire pool, notwithstanding its filth, to retrieve their prized pellets, even in the dead of winter, when the water was colder than it was dirty. Another hole required a harrowing blind shot over a kitchen in which Germans were working.

The golfers were not particularly popular with the nongolfers among the prisoners, inasmuch as they weren't especially accurate. The course was simply too expansive for such a confined space, and it brought too many human beings into play. One was a German *Unterofficier,* or noncommissioned officer, who was sitting on a toilet, quietly taking care of his business, when a golfer shanked his shot. The ball shot straight right and crashed through a window of the building in which the German sat, evoking raucous laughter from the golfers outside. Fortunately, the German was unperturbed. The golfers were asked only to move the tee area to prevent a repeat occurrence.

One of the golfers, Norman Thomas, borrowed a spade from the Germans, and in an area eight by ten yards fashioned the first green, which wasn't green at all, of course, but was brown leaning to yellow. After the stones and stumps were removed and the ground leveled, it was covered with a yellow sand that was smoothed with a homemade squeegee. The green putted relatively true, particularly after a rainfall had firmed it up. The cup was a powdered-milk can inserted into the ground. Nine greens were eventually built for a course that measured around 850 yards and played to a par of 29. The longest hole was 140 yards.

The mounding around the greens, designed to give the course a modicum of definition, required dirt, hauled in from elsewhere. Naturally, this aroused the Germans' suspicions; they wondered whether the dirt was coming from an escape tunnel under construction beneath the camp. The prisoners finally convinced the guards that their actions were innocent, and the guards allowed the POWs to continue to play their quirky game, at least until three wily men escaped via a tunnel dug beneath a wooden gymnastics vaulting horse. It was an ingenious plan, better than most hatched in Stalag Luft III, where imaginations worked overtime devising ways by which POWs might escape to freedom. Escape was something of a game between the Germans and the Allied airmen. The latter would begin digging a tunnel and the former would discover it before its completion. The wooden horse was the exception. Each day, it was carried into the yard. The diggers were hidden inside. The horse was placed directly over the hidden entrance to the tunnel they were digging. The prisoners disposed of the yellow sand they were excavating by carrying it in pouches inside their trousers. Attached to the pouches were drawstrings. They'd walk along, pull the drawstring, and release the sand down their trouser legs and onto the ground, undetected.

When the three men escaped and the tunnel was discovered, the Germans were none too happy. They immediately destroyed the golf course, having concluded that tunnel dirt had been used for the mounding around the greens after all. Their suspicions were amplified by the fact that the wooden horse and the tunnel stood between the trip wire and the sixth green.

A few weeks later, the POWs finally convinced the Germans that their course had not been built with dirt from the tunnel. The guards acquiesced, allowing them to build another course. Timmy Biden, whom the other Sagan Golf Club members referred to as the head "brownkeeper," set about restoring the Sagan layout, sans the yellow sand. As a result, the greens were closer to black than brown and they were considerably bumpier than they had been when they were top-dressed with yellow sand.

The decline in the quality of their course did not dampen the prisoners' enthusiasm for golf. Some of the better players gave lessons, even exhibition matches. Danny O'Brien and Ronnie Morgan were unofficially Sagan Golf Club's teaching professionals—their expertise was sought by growing numbers of prisoners looking to improve their fundamentals. Under the tutelage of O'Brien and Morgan, men who had never swung a golf club before developed a level of competence that would serve them well once the war ended.

Many of them played in the first Sagan Golf Club Championship, which featured an individual competition as well as a four-ball. Predictably, the players decided to play for something more than pride. There was even a bookmaker to supervise the action, Bill Skinner, who bounded into Green's barracks one evening looking for action on the foursomes competition.

"What's the price on Norman Ryder and myself?" Green asked.

Skinner pondered their skill for a moment.

"Fifty to one," he said finally.

Green immediately bet 100 marks on his own twosome. When he and Ryder indeed prevailed, Green collected 5,000 marks and in turn paid Ryder 1,000 marks for his partnership effort. It was camp money, which rendered it virtually worthless beyond its limited purchase power in securing food and bottles of German scents. At that, the latter were worthless, save for the bottles; the prisoners discarded the scents and refilled the bottles with home-made plonk, an intoxicating beverage that came up easier than it went down.

Challenge matches became part of the golfers' routine. One day, O'Brien and his partner, an Australian named Samson, challenged any two golfers in Stalag Luft III to a match that included a thirty-six-hole four-ball and two thirty-six-hole singles matches, for a sum of fifty marks. Ronnie Morgan and George Murray Frame accepted the challenge, then won the four-ball. Each of them lost his singles match, however, giving O'Brien and Samson the victory.

Ward-Thomas chose to write a brief account of the matches for the camp newspaper, which was nothing more than a couple of pages posted on a bulletin board. Ward-Thomas so enjoyed recounting the match on paper that he immediately began pondering the possibility of a career writing about sports. A few weeks later, Ward-Thomas laboriously reconstructed the camp's golfing adventures in a fourteen-thousand-word story that he and a few of his campmates agreed might be of interest to readers back home. They were uncertain how they might get it published, however. Finally, someone suggested sending it along to Henry Longhurst, a noted golf writer and the author of a book with which they were familiar, *It Was Good While It Lasted,* published in 1941.

German censors removed only a passing reference to the wooden horse escape; otherwise the manuscript arrived intact. When Longhurst received the story, he was indelibly impressed, to a degree that he attempted to convince the Red Cross to publish it in a booklet form.

Ultimately, the story of golf in Stalag Luft III was told as a result of a letter Ward-Thomas wrote, to the Royal and Ancient Golf

Club of St. Andrews. His purpose was to ask whether the organization could see fit to send some clubs and balls its way. The R & A
dutifully complied, meanwhile passing the letter on to Bernard
Darwin, the renowned British golf writer. Subsequently, Darwin
wrote about golf in a POW camp in a piece that appeared in
Country Life magazine. He recounted as well how golf had similarly become a diversion for captured airmen in the First World
War. "So erratic were their shots," Darwin wrote of POW golf in
the first World War, "that on one occasion the German comman-
dant, a portly and pompous old colonel, advanced to the middle
of the playground, possibly to protest, and was driven into highly
undignified flight. The airmen were no respecters of persons and
pursued him relentlessly with a creeping barrage of cleek shots.
He did not apparently bear any malice; so there must have been
one German colonel for whom something good could be said."

Ward-Thomas's letter was as productive as it was entertaining
and enlightening. Among the clubs that the Royal and Ancient
sent along was a modern driver, equipped with a steel shaft. The
POW course was too short, the grounds too confined, to actually
use it, though Ward-Thomas snuck outside with it one bitterly
cold winter day, when everyone else was huddled inside attempting to stay warm. Curious as to how it would perform, as well as
aching to hit a real drive, Ward-Thomas teed a ball and gave it
his best swing. The ball cleared the kitchen, but crashed through
a window on another building, sending glass flying and the
Germans inside diving for cover. None were hurt, and, miracu-
lously, they weren't angry. They even agreed to return the ball to
a relieved Ward-Thomas. Darwin's World War I colonel was
not the only benevolent German discovered in a POW camp, it
turns out.

The shot was pleasing to Ward-Thomas, or was once he determined that there would be no punishment attached to the

broken window and terrified Germans. He even began entertaining thoughts about freedom and the day he could return to a regulation golf course, and hit such shots with impunity. He wondered how large the greens would appear after a few years of attempting to hit minuscule targets.

Oliver Green similarly pondered the future, only he was determined to hit the ball close to the pin without regard to the size of the green. Toward that end, he took to standing in front of a mirror and swinging a club for hours on those days when he wasn't playing. He was attempting to groove his swing in anticipation of the end of the war and golf played on real golf courses with modern equipment.

Life in the camp was bleak. The loss of liberty was debilitating and the prisoners' misery was compounded by the unavoidable guilt they burdened themselves with for somehow letting down their countries. There was never enough to eat, and hunger was among the more compelling reasons that prisoners hatched escape plans. One of the most ambitious in the history of the war involved the building of three tunnels beneath Stalag Luft III. They were code-named Tom, Dick, and Harry. Only Harry was intended to be used for escape. Tom and Dick were built in innocuous areas and led nowhere, but once they were completed, the prisoners then had tunnels that allowed them to dump the dirt excavated from Harry. It was an ingenious plan that allowed them to dig undetected. Eventually, Harry extended to three hundred thirty-six feet, the longest escape tunnel dug during World War II.

On the night and early morning of March 24–25, 1944, two hundred twenty prisoners were poised to make their escape. Seventy-six made it out in what came to be known as the Great Escape. Initially, it was thought to have been a significant success. However, seventy-three of the prisoners were recaptured.

Fifty were duly executed by shooting under orders of the Führer, who was outraged and embarrassed by the escape.

The night after the Great Escape, Lieutenant Robert Laubach arrived at Stalag Luft III and was placed in the American compound, on the other side of the camp from the British airmen. Early on, Laubach recognized that the only freedom that could not be taken from him was the freedom to control his attitude. He watched disconsolately as dispirited men sat by idly, staring blankly ahead, doing nothing other than pondering their fate. Eventually dementia set in and the guards would take them away, reporting later that they'd died of pneumonia.

Laubach intended to avoid a similar fate. He joined a group of prisoners who decided to build a golf course between the barracks, without knowing that their British counterparts had done so in another part of camp. They laid out a six-hole course, no hole measuring more than fifty yards. They sank powdered-milk cans into the ground to replicate holes. One of them was placed on a patch of dirt on the other side of a sixteen-hundred-square-foot hazard of filthy water that was to be used in the event of a fire.

The men set about manufacturing their own golf balls, similar to how they were making them in the British compound. They used scraps of shoes and worn-out softball covers. They began holding contests to see who could make the best golf balls, which they steadfastly refused to share. Too much time and effort went into the making of a single ball to allow another to use it. The YMCA provided them with three clubs that they were required to share. The balls were aerodynamically abysmal, and they did not carry far. Nor did they roll straight, which mattered not a whit on bumpy ground that was determined to knock a putt off-line anyway. Golfers with money at stake would putt and pray.

The Germans watched with tepid amusement, deducing that a game that kept the prisoners occupied diminished the time they might otherwise be devoting to escape. In this part of the camp, an errant shot could result in disciplinary action. The golfers took great care to avoid breaking a window, which would have been an affront to German guards who considered Reich property sacred.

The golf may have been crude, but Laubach quickly developed an affinity for the game, even as his weight began dropping precipitously. Golf diverted his attention from the gnawing hunger that was a constant source of discomfort in Stalag Luft III. Prisoners received a single eleven-pound Red Cross parcel per man per week. It contained cans of corned beef, salmon, Spam, and powdered milk, soap, three or four packages of cigarettes, Nescafé, crackers, a box of prunes or raisins, and a can of margarine. In the morning, the Germans would provide them a slice or two of bread. They had a potbelly stove with flat sides. For toast, they slapped their bread against the side of the stove, where it would stick. When it was toasted, it would fall off. Then they would similarly toast the other side. The bread was heavy and dark, as was the custom in Germany. The prisoners suspected that it had been leavened with sawdust.

Lunch was typically a thin broth. As the war began to go poorly for the Germans, the quality of the soup (such as it was) deteriorated, to the point that dead worms would float to the surface. Dysentery was rampant. At Stalag Luft III, the prisoners were often reduced to starvation rations of food, maybe a fifth of an average-sized loaf of bread and a half liter of soup. Some prisoners would take a razor blade and carefully carve their portion of bread into twelve slices so thin that light could pass through them. They'd eat four for breakfast, four for lunch, and four for dinner, in a vain attempt to convince themselves that they were being adequately fed. On such occasions, they became preoccupied by food, the subject dominating their thoughts and threatening to undermine their survival. Golf, even in this elementary and rudimentary form, worked as a passable distraction, allowing them to focus on something other than their next meal. Green and the other golfers were uninterested in whiling away their time in other activities, so for them golf became their lifeline, a means by which to forge ahead, fending off madness one shot at a time.

It was no way to go through a war, but it was all they had, and they made the most of it. Ward-Thomas, incidentally, estimated that the Patrick of Leven mashie with which they began their obsession probably hit more than two hundred thousand shots during its time in their possession, its durability exceeded only by those who had come to rely on it for their very survival.

12

D-DAY

Golf and Operation Overlord

The game never looked so small, so nakedly bereft of importance, as it did in the context of D-day. It was here that
Churchill's words, spoken two years earlier, resonated loudest:
"In this strange, terrible world war there is a place for everyone,
man and woman, old and young, hale and halt. . . ." Every walk
of life was to be represented in the Allied Forces' D-day invasion
of France, a plan that if executed successfully would bring the
fall of the Third Reich, the beginning of the end. The irony for
golf was that even in its diminished state—forced by circumstance to acknowledge its elementary appeal, its child's-play
quality of hitting a stone with a stick—it had a commanding presence in the most critical battle of the war.

An inveterate, albeit inexpert, golfer had been called upon to
orchestrate the invasion. On December 24, 1943, General Dwight

Eisenhower received word that he was to direct Operation Over-lord, the code name of the invasion of France. Less than a month later, on January 16, 1944, he assumed his duties as the supreme commander of the Allied Expeditionary Forces.

This was a promotion that again landed him in London, where once more he took up residence at Telegraph Cottage in Coombe Hill, outside the city. It was the most important assignment of his life—indeed the most significant mission anyone of his generation had ever had. The pressure on Ike was enormous, but again he had the Coombe Hill Golf Club on which to enjoy an hour or more of solitude. Occasionally, he'd sneak out to play the same five holes he'd played during his stay two years earlier—fourteen and fifteen, then cutting over to play eleven, twelve, and thirteen, which returned him to the back gate of Telegraph Cottage.

The course, like so many around the world, had fallen into disrepair. A herd of twelve goats had joined its grounds crew, grazing at will on the rough, keeping it in check, while also contributing a dozen quarts of goat milk each day. It was no way to maintain a course, but with the labor shortfall brought on by war, the goats were an acceptable alternative to allowing it to go to seed. Ike didn't mind. He seldom hit his target anyway. Whether it was groomed properly was of no consequence to him in this time and place. It was golf, and it served its purpose by clearing his mind.

The game in various forms was involved in the planning and execution of D-day. Several hundred miles from Telegraph Cottage, on the northern coast of Wales, a massive secret project was nearing completion. The project had begun in early 1943, when nine hundred workers descended on the town of Conwy and began a construction project that required the Conwy Caernarvonshire Golf Club, founded in 1890 and among the oldest in

Wales, to surrender its marvelous short par-4 ninth hole, effectively transforming the course to the finest seventeen-hole layout in all of the United Kingdom.

Conwy Caernarvonshire Golf Club already had a history of contributing to Britain's war efforts. In the First World War, the course was closed and virtually destroyed after it had been requisitioned as an Army training camp. At the conclusion of the war, the course was restored, with improvements.

Now, on the ninth hole, workers constructed sections of Mulberry Harbors, a remarkable feat of engineering performed under the duress of war that included occasional bombs falling on the area. These were artificial harbors consisting of one hundred forty-six caissons, thirty-three jetties, and ten miles of floating roadways that would allow the Allied forces to transport their war machinery from ship to shore on D-day. The sections constructed at Conwy Caernarvonshire Golf Club would be slipped into the Conwy River, tugged out to the Irish Sea, then down to the English Channel, and finally to Omaha Beach at Normandy, France, where they were to be fitted together with sections built in other parts of Britain.

There were also golfers eager to participate on behalf of the Allies. A few days after New Year's Day, 1944, Major Bobby Jones arrived in London, ready to serve. He was immediately recognized, as he stood awaiting a train in Waterloo Station. "Aren't you Bobby Jones from Atlanta?" Lieutenant Morris McLemore asked.

"Yes, I am," replied Jones politely.

Prior to joining the armed forces, McLemore had been a member of *The Atlanta Journal* sports staff, which was perhaps the only reason that Jones had been recognized. He was traveling in England incognito, which is to say without his golf clubs, a first for the man who had constructed his legacy in large part on his achievements in Britain. The clubs had remained home in America, gathering dust. "Playing golf is like eating peanuts or going to ball games," Jones told McLemore. "If you play several times you want to play more often, and if you don't play at all you get out of the notion."

During his brief time on this particular visit to Britain, he had seen golf courses only from the window of a moving train or motorcar. The courses were devoid of players, which helped quell his own desire to play. It reminded him that he was in London to work, and not only was he fine with that, but he welcomed the opportunity ahead of him. "I was tired of fighting the battle of the Atlantic seaboard," he said, explaining why he was there. "When I entered the Army, it was with the hope of seeing really active duty. That's why I'm glad to be here."

His arrival in London allowed him to renew several friendships. He dined with his Georgia Tech classmate Major Al Staton and encountered Major Allen Watkins, whose wife worked with Jones's law firm in Atlanta.

ANOTHER GOLF AFICIONADO, Army sergeant William Powell, had arrived in London via the *Queen Mary*, one of twenty-three thousand troops aboard the legendary ship. The *Queen Mary* was an inviting target, given its size and stature and the human cargo aboard. Hitler was even offering a reward to the crew of any German U-boat that could sink the renowned ship. The *Queen Mary*, fortunately, avoided the German Navy altogether in its trek from New York to London.

Powell was an accomplished golfer, though one of no particular repute beyond his hometown of North Canton, Ohio. His was not a game that graciously welcomed people of color. Powell was black, seemingly a greater obstacle to mastering golf than even a dearth of inherent talent. There was the time he decided to play in a prominent junior tournament at the prestigious Orchard Hills Country Club in North Canton. Though the tournament had no rule forbidding black kids from playing, it was generally understood that they weren't welcome. Undeterred, Powell hitched a ride to the course, twenty-one miles, with golf clubs in tow. When he arrived, tournament officials were uncertain what they ought to do with "the colored boy" who wanted to play. They knew him to be a quality player and were aware that he had a following among the members, many of whom had employed him as a caddie. Reluctantly, the tournament officials decided to allow him to play. In the qualifying round, Powell shot the best score of the day, earning him an invitation to return the following day for the thirty-six-hole stroke-play tournament. When he arrived the next morning, he learned that he had been paired with the two boys who had shot the highest qualifying scores, an apparent attempt by tournament officials to distract him and prevent him from contending by having him play with largely unskilled players. Their mission, if that indeed was what it was, failed; Powell eventually finished third.

Powell went on to play golf at Wilberforce College in Xenia, Ohio, and was involved in the first interracial golf match in collegiate history, between Wilberforce and Ohio Northern University.

In Britain, Sergeant Powell found it liberating that the prejudices that blacks encountered in the States were nonexistent in Britain, where most people had never before seen a black man. Everywhere he was stationed in Britain, he sought out golf courses, most of them allowing him to play without restrictions. A few, Inverness in Scotland among them, required that he play with a member, which was fine with Powell. He had access to

Ipswich, Southampton, Cambridge, and Bury St. Edmonds, among other English courses.

His skill level was such that he was occasionally asked whether he intended to pursue PGA golf once he returned to the States. Initially, he attempted to explain that that was not possible, given the color of his skin and a PGA that had a Caucasians-only rule. The only option available to black professionals was the United Golf Association Tour, which played only on second-rate courses for paltry sums of money that wouldn't pay the bills, particularly for those with a family to support. Eventually it became too tiresome, as well as depressing, to explain the racism that would not allow him to pursue the game in the country for which he was fighting.

Powell was playing one day at Southampton Golf Club, near the base at which he was stationed in Basset. He was playing so well that after making a tap-in birdie 2 at the par-3 eleventh adjacent to the clubhouse, he had developed a crowd to watch him play. The ability to play without the shackles of racism had inflamed his love for the game. His recovered enjoyment renewed his resolve to continue to pursue the game at home once the war was over, notwithstanding the color of his skin.

In the meantime, he had an important job to do. Powell was a technical sergeant with the 1517th Quartermasters Mobile Aviation. Powell's assignment was to organize truck convoys that kept Army Air Corps and Royal Air Force bases in England supplied with bombs and other munitions. As D-day approached, Powell's unit was transferred to Ampfield Woods, just north of the port city of Southampton. Ampfield Woods was a staging area for the imminent invasion of France. Powell's unit began transporting troops to the area, employing more than a thousand trucks operating twenty-four hours a day. The activity did not escape the notice of the Germans, who began nighttime bombing runs to the area.

ANOTHER GOLFER, this one of national note, was also preparing to join the D-day invasion. Lloyd Mangrum had won three tournaments in 1942, after which the war interceded. He was a star on the rise, who could have used his growing reputation to avoid combat. He was offered an opportunity to become the professional at the Army's Fort Meade golf course, but he declined, to the astonishment of most from his industry. "I'm in the Army to fight for my country, not to play golf," he said defiantly.

Mangrum was originally in the infantry, though he grew tired of walking, generally, and marching, specifically. He wrangled a transfer to a reconnaissance unit, which allowed him to ride instead. He wrote a letter to his wife, informing her of his good fortune, and she, too, was pleased, for about a week, until she learned that the role of a reconnaissance unit was to examine an area in advance of the troops. "I could have killed him," she said, overtly concerned that the Germans would beat her to it.

On June 6, 1944, Operation Overlord came to fruition. Mangrum entered the fray at Omaha Beach on D-day. He stormed the beachhead as part of the second wave of soldiers. In the mayhem, his jeep overturned. He sustained a broken arm in two places, an injury that temporarily ended his combat venture one day into it. The arm would require several months of rehabilitation, and Mangrum was sent to a hospital in perhaps the most appropriate place for a golf professional to heal, St. Andrews, Scotland, the town in which the game was said to have been invented. It was not a holiday, however. Mangrum was predictably concerned that he would never play competitive golf again. The doctor informed him that, once the cast came off, if he was able to lift his arm elbow high he'd play golf again.

"I have to be able to play as well as I ever did or it won't matter," Mangrum told the doctor, who was unable to give him the assurance he wanted.

Powell's work, meanwhile, intensified with the invasion, but rather than running troops to the staging area, his trucks took on the grisly task of picking up the Allied dead that had been collected from the French beachheads and taken to the port and bringing them back to refrigerated tents, where they were stored.

ON D-DAY PLUS ONE, Bobby Jones's wishful thinking became a reality. His unit had been converted to infantry, requiring that it go ashore at the outset of the most important military operation of the war. Its mission was to make its way inland about twenty miles, to an airfield it was asked to secure.

Jones, forty-two, married and the father of three, one of the most famous athletes in the world and an enduring American and British icon, found himself engaged in combat, under intense enemy fire for two days. He was a high-profile target for the enemy as his death would have had a demoralizing effect on Allied troops. Jones lived, though not to tell about it. The horrifying nature of combat often turned soldiers into mutes on the subject of their own experiences, Jones among them.

His combat duty was short-lived. Jones was eligible for a discharge based on his age—those over thirty-eight were given a priority. Moreover, his father, Big Bob Jones, had taken ill at home in Atlanta, and he wished to be there with him. His father was eager to congratulate his son personally for his promotion to lieutenant colonel, a rank that carried special significance in the Jones family. Big Bob was frequently called Colonel Jones, though he had never been a colonel. Bobby Jones's promotion meant that the Jones family finally had a legitimate colonel.

Jones had noticed that the Army had a surfeit of overage officers, of which he was one. Moreover, his contributions to the war
effort were essentially behind him, and he realized that his father needed him home more than the Army needed him abroad.
So he entered a replacement pool and awaited his orders to return home. In the meantime, he reported to Warton Air Base,
which was only a short distance from Royal Lytham and St.
Annes, where in 1926 he had won the British Open for the first
time. The proximity was too tempting for Jones, who made a so-
journ to the site of one of his greatest accomplishments.

He spent a week at Royal Lytham and St. Annes, playing golf
and visiting with its members. During Jones's visit, Henry Cotton,
the British golf legend, suggested that a plaque be installed on the
spot from which Jones had hit the mashie-iron shot that had won
the Open for him in '26. Jones agreed to pinpoint the spot for the
members.

Jones had no clubs with which to play, so he borrowed those
of a member, Donald Beaver, who was off serving the British military. One day, he played an exhibition match against a member,
Johnny Bradbury, to raise money for the Red Cross. To spice up
their match, they wagered a pound that Jones eventually lost.
Bradbury asked Jones to sign the one-pound note for him. Jones
complied, and Bradbury proudly displayed his most prized trophy, a one-pound note with Jones's signature, on his living room
mantelpiece.

Upon his departure, Jones presented the club with a copy of
his book, *Down the Fairway*. His inscription read: "To the Members of Royal Lytham with my grateful thanks for their many
kindnesses to me during my visit." It was signed Robert T. Jones,
Jr., and dated 6 August, 1944.

Less than three weeks later, a Liberator bomber was struck by
lightning just after takeoff and crashed onto a school in nearby

Freckleton. Thirty-eight children and two teachers were killed and many more were injured.

Days after the tragedy, Bing Crosby was in Great Britain to entertain the troops, principally, but while he was there he intended to play a little golf, too, on some of Scotland's historic courses. Moved by the Freckleton tragedy, Crosby paid a visit to the injured, including a five-year-old girl who had been badly burned. He spoke to her for a few moments, after which she asked him to sing his hit song, "White Christmas." The request overwhelmed him, and Crosby dashed from the room in tears, requiring several minutes to compose himself. Still unsure whether he would be able to maintain his equanimity, he returned to her room and sang the song for her, more his pleasure than hers. Golf also looked small in the context of a severely injured child.

BY THE END OF AUGUST 1944, Colonel Bobby Jones was back home in the United States, his war service effectively over. He left New York via train and arrived at Peachtree Station in Atlanta. His wife, Mary, was there on the platform awaiting him, as were his daughters, Mary Ellen and Clara Malone, and his son, Bobby III. The other Colonel Jones, his father, waited for him in the car.

He declined to comment on his war service. "Can't talk about those things, you know," he said, reminding a reporter that he had been serving in Army Air Corps intelligence. He was taken directly to Fort McPherson in Atlanta, where on August 26, 1944, he received his separation papers. He was a civilian once again.

The hero's welcome home was generally avoided by Jones, who in this instance would have loathed it. What had he done other than what other Americans had done? He had answered the call, performed to the best of his abilities, witnessed the horrors of war, and come home.

A columnist in *The Augusta Chronicle* celebrated his homecoming, and salivated at the possibility that the Masters could be resumed in 1945 and that Jones could contend for the title, nearly fifteen years after he had last played serious competitive golf. This was reverie that routinely emanated from a newspaper sports department, where fantasy was fueled by the occasional athletic miracle. The columnist reasoned that Jones might prevail, in the win-one-for-the-Gipper vein, because he was twenty pounds lighter than he had been before joining the service, weighing in at a svelte one hundred fifty-five pounds. "One in Augusta cannot think of Bobby Jones and not allow his mind to backfire on memories of the Masters Golf Tourney. . . . One cannot help but let his mind dwell on Bobby Jones's weight—155 pounds! Wow, with Bobby in condition, what a show he'd be in the Masters next year! . . . You can't help but think of Jones in here weighing 155 pounds, hard as nails and swinging away for just one Masters' title before he quits."

THE WAR WAS NOT YET WON, which was the condition under which the Masters would resume. The Allies had the Germans on the run, however, giving Lloyd Mangrum another shot at the enemy. His arm fortunately had healed properly, and so he returned to the front lines, this time in Germany, near Frankfurt, where he engaged the retreating German Army in the Battle of the Bulge. Amid a noisy firefight, Mangrum somehow heard a friend yell his name. He turned his head, just as a bullet passed through his helmet, where his face would have been had he not swiveled. He was lucky once, but not twice. Moments later, bullets struck his shoulder and his lower leg, felling him. His injuries would have ended his life had he not been rescued a short time later. He would receive two Purple Hearts for his injuries, which he would explain were the result of "tripping over a whiskey bottle while running out of a whorehouse in Paris."

Those who knew him considered it a plausible explanation. But it was an unseemly one. It diminished the selfless nature of his decision, to forgo the golf option to join fellow Americans on the front lines in a critical and dangerous exercise.

13

SOLDIERING ON, HOLE BY HOLE

Golf Keeps Up the Fight

Robert Moses was perhaps the state of New York's most powerful man, and his most glaring weakness was that he knew it. The New York City parks commissioner, Moses was responsible for the construction of bridges, roads, parks, even golf courses. He was a ruthless man; witness his advocacy of the automobile as the principal means of transportation and the manner in which he promoted it: Highway overpasses constructed on his watch were said to have been purposely built too low to allow buses to pass underneath. New York City mayor Fiorello H. La Guardia considered him so arrogant that he referred to him as "His Grace."

His power was based on his having advanced enough good ideas that his haughty manner was largely tolerated. One of them was for Nassau County to purchase the vast property of the late railroad tycoon Benjamin Yoakum. It included a golf course, Lenox Hills Country Club, that after the sale was renamed Bethpage Golf

Club. Moses thought on a large scale; his idea was to build a massive golf complex. The result of his vision was Bethpage State Park, which featured four golf courses, including the difficult Bethpage Black.

Moses's arrogance caused him on occasion to talk through his high hat, as he did one day in 1944 via a letter to the editor of the Long Island newspaper, *Newsday*. The paper was concerned that thousands of soldiers at military posts in the area had no place to play golf. It began campaigning to allow them to play Bethpage State Park's four courses for free on Sundays and holidays, a proposal to which Moses, as the president of the Long Island State Park Commission and the ruling authority of the courses, took umbrage, no doubt because he considered *Newsday's* campaign an attempt to usurp his power. Moses responded with an inflammatory letter that touched off what *The New York Times* called "a controversy of global proportions."

"The statement in your editorial that our decision on this matter was arrived at without proper thought or information is unwarranted," Moses wrote. "There is no basis for your assumption that there are thousands of soldiers at near-by camps who are being deprived of an opportunity to play golf.

"As a matter of fact, experience has shown that most of the service men who play golf are officers who can afford a reasonable fee, and that the average soldier at camp does not include golf sticks and golf lingo in his equipment. The average doughboy regards golf as a sport of toffs and gentlemen, and doesn't know a divot from an Attic tomb inscription.

"On the other hand, large numbers of trucks and buses with soldiers are regularly sent to other parts for swimming and other recreational facilities which appeal to the G.I. Joes."

His letter leaked condescension. It was an astonishingly elitist point of view that was as wrongheaded as it was boneheaded.

Newsday responded accordingly, taking Moses to task and defending the soldier/golfer in an editorial.

"With respect to Mr. Moses and the wonderful job he has done in the many enterprises with which he has been connected, we think he is all wet here," the paper wrote. "Our G.I. Joes aren't drawn from any special strata of society. They include every bracket from millionaires to paupers. They play golf, squash, tennis, horseshoes, badminton, bridge, chess, polo and what have you. For most of the men who can walk without falling down are in the armed services. To single out that great mass of American humanity and say that they as a group regard golf as a game of 'toffs and gentlemen' is an extraordinary statement."

The controversy resonated with the community. Several area clubs weighed in by establishing programs for uniformed golfers of every rank. Piping Rock Club in Locust Valley, one of the more exclusive clubs in the region, allowed servicemen of any rank to play free on Mondays, Tuesdays, and Wednesdays as long as they were stationed at nearby Mitchel Field. At the private Cherry Valley Club, seventy-five uniformed men of all ranks were permitted to play gratis during the week. Even Bethpage State Park's courses at the center of the controversy acknowledged that course officials there had been providing enlisted men with free golf during the week since the Pearl Harbor attack.

An upshot to the brouhaha was that Nassau County executive J. Russel Sprague announced that all uniformed personnel were invited to play the county-owned Salisbury Golf Course in Westbury every day, free of charge, and even included the use of a locker. Moreover, he was making twenty-five sets of golf clubs available for use by uniformed personnel. Prior to Moses's claims, soldiers had been charged a reduced rate to play the course.

The fact was that soldiers in substantial numbers were playing golf whenever they could, wherever they could, anywhere a club and a ball turned up. Golf was growing in popularity at military posts across the country. Soldiers had undertaken the task of building a nine-hole course at Camp Gordon in Augusta, Georgia, to go along with the practice range and putting green that the Augusta National Golf Club membership had built for them. Augusta National continued its support of the camp by providing the expertise required to build the nine-holer, which became the Enlisted Men's Golf Course.

Professional golfer Bill Lynch, an Army private first class, was given the job as pro at the course. Among his assignments was providing the soldiers there with golf lessons. Lynch also stocked his golf shop with a variety of golf magazines that quickly became tattered from overuse by soldiers leafing through them in search of tips that might help their golf progress. Lynch also put out a plea for used golf balls. "We're in great need of some old golf balls," Lynch wrote. "If we could get some more the boys would have a hell of a swell time from golf as a relaxation from hard work at soldiering."

Convalescing soldiers there, under the direction of Lieutenant Anthony Reiger, also frequently used the golf facilities, recalling that in the First World War, Major Tommy Armour vigorously pursued the game as part of his own rehabilitation from injury and evolved into one of the game's better players.

Golf was the inspiration behind the most unusual nine-hole course developed by the military, the Camp Chafee Grenade Golf Course at Fort Smith, Arkansas. The course was designed as a training ground for tossing hand grenades, nine "holes" that featured targets such as an effigy of Hitler, a .30-caliber machine-gun pillbox, a miniature railroad car, and a 155-millimeter howitzer. The "holes" measured from twenty yards to sixty yards. A direct hit with a grenade counted as an ace, one stroke; probables, within five feet of the target, counted as two strokes; possibles, within ten feet of the target, as three; and misses as four. Par for the course was 21. "Grenade golf is played from standing, kneeling, or prone positions," wrote the *Service Sports Clip Sheet.*

Hitler was an enticing target across the military spectrum, especially for uniformed golfers. A caricature of the mustached face of the enemy adorned the large two-hundred-yard target on the driving range built for the soldiers at Camp Croft, South Carolina. Beneath the caricature were the words FIRE AT WILL.

Elaine Rosenthal had once been a golf star, who during the First World War traveled with a young Bobby Jones and U.S. Women's Amateur champion Alexa Stirling, giving exhibitions on behalf of the Red Cross. Her well-heeled mother, Mrs. B. J. Rosenthal, donated the funds necessary to build and maintain a nine-hole pitch-and-putt course at Fort Sheridan, outside Chicago. Edward B. Dearie, an associate of Donald Ross, had built the Fort Sheridan Golf Course six years earlier, and was assigned the task of delivering the pitch-and-putt course on which soldiers could learn to play sans much of the frustration from attempting to navigate around a championship-length course.

Camp Roberts near San Luis Obispo, California, featured a story in the camp newspaper, beneath the headline GOLF FOR SOLDIERS IS CAMP'S OBJECT. It read: "A spirited drive to revive golf among soldiers stationed at this vast training center is in full swing. Dynamite in the drive to blast soldiers from their barracks and onto the fairways was furnished by Sgt. Art Gonzales and M/Sgt. Bobby Walsh."

Golf was popular at Camp Callan, an antiaircraft artillery training center that had opened on Torrey Pines Mesa, a bluff overlooking the Pacific Ocean just north of San Diego. As military installations go, few offered a better view. The camp sat among a forest of rare Torrey pine trees, which were found only one other place in the world, on Santa Rosa Island, part of the

Channel Islands off the coast of Santa Barbara, California. The Pacific Ocean stretching out beyond the bluff also provided a perfect place to practice shooting antiaircraft artillery. Planes towed targets out over the Pacific, while 90-millimeter shells were shot toward them. Those that missed fell harmlessly into the ocean. The officers and enlisted men at Camp Callan had access to La Jolla Country Club nearby. The club even agreed to host the All–Camp Callan Golf Tournament and provided clubs to boot.

Golf was played by soldiers and sailors abroad, too, among them Technical Sergeant Frank Strafaci, an accomplished amateur golfer, who in 1935 had won the U.S. Amateur Public Links Championship. He also won the prestigious North and South Amateur in 1938 and '39, and had defeated U.S. Amateur champion Willie Turnesa in the final of the 1938 Metropolitan Amateur. The sergeant was part of the DUKW Command in the Philippines. A DUKW—or Duck, as it was commonly called—was an amphibious vehicle used to ferry ammunition, supplies, and troops to beachheads, an invaluable vehicle for shorelines without docks. DUKWs had played a critical role in the D-day invasion of Normandy in the European theater earlier in the year, and they were exceedingly successful in the U.S. effort in the Pacific, including the Philippines.

In addition to his prowess at golf, Strafaci was a prolific letter writer. Letters, of course, armed the combat soldier for the psychological war with himself, the means by which he could remain connected with the world he had left behind. For Strafaci, it was a small world that he had left behind, no more than seven thousand yards, typically, the distance from the first tee to the eighteenth green.

So it was that when a morning of quiet unexpectedly presented itself in the war-torn Philippines, Sergeant Strafaci sat down with pen and paper and wrote a letter to his friend Morton Bogue, president of the United States Golf Association. Golf was in Strafaci's blood, which to his good fortune he had not been required to shed on behalf of the Allied war effort. He was deft at dodging bullets, as his letter would reveal, but their fleeting proximity to his skull as they passed by got him thinking. Thinking about what? Golf, naturally.

Even between dodging bullets, Strafaci found time for golf, which he recounted in his lengthy letter to Bogue. He also reinforced the notion that golfers are daft. Wherever they are, whatever the peril, they invariably manage at least a thought or two about the game.

The letter was dated November 4, 1944. It read:

Dear Mr. Bogue:

Just received your letter and it's the first one in 7 weeks, so I enjoyed reading it a great deal. Before I left Brisbane I got a letter from an American Red Cross official, expressing his thanks for the golf balls he received from the USGA. I'm sure they can make very good use of them.

As for golf news, when I get back to the States I hope to present the USGA with a golf ball that has already traveled over 43,000 miles and been used for 52 rounds of golf. It was used in America, Australia, Dutch New Guinea, I expect soon to use it in the Philippines, China, and Japan. I used it for the first time at my club Sound View, and from there it went to Omaha, back to Sound View, then to Frisco, Adelaide, Australia, Melbourne, Townsville, Cairns, Sydney, Cairns, Brisbane, Cairns, Brisbane, Dutch New Guinea (I didn't have a club, I batted it around with a club made out of a branch).

At present things are pretty hot here. Col. Grimm and I landed

15 minutes after the first wave D-day. The front line was already being established ten yards in from the beach, and for the next two hours we carried shells. I say "we" because the Col. and I were together for the first five days, and wherever he went I tagged along. The reason why he had to haul ammo was because, there weren't sufficient men on the beach at that time, so we all had to pitch in. We got out of that detail oke. As we were resting, we got a big thrill. General MacArthur, President Osmena, and lots of other brass came ashore right in front of us.

The second day we headed for a town, our mission being to contact the Mayor and the Governor, and take intact a certain building where we were to place guards to protect it from the enemy. We hiked many miles when we finally reached a spot one mile from our destination. We were held up for two hours; the town was being shelled. We finally got started, moving in with the infantry. As we reached the town, many people came towards us, they hugged and kissed us, some were crying of happiness. It sure did make me feel funny inside.

The Mayor invited us into his home where we were given some good chow and beer. After the Col. told the Mayor what was expected of him, we left and headed for the other sides of town, where the particular building we were interested in was located. Just before we reached it many civilians were running our way. One boy, about 16 years old, stopped us and told us that there were many snipers ahead, couldn't we give him a rifle. I was thinking that it wouldn't be a bad idea if I gave him mine, I hadn't fired one in so long, that he probably would have done a lot better than I hoped for. He decided to tag along, and we continued on our way. We got within ten yards of the building when the Nips opened up at us. I finally got behind a tree. The Nips were a couple hundred yards away, up on the side of a hill.

I couldn't see them and so I held my fire, and it was at this time that I got to thinking of the five foot putt I had to make to tie the 8^(th) hole in an exhibition golf match played in Brisbane only a few weeks ago (Captain Bud Ward came down from Dutch New Guinea for five days, and I arranged for a match for the benefit of the Australian Red Cross, which we lost 3–2). Our opponents, Alex College and Dick Coogen, played a bit too good for us. I thought of what a tough spot we would have been in if I missed the putt. I can assure you I'll never try hard for another putt as long as I live, at least it won't seem like trying.

We were there only five minutes when the infantry came up. They proceeded ahead and blasted hell out of those monkeys. After placing a guard around the building we headed back for the Mayor's house, but only before that native lad talked me out of my rifle for one hour. He certainly did have a happy look on his face. I checked my rifle and only three shots were fired; not bad shooting. The last I heard of my friend was that he and two other boys were headed for the hills. They hate the Japs as much as we love our country.

That nite we stayed at the Mayor's home, and the following day we were treated to one of the finest Chinese dinners I ever had. The head of a Chinese village was the host. We had roast duck, fried chicken, rice, wine, whiskey, and it was topped off with a Filipino cigar soaked in rum. The next few days I rested up, my feet were shot to hell, and I stayed at an actor's home. Finally I was given an assignment, which I'm still carrying out.

The past ten days have been hell on wheels. The Nips have been coming over night and day, throwing everything at us. And I must say they are the stinkos of all time. Don't get me wrong; I'm not complaining. Last night was tough. They started at 9 P.M. and every 10 or 15 minutes they came over and dropped their eggs. They finally went away at 8 A.M. Our planes came around, and the Nips are in no mood to mess with our flyers.

That's the way things stand at the present time. Until this

Bomber's moon goes away, we'll continue to catch it. So far I've had five narrow escapes, but the only thing that connected was a scorpion bite on the night of the Typhoon. The Nips didn't come over that night. I'll take them any time in preference to that bit of rain and wind, and the everlasting scared out of me, too many times to mention. Even so, I believe all will be well with me, my name is pretty hard to spell.

Sincerely yours,
Frank Strafaci

A war, as Strafaci had discovered, was good for the perspective business. There was nothing like a passing bullet to initiate a reevaluation of the importance of a five-foot putt in the context of life and death.

THE GAME FREQUENTLY TURNED UP in war zones, often on captured islands in the South Pacific. At Guadalcanal in the Solomon Islands, Marine Corps private Howie Miller, the 1941 club champion at Wykagyl Country Club in New Rochelle, New York, fashioned a golf club from a tree limb and belted stones around between combat activities. Smiley Quick, a prominent amateur from southern California, an electrician's mate in the Navy, played five-hole rounds on the atoll of Betio on Tarawa, an isolated chain of coral islets in the Pacific that the Navy had taken. Quick found a Japanese-model putter on Betio and cobbled together a second club from a radio antenna and the wreckage of a landing craft. Finally, he scrounged together five worn-out golf balls, giving him a set of equipment that, given the circumstances, worked wonderfully to reconnect Quick with the game he'd left behind.

On another island in the South Pacific, a nine-hole course was carved out by a U.S. Navy Seabee construction crew, which dubbed it the Yankee Bee Country Club. Existing bunkers were filled with sawdust, though Japanese bombs often created bunkers faster than the Navy men could fill them. The men built their own golf clubs, using whatever scrap metal was available for the clubheads and pickax handles for shafts. The group had only four old balls, which demanded that they possess a degree of accuracy that at least would prevent the loss of one. A local rule was established for those losing a ball: loss of playing privileges for a month. The sailors kept the greens cut with an old-fashioned mower, also known as a goat, whose rank was CGK, for Chief Green Keeper. The goat was tethered to a long rope that was moved each day, to allow uniform eating of grass around the course.

Forty-five men coughed up the entry fee of fifty cents for the first Yankee Bee Country Club Championship. "Nothing could compare with the tournament put on by the Yankee Bee's jungle course," Marine Corps correspondent Ralph Peck wrote. "Stateside tournaments find the gallery heading for the clubhouse at the outbreak of a rainstorm. Here, an occasional bombing from the Japs adds to the many hazards, sending players and spectators scampering into the many foxholes nestled about the course."

First Class Metalsmith Timmy J. Sullivan, from Elsford, New York, won the club championship, defeating another first class metalsmith, Emil Corrente, of Springdale, Connecticut, in the final. The trophy was hammered out of a 105-millimeter shell.

Though Puerto Rico was safely removed from a war zone, servicemen there also engaged in a tournament, at the Berwind Country Club. "Previous experience not necessary," the entry form said, a risky proposition that invited the possibility of extensive damage to the course. In advance, the Navy boys waylaid such fears by volunteering to repair any damage they caused. Chief Petty Officer C. V. Tarter won the Services Tournament, shooting an eight-over-par 80 that bettered Seaman Second Class John M. Sokash by one. For his effort, Tarter received a watch valued at $50 from the Bacardi Corporation, while Bacardi paid out additional prizes in "other suitable awards," presumably of the liquid variety.

The ball scarcity was the most frequent impediment to servicemen playing golf, at home or abroad. In the States, soldiers were asked to exercise care. Among the more creative ways of keeping the scarce supply from diminishing further was the one devised by a WAC, who was in charge of golf equipment at the nine-hole course at Fort Dix. She began requiring a twenty-five-cent deposit on all golf balls, which resulted in a precipitous decline in the number of lost balls. Abroad, soldiers were asked to exercise patience. It might take months to find even a small supply of golf balls in pitiful condition. Strafaci again sent off a letter, this one to a couple of acquaintances at the United States Golf Association, imploring them to send golf balls. "People here have been very kind to all of us," Strafaci wrote. "This particular place I'm at is doing everything possible to make us feel at home. A golf course is here and many of the boys can use it. Many would like to play but golf balls are very scarce. A few hundred balls would be priceless here. There isn't much one can do on his time off and if some golf balls were to be had, I'm sure the boys would appreciate it a great deal. The Red Cross asked me if I could help them. I told 'em I'd do my best."

The request resonated with the USGA, which promptly gathered the balls that equipment companies had sent for testing purposes, to see whether they conformed to the rules. They collected nearly fifteen hundred balls, virtually all of them in excellent condition. They were presented to the Red Cross for shipping overseas for use by soldiers, sailors, toffs, and gentlemen, who may or may not have known a divot from an Attic tomb inscription, but knew they wanted to play golf.

Moses, as it turned out, had only one ally (or at least one club that could appreciate his position) in his quest to rebuff *Newsday*'s golf campaign on behalf of enlisted personnel. It was a private club on Long Island, which all along had allowed only officers to use its course. It responded to the controversy by inviting soldiers to caddie at the club in their spare time, to help alleviate a caddie shortage brought about by the war.

It was the least they could do.

14

THE FLYING DUTCHMAN AND COW CHIPS

A Game's Resilience

Fred Corcoran, the Tournament Bureau manager for the PGA, was a promoter, paid to separate people from their money by whatever legal device his vivid imagination could concoct. Early on, for instance, Corcoran saw an opportunity in perpetuating the image of Sam Snead as a hayseed, arousing curiosity that eventually would manifest itself in boosting a gate. When Snead was told that his photograph had appeared in a New York newspaper, he reportedly said, "How'd they do that? I ain't ever been to New York." That was Corcoran's handiwork, not Snead's naïveté, though the latter was a willing accomplice to the ruse. Tour pro Dutch Harrison called Corcoran "the Persian rug dealer of golf tournaments." He meant it as a compliment, but the inherent warning was to listen to his sales pitch at your own risk.

Late in the summer of 1943, Corcoran returned from a tour of England, where he said he had witnessed the restorative power of golf played by wounded soldiers. It convinced him, he said, that with the war finally having turned in favor of the Allies, efforts should be made to resume the tour, to help stimulate interest in the game. No doubt there were restorative powers when wounded soldiers played golf, and surely Corcoran had witnessed them. But that could only have been a secondary concern to his wanting to resume professional tournament golf. The overriding reason, of course, was that that was how he got paid.

Tournament golf had been virtually suspended in 1943, so Corcoran had gone to work as a volunteer for the American Red Cross. The PGA continued to pay him his salary, though pressure was mounting to cut off the flow of money for work not performed. George R. Jacobus, a member of the PGA Finance Committee, was at the fore of the movement to suspend Corcoran's pay pending the resumption of the tour. An article he wrote for the *Professional Golfer of America* magazine carried the headline:

P.G.A. SHOULD NOT PAY CORCORAN $100 PER
WEEK FOR VOLUNTARY RED CROSS WORK

Jacobus's point was that people everywhere had surrendered their salaries to do the nation's work, and Corcoran should not be an exception. "I firmly believe that the money that would be paid to Fred Corcoran could be put to much better use for the greater benefit of the Association and its members," he wrote.

Corcoran was able to deflect the criticism and the potential salary suspension because PGA officials, of which he was one, elected to resume tournament play in 1944, despite the projected absence of representative fields. He also had the obvious support of the players who weren't engaged in war work. "The tour, I feel, not only will help the war effort but also will stimulate interest in golf," Jug McSpaden said. "Some of our best friends in service—Ben Hogan, Jimmy Demaret, Sam Snead, Jimmy Thomson, Lawson Little, Paul Runyan, Horton Smith—have asked us to play as much as we can in order to keep the game going for them."

So Corcoran went back to work, doing what he did best—finding money. He began soliciting bids for tournaments, and anyone willing to ante $10,000 could secure a date on the tour schedule. The likelihood of a host of tournaments stepping up seemed remote, given the unresolved status of the war and the dearth of marquee talent available. Yet Corcoran worked his magic and stitched together a schedule that could accurately be described as a tour, twenty-three tournaments, or twenty more than were played in 1943.

His greatest feat was securing a bid of $20,000, double the going rate, from the Spokane (Washington) Athletic Round Table to host the 1944 PGA Championship, the first major championship to be played in two years. Anything less might have been a stumbling block to taking the PGA's signature event to a sparsely populated region as remote as any in the country. The Round Table was comprised of a group of influential businessmen from Spokane with a passion for golf. The men were flush with cash from a legal slot machine operation, and they saw an opportunity to bring a major sporting event to their remote town, 275 miles east of Seattle and so far removed from civilization that the PGA could not promise that even the best players not otherwise occupied with war-related commitments would attempt the journey. The idea was to play the tournament at the Manito Golf and Country Club, south of the city. *Manito* is an Algonquin word that translates to "magical power," fittingly, considering that the Round Table's cash was the magical power for luring professional golf to a city as remote as Spokane.

Once the tour resumed, Corcoran's job was simplified by the

emergence as a major figure of E. J. Harrison, as newspapers referred to him in their scoring roundups, though he was better known as Dutch. Harrison was a gregarious tour professional from Little Rock, Arkansas. He had a southern accent, a folksy charm, and an innate ability to spin a yarn for any kind of audience. Dutch Harrison had spent most of the war in the Army, though the majority of his marching was done down a fairway. A man with his ability to hit a golf ball so well and a personality warm enough to melt the Army brass could virtually depend on receiving orders to report to a golf course.

He was so engaging, in fact, that he talked an Army general into loaning him his military aircraft. At the outset of the summer of '44, Sergeant Harrison was transferred to Wright Field in Dayton, Ohio. The commanding general at Wright Field was charmed to a degree that he allowed Harrison the use of a B-17 to ferry him to tournaments around the country. Harrison's mode of transportation naturally earned him the sobriquet "the Flying Dutchman," as well as the admiration of his competition, which was relegated to traveling by automobile or train.

Early in the year, Harrison won the Charlotte Open while wearing GI trousers, a white T-shirt, and a garrison cap that was tilted on his head. The crowd was smitten, beyond the fact that his was the first PGA victory by an active serviceman. Former Masters champion Craig Wood called it the best thing that had ever happened to golf, an obvious overstatement, but one that accurately conveyed the importance of a victory that declared to the sporting public that professional golf had returned.

Byron Nelson and Jug McSpaden were the PGA headliners in 1944, the two of them winning with such frequency that they became known as the Gold Dust Twins. They had the advantage of competing on a tour without Hogan and Snead, neither of whom was able to extricate himself from service commitments.

When the PGA Championship came around in August, their competition was so light that Olin Dutra and Lighthorse Harry Cooper, both fading stars, were included among the notable players entered, as were Sam Byrd and Craig Wood. Few established tour professionals were available for a tournament so remote, and as a result the anticipated field of one hundred forty was trimmed to one hundred, then to eighty-five. When the tournament finally began, only sixty-six players were on hand, eight of whom were culled from Washington state club pro ranks to give the field a bit more heft.

Nelson and McSpaden predictably qualified one and two for match play. McSpaden bowed out early, however, leaving Nelson to defend the honor of the tournament. Nelson advanced to the thirty-six-hole final against Bob Hamilton, a relatively unknown pro from Evansville, Indiana, a player who had yet to establish his credentials as a bona fide tour player. Accordingly, he was established as a ten-to-one underdog.

In the final, Hamilton set out to reduce the odds against him by engaging in the art of gamesmanship. He had a tendency to clear his throat when Nelson was ready to stroke an important putt. Eventually, Ed Dudley, the PGA president, warned Hamilton to cease and desist, lest he be penalized, or even disqualified. Nelson missed a two-foot putt on the first hole, a four-footer on the second hole, and a three-footer on the ninth hole. Ever the gentleman, Nelson declined to complain about the propitiously timed noises coming from the direction of his opponent. He acknowledged that he was aware of Hamilton's attempts at the time-honored tradition of rattling his competition. Yet Nelson blamed his miscues on himself. "I didn't putt very well," he said.

The match was even through thirty-three holes as a result of Nelson's benevolence with the putter. On the thirty-fourth hole,

Hamilton made a thirty-foot birdie putt to go one-up with two to play. They halved the thirty-fifth hole, then on the thirty-sixth, Nelson finally holed a putt, an eighteen-foot birdie, to transfer the onus to Hamilton, who now needed to two-putt from the fringe to win. His first stopped twenty inches from the hole. "I putted that last one as quick as possible," he said. "It was less than two feet, but the longer I looked at it, the longer the distance seemed." He rapped the putt, though later he said he could not recall the putter even striking the ball, only that the ball seemed to be magically drawn to the hole. When it fell, Hamilton threw his putter in the air.

Hamilton was such an improbable winner that newsmen labeled it "the most spectacular upset in the history of the tournament." One New York columnist, Jim McCulley, suggested that Nelson's defeat at the hands of an unknown spoke to the need to expand the size of the hole. He reasoned that since Nelson was superior in every other facet of the game, but was at best an average putter, he was beaten only when confronted with "a hot or lucky putter," McCulley wrote.

"Wouldn't golf be just as fine a game, a much finer and fairer game, perhaps, if the stress were taken off putting?" his column asked. "Why should the harmony of a fine drive and approach be disrupted by the thought of missing an eighteen-inch putt? Was the four-and-one-fourth-inch-hole rule in the game so that it would be possible for the Hamiltons to beat the masters like Nelson? If so, why? Would baseball have benefited if it had built thousand-foot fences to stop the likes of Babe Ruth? I'm for bigger and deeper holes in golf courses."

A pertinent point that escaped McCulley was that Hamilton won because his own skills were considerable, for which Dutch Harrison could have vouched. Harrison and Hamilton had spent many an afternoon in their formative professional careers hustling unsuspecting victims. Talent and virtual anonymity were a hustler's best weapons, and Hamilton had used them to sneak off with the first major championship played in two years.

Moreover, it wasn't that Nelson's putting woes were derailing what otherwise would have been a remarkable career. In 1944 alone, he won eight tournaments and finished in the top three in eighteen of the twenty-one events he played. He played so well, in fact, that he lost his job as a result. Late in the year, Nelson began to hear murmurings that members at the Inverness Club in Toledo, at which he was the professional, had begun to resent the amount of money he was making from tournaments and exhibitions, and were wondering aloud why the club had to pay him as well. He solved that problem for them. He resigned.

ONE CLUE THAT GOLF was regaining its equilibrium was the return of professional golf, even in a depleted state. Another was hidden in a small southeastern newspaper, between antacid and aspirin ads that, according to their curious placement on the newspaper's obituary page, seemed to suggest that the readers' own demise might be thwarted by the use of these products. The clue was part of an obituary of another sort, a two-column ad recounting the not untimely deaths of a group of barnyard animals (as well as the impending deaths of others of their ilk).

The ad first appeared in the November 20, 1944 edition of *The Augusta Chronicle* of Augusta, Georgia, prior to Thanksgiving. The ad read:

TURKEYS!

- ON FOOT
- FEATHER PICKED
- DRESSED AND DRAWN

O.P.A. CEILING PRICES

NO DELIVERIES

AUGUSTA NATIONAL GOLF CLUB

WASHINGTON ROAD

PHONE 3-7247

The ad appeared the following day as well, and again one week before Christmas. Augusta National Golf Club was divesting itself of its farm animals and preparing to abandon the meat business to return to the business of golf. In addition to the well-publicized herd of cattle the club had acquired to assist it in keeping the grass in check and in alleviating the meat shortage brought on by war, it had purchased 1,423 day-old turkeys on the advice of its superintendent, Simk Hammack, whose diversified resume included experience raising turkeys. More than a thousand turkeys survived and were raised to edible size. Many of them were sold toward the end of 1943. Clifford Roberts, who cofounded the club with Bobby Jones, also decided that a turkey ought to be given to each member at Christmas, 1943, when meat was still rationed. Now the remainder of the turkeys had gone on sale, signaling an end to the venture. The club had already sold its herd of cows, ultimately absorbing a $5,000 hit on the enterprise, at that without factoring in the damage the cows caused to the course. The club did better with the pecans it picked from its own trees. It donated half to an Army canteen and sold the other half to members.

The final accounting showed that the club's success with turkeys offset its failure with cows. The lesson that Roberts took away from this farming experience was that the club would do better focusing only on golf in the future.

Golf, indeed, was again in Augusta's future, as the Allied forces continued to close in on victory. On November 19,

1944, the Augusta National Golf Club announced that it was reopening to members on December 23, while also announcing that the Masters would not be played in 1945, out of deference to those still waging war on America's behalf. Only when victory had been achieved would the club resume hosting the Masters.

To prepare for the reopening, forty-two German soldiers, held as prisoners of war at nearby Camp Gordon, had been working for six months to return the course to its former glory. The club provided transportation to and from Camp Gordon, picking them up each morning and delivering them back to the camp each evening. The POWs had been with the engineering crew serving with Rommel, the Desert Fox, in North Africa, part of the Panzer division responsible for building bridges that enabled German tanks to cross rivers. It was a useful skill for the renovation work to be done at Augusta National. The Germans were asked to erect a wooden bridge over Rae's Creek adjacent to the tee box at the thirteenth hole.

They were also employed to repair the damage done by the club's beef venture. The voracious cows had devoured much of Augusta National's character—its stunning flora—while littering the premises with cow chips that neighborhood boys used to fling at one another, when they weren't chasing the cows or swimming in the pond that fronted the twelfth green.

Augusta National's reopening generated interest beyond the confines of the club's membership rolls. It was a signal to the golf world at large, a demonstration of the game's resilience (even when encumbered with a rubber shortfall). The war had tested the game's elasticity, to be sure, and it would require time to return it to what it was before the war, but the damage assessment was already under way, the first step to full recovery.

———

ONE FORMER CLUB PROFESSIONAL who had joined the war effort stood as a wounded testament to the state of the game. When he returned home from his overseas assignment he took inventory of his health and discovered a mixed bag; his injuries warranted a medical discharge but were not severe enough to prevent a full recovery. Then he took inventory of his golf equipment—metaphorically, at least—and discovered that it had not similarly survived the ravages of war.

"My present invoice of equipment to start back to a pro career," he wrote anonymously in a letter to a magazine, "is a bent screw-driver, a well-worn pair of golf shoes, seven worn out shoe-calks, a torn rain jacket, a set of clubs in a bag I'm no longer strong enough to lift, and a golf ball in poor condition. I tried to buy a new ball last summer. My biggest chance was the day I got up to $2.35 in the bidding. Had I have been a Sgt. or a 2nd Lt. I might have made it. My last report from the manufacturers was that no matter how many times they tried to make a No. 2 iron it always came out a machine gun."

It was evident that by the end of 1944 the game was in a state of disrepair. Neglect had it merits, certainly, in having forced the game to forgo its elitist ways temporarily. Golfers at prestigious clubs whose caddies and maintenance crews were off at war were often required to carry their own bags over grounds that weren't manicured to their standards. Among the affected clubs was the exclusive Winged Foot Golf Club in Mamaroneck, New York, which lost three hundred caddies to the armed forces. Private club members, reluctantly and ignominiously, were getting a whiff of the public golf experience, playing on courses where grooming was overlooked, with balls of the refurbished variety.

The ball shortage that had plagued the game from the outset

of the war in fact had reached epidemic proportions around the world. A former employee of the Acushnet Company, manufacturer of the Titleist golf ball, wrote to friends at the company of a conversation he had had with a local golfer from Fedhala, near Casablanca, on the Mediterranean Sea. The Fedhala man was a regular at the golf course there. "I would like to get my hands on about a half-dozen of those Acushnet Titleist balls!" the man said.

The obvious response: "Who wouldn't?"

The story was the same from continent to continent. In Ireland, new balls left over from before the war were selling for $75 a dozen. In India, the cost for a new ball reached twenty rupees, or $6.04 each, according to Private First Class Joseph D. Orchard, who was with the American Air Depot Group there. He wrote a note to the Wilson Sporting Goods Company, seeking to purchase new balls:

Golfers in the American Army Air Forces stationed in India find it almost impossible to obtain golf balls. A few new balls are available in the near-by city at an exorbitant price of Rupees 20 ($6.04) each. Reclaimed balls, sold by merchants here in India for Rupees 8 ($2.40), each are in worse condition than those which were being sold by caddies before the war.

Therefore, we are appealing to you directly to help make it possible for us to continue to enjoy this grand old American sport.

Our golf club considers this strictly a business proposition and will pay for all balls you can send us (preferably re-processed balls).

Attached you will find a score card of our course. With the help of Indian coolie labor we constructed this course in our spare time in four months. The layout may be quite different from the championship courses in the States, but we enjoy the course as though [we] were playing on Merion Cricket Club.

A joke frequently told to American servicemen regarding an ornamental rock structure on the King's Course at Gleneagles, Scotland, was that it was a monument to a caddie who died of starvation attempting to locate a ball lost by Sir Harry Lauder.

R. E. Anderson, with the U.S. Army in England, wrote a letter to a friend regarding the golf ball shortage in the United Kingdom:

> Well, Jack, I've seen fellows over here playing with balls that you wouldn't even bother to knock away—you'd just leave them, they were so bad. Fellows over here have played with balls that must have had at least six or seven good nicks in them. I've seen one Englishman with a ball that's had a piece of the cover cut off by a knife, so the loose piece cut off wouldn't interfere too much with his putting. I picked up an old scab in the middle of the fairway that was so bad that I took my No. 5 out and belted it off the course and when a fellow came up looking for the ball he had hit in that vicinity, I had to fess up that I knocked it away and give him a good one to replace it. Heck, the ball I hit away was almost square—no fooling.
>
> When you see the lack of equipment over here and realize the difficulties these people have in maintaining some semblance of play, you're glad you belong to a fraternity that takes the game so seriously. As long as there are fellows who will put up with conditions such as these to play golf, there will always be golf—the best game in the world. You can rest assured that your golf balls will have their covers knocked off before they're discarded over here.

The Royal Air Force actually made an appeal for golf balls, new or used, on behalf of its pilots. The RAF reasoned that pilots spent so much time focusing on distant horizons that to keep their eyesight strong from any distance they needed to engage in an activity that required that they focus on an object at short range, i.e., a golf ball.

American golf writer Herb Graffis traveled to London in the summer of '44 to report on the state of British golf. He ventured past a dilapidated store near Waterloo Bridge in London one morning and noticed a pair of used, beaten, dirty golf balls in the window. When he passed the same store later in the day, the balls were gone. Curious, Graffis entered the store to find out what had happened to them.

"I sold them," the clerk said. "I can sell any kind of ball I can get."

An advertisement appeared in *Golf Monthly,* an Edinburgh, Scotland, publication:

WHISKY FOR GOLF BALLS.
BOTTLE FOR 4 PRE-WAR; 1/2 BOTTLE FOR 2.

The scarcity of golf balls was an amusing problem, at least until it turned deadly one day. A British Army officer on leave was playing golf on a seaside course that had been mined to fend off an enemy invasion. He ventured into a wired-off area to retrieve a ball he had hit there and stepped on a land mine, killing him.

Golfers carried on in the UK, notwithstanding the proximity of the war and its demoralizing effect, and the diminishing ball supply. A British munitions worker attempted to make up for lost time during a day off early on during the Normandy invasion. He played eight rounds, 144 holes, in a single day.

American servicemen in Britain also frequented the courses there. They generally were provided unlimited access to British courses as a show of appreciation for their efforts on the Brits' behalf. Army brass recognized a potential for mischief to arise from the Brits' largesse, however, and lectured the troops on their responsibility to demonstrate proper decorum. U.S. Army headquarters issued an order for service personnel playing on British courses:

> To us as Americans there is a most important phase of the game, universally known as etiquette. It governs our actions from the first tee to the 18th green and even follows us into the clubhouse. A few points are listed below:

> (a) Replace all divots. (Turf dug up by clubs.)
> (b) Smooth all sand-traps of both club marks and footprints after making a shot.
> (c) Always be courteous; let people behind you play through if they appear to be playing faster than you are.
> (d) Be quiet on the course. Both here and at home golf galleries at championships are marveled at by laymen because of the fact that three thousand people never utter a sound during a shot.
> (e) You are requested not to enter a bar except by invitation of a member and under no circumstances whatsoever to enter a dining room.

> The reasons for the above, in a land of rigid rationing, require no further explanation.

> The British people are extremely fond of their courses. They are lending us their sons' clubs and in many cases their own. Treat both carefully. Nearly 40 per cent of their people play golf and love it. Let us show them that golf and manners as well are on the same high plane in the United States as they are here.

The Scottish publication *Golf Monthly* took note of U.S. efforts and expressed its appreciation. "We assure United States readers of *Golf Monthly* that their soldier sons have lived up when here to the etiquette and the traditions of the game."

American servicemen were warmly embraced by the Scots, whom they had come to regard as "the Texans of Great Britain"— generous to a fault if they're for you, determined to rain misery on you if they're against you.

Yet not every American was enamored of the legendary British links. One Army airman wrote in a letter home about his impression of St. Andrews, the birthplace of golf: "After all I'd heard at home about St. Andrews I expected to have to take my shoes off as though I were entering one of the holy places south of the Mediterranean. We got up to play it and for my money we have several better courses around Chicago. Some of the greens are so big you have to pivot on your putts and the greens are much faster than ours at home. The wind makes it a tough course. But we had a great time and that is the answer to everything. The Scots we met would turn themselves inside out to see that we enjoyed ourselves."

The game was recovering, but in fits and starts. Olympia Fields Golf Club in suburban Chicago, host of the U.S. Open in 1928, lost so many members during the war years that it no longer had enough of them to support its four golf courses. It closed two of them but was still unable to pay its bills. On January 4, 1944, it filed for bankruptcy.

Otherwise, golf's vital signs were generally good, which boded well for the sport once the messy business of war was finished. *The Wall Street Journal* concluded as much in an editorial, beneath the headline *Golf Will Survive*. The editorial, addressing a news story that it had published a day earlier, read in part:

Monday's issue of *The Wall Street Journal* reports that golf has a better chance of surviving the rigors of wartime than does tennis . . .

The game of golf is the quintessence of futility. There is the reason it will survive. It furnishes a relief without which a large percentage of the population might easily become candidates for the insane asylum.

There is some logic to the game of tennis. Two players evenly matched, even though they are far from experts, can get onto a court and engage in an interesting contest. If they are just reasonably good, their efforts will not appear ridiculous.

Nothing like that happens in golf. Two men may have ever so close and interesting a game, but is the winner happy? He is not. He thinks back how he could have lowered his score and goes home with the thought tormenting him. Professionals shoot 18 holes in sixty odd strokes, a feat which only a few years ago was considered miraculous, if not impossible. And what do the sportswriters report the next day? They talk about the one or two mistakes the professional made. . . .

Our news story speculates darkly about a shortage of golf clubs. It's of no consequence. A man who can play golf can rip a picket off the nearest fence and beat an inept man with a bag of all the clubs that have ever been invented. . . .

Of course golf will survive. It may go back to the days when people battered feather balls about a pasture with crooked sticks, but it will be there.

15

BEN WHO?
AND LORD BYRON

The Greatest Streak in Golf History

Lieutenant Lance Anderson quickly came to realize that there were only two jobs worth having in the Army: general or a general's pilot. By virtue of his having joined the Army Air Corps and learned how to fly, Anderson became the latter. It was a cushy job, he reasoned, principally because generals weren't typically reporting to the front lines. Their responsibilities were to direct the war from a safe distance.

Or so he thought. Lieutenant Anderson was stationed in London when the Germans introduced their new V-2 to the Allied Forces in the UK. The V-2 was a guided missile the Germans had developed and began employing in September 1944. It could transport 1,650 pounds of explosives two hundred miles, a range that made London accessible from a wide swath of coastline on the European continent. The Germans began using the V-2 as part of a last-ditch effort against the Allies, principally targeting

London and other British cities. More than 2,700 British civilians were killed in the V-2 campaign.

On December 31, 1944, Lieutenant Anderson found himself in the vicinity of an incoming V-2 missile. The ensuing explosion broke his left wrist (as well as his neck, though this injury was not detected until much later), effectively bringing his service in the armed forces to a conclusion.

John Searcy might have considered Anderson lucky. Searcy was a navigator on a B-24 Liberator, part of the Army Air Corps's 389th Bomb Group, 567th Squadron. On one bombing run over Germany, antiaircraft fire riddled his plane, one bullet hitting Searcy in the mouth, knocking out six teeth. The injury earned him a two-week hiatus, after which he returned to combat. En route home from another bombing run to Germany, his plane again was a target of antiaircraft fire. The plane's fuel tank was struck and exploded, crippling the aircraft. Searcy suffered first-, second-, and third-degree burns on his face. He had also taken five slugs in the back and his knee was shattered. He managed to limp toward the bomb-bay door, from which he intended to bail out. Flames repelled him, however, forcing him to frantically seek an alternative escape hatch. He eventually rolled out of a hole where the nose-wheel assembly had been, escaping intact, more or less, from the doomed aircraft.

Searcy began his free fall, then pulled the ripcord only to find that his parachute would not open. He pulled again, and again the chute failed to open. Plunging toward earth, Searcy reached over his shoulder and jerked the chute loose, but the speed at which he was descending caused his arm to snap. The chute finally came free, but it failed to appreciably slow his descent; the flames from the plane had burned holes in the silk, depriving it of much of the wind resistance required to allow him to float to earth. He was plunging toward a stand of trees and certain death, when the chute caught some branches of one of the taller trees, breaking his fall and saving his life, a fortuitous turn, he figured, until three German soldiers quickly found him and trained their rifles on him. Searcy became a prisoner of war at that point and spent nine months in a German stalag.

Lieutenant Anderson was sent back to the States, to the 14th Army Air Forces Regional and Convalescent Hospital, formerly the Biltmore Hotel, in Coral Gables, Florida. The Army had converted the Biltmore Hotel into a hospital, providing the injured airmen there with first-class accommodations that even included a Donald Ross–designed golf course, adjacent to an orange grove. Shortly after arriving at the Biltmore, Lieutenant Anderson went for a walk one morning and saw several patients gathered at the first tee of the golf course. One at a time, they flailed at the ball, sending it at odd angles and trajectories away from the fairway, in the event they hit it at all. Anderson considered himself a skilled athlete and a pretty good hitter in baseball before the war. To that point in his life he had never swung a golf club, but he was intrigued by the patients' play, and he decided to try it the next morning, after obtaining some clubs and balls from Special Services. He got in line at the first tee, notwithstanding the cast on his left wrist. When it was his turn to hit, he took an untrained swing at the ball, which went soaring down the middle of the fairway.

"One thing about it," said a bystander, a short, slight man watching the airmen tee off, awaiting his turn to play, "your left wrist can't break down."

A short while later, Lieutenant Anderson asked another airman who the first lieutenant at the first tee was.

"Ben Hogan," came the reply.

The name meant nothing to Lieutenant Anderson. In the course of a walk on another morning, he spotted the same little man hitting golf balls toward his caddie, who was stationed down by the edge of the orange grove. Anderson decided to watch for a while, transfixed by the consistency of the shots. Hogan's caddie was collecting the balls and dropping them into a canvas bag. The caddie never had to range more than a few feet in either direction to gather a ball. Each morning, Hogan was out hitting balls, as many as five hundred. He lunched virtually every day with his wife, Valerie, then played a round of golf, either with military brass or with well-heeled businessmen at Miami Springs Golf Course, high rollers who had no aversion to losing money. When Hogan's round was completed, he returned to the side of the orange grove and resumed hitting balls.

Eventually, Lieutenant Anderson (a second lieutenant, or First Lieutenant Hogan's subordinate) began striking up conversations with Hogan. He was keen enough to observe that interrupting the man during the midst of his morning routine was not wise, so he waited for a break before approaching him. One day they were discussing the golf-course conduct of some of the airmen, who had not played the game before. "Remember," Hogan told Anderson, "golf is a gentleman's game, though not all golfers are gentlemen."

Lieutenant Anderson eventually determined that Hogan's Army Air Corps job description was "golfer," that he was a professional of some note, though details were sketchy. Virtually all the golf Hogan played during the war was with other uniformed personnel. He had not played tournament golf in 1943 and only played in three tournaments in 1944. Essentially he played only when the tour came to him, as the Miami Open was preparing to do in 1945. Hogan entered the tournament, and Anderson was there for the final round, walking alongside Hogan shot by shot for eighteen holes. The following morning, Anderson again ran into Hogan, who had resumed hitting golf balls, per his daily routine, alongside the orange grove. Anderson casually mentioned how much he had enjoyed watching Hogan play the previous afternoon.

"You were there?" Hogan asked. "I didn't see you."

Anderson understood immediately that it was not an insult, that Hogan had simply been focused on his work, to the exclusion of everything around him. It contributed to his intrigue at Hogan's commitment, at his dogged pursuit of a game Anderson had only recently discovered. The conversations with Hogan piqued his interest in the game and helped foment a passion for it. Anderson even attempted to replicate Hogan's swing after concluding from watching the remarkable consistency of its results that it was the proper way to go after a golf ball. Anderson's own wildly fluctuating results indicated that he still had work to do.

JOHN SEARCY WAS MISSING in action and the Army assumed him dead. It even sent a telegram to his mother, expressing its sympathies for her son's death. When Germany surrendered to the Allies on May 8, 1945, Searcy was among the first group of prisoners repatriated. When a short time later he walked into the family's Hot Springs, Arkansas, home, unannounced, his brother fainted.

After a short reunion, Searcy was sent to an Army convalescent hospital, the Don Cesar Hotel, on the waterfront in the Gulf Coast town of Pass-A-Grille, Florida, near St. Petersburg. The Don Cesar's luxury accommodations had once served as the New York Yankees' hotel headquarters during spring training. The Army had condemned it, however, buying it for $450,000, then modifying it to serve as a hospital. It opened in 1942 and two years later became the Air Force Convalescent Center, though it remained a temporary home to at least one Yankee. Joe DiMaggio, suffering from a duodenal ulcer, was there in 1945 until he received a medical discharge from the Army.

The patients seemed to lack the initiative to expedite their rehabilitation, so hospital workers intervened. They informed the patients that they needed to find an activity to give them something to do other than feeling sorry for themselves, ordering them to choose from a list of activities posted on a bulletin board. On a whim, Searcy signed up for golf, although he'd never played the game. He viewed it as an opportunity to escape the dreariness of the hospital and to get outside. A dozen other patients signed up for golf as well.

On the morning they were to start, they boarded a bus that transported them to a nearby golf course. An instructor was waiting for them on the practice tee.

"I understand you want to learn how to play golf," the man said. "I'm your instructor. Let me introduce myself. My name is Captain Ben Hogan."

The man's rank (Hogan had recently been promoted) commanded Searcy's respect, but his name meant nothing to him. Twice a week, Searcy and his wounded compatriots took lessons from Hogan, who carefully explained the fundamentals of a sound golf swing. One day he'd address the grip, another the setup. Searcy eventually learned that Hogan was a golf pro, though from his perspective he was not one of any particular renown. He was just another civilian who had been caught up in the war and was doing his part to help. Hogan worked with each of them individually and occasionally staged an exhibition for them, hitting shots with greater precision than a drill sergeant expected in a boot camp march. Searcy's lessons from Hogan began to pique his interest in this game that heretofore had held no special attraction for him. Once apathetic at the prospect of hitting a golf ball, Searcy began looking forward to sessions on the range. He marveled at his instructor's apparent expertise, without once considering its possible utility in the outside world.

By the middle of the summer Captain Hogan was gone. He had returned to Miami, where, on August 5, 1945, he was discharged from the Army Air Corps. He had served honorably for two and a half years, and in the end, his contributions were quantifiable after all. Hogan left behind at least two men who were grateful for his having introduced them to a game that had become more than an integral part of their rehab. Golf was now an important part of their lives as well.

BYRON NELSON HAD no such military obligations, allowing him to return his focus to the bottom line. Golf was never only a game for Nelson; it was also a business at which he did very well, demonstrating a keen marketing acumen over the years. In 1940, when he was augmenting his income with a job as the professional at Inverness Country Club in Toledo, Ohio, Nelson struck upon an idea he thought might help boost shop sales. Historically, golfers interested in buying a new pair of golf shoes examined the models available, then ordered a pair in the proper size through the golf pro. The new golf shoes would not arrive for a number of weeks. Under such a primitive system, sales to customers who tended to buy on impulse were lost. Nelson took the bold step of stocking shoes in a variety of sizes, the first club pro in the history of the industry to do so. As a result, he sold more shoes and made more money. Emboldened by his success with footwear, he went to an American umbrella manufacturer and instructed its designers how to make a better golf umbrella. Until then, golf umbrellas were made exclusively in Europe and were largely inadequate by Nelson's estimation. His handiwork and business expertise earned him a vice presidency with Haas-Jordan Umbrella Company.

Nelson approached playing the game as a business too; he donned his business attire, in this case golf clothes, at his home or hotel, then reported to work at the golf course. When his work was done for the day, he never loitered at the club, instead returning immediately to his home or his room, meanwhile forgoing tournament parties at which he was never entirely comfortable anyway, given the fact that he neither drank nor smoked.

Sportswriters referred to him as a golf robot, because of the businesslike approach he brought to the game and the consistency it engendered. Accordingly, he always kept a close eye on his finances. Nelson was as likely to know how much money he had earned in a season as he was how many tournaments he had won. He was an inveterate note taker, carrying a small black six-ring binder, which he filled with his tournament results and earnings and expenses, earning him yet another nickname, "the Bookkeeper," from newspapermen. Beneath his entry for the 1944 Phoenix Open, for instance, he wrote:

71-66-71-65-273

Tied McSpaden

Lost in playoff—shot 72

Won $1,325.00 Bonds

The more important numbers to Nelson had dollar signs attached to them, as a result of retirement assuming an even higher priority for him. He would turn only 33 in February of 1945 and was the dominant player in the game, with as much of his career ahead of him as behind him, though he did not intend to play until his talent ran out. His nerves were already eroding, and he admitted to becoming nauseated while standing over the short putts on which his livelihood depended. He also knew that the situation was likely to worsen over time.

Nelson and his wife, Louise, owned a fifty-five-acre ranch in Denton, Texas, north of Dallas. He ran modest herds of cattle and sheep on the ranch, but his wish was to acquire a substantially larger spread, with more livestock, so that the ranch could help support him and his wife, and a tenant family to run it. Another productive year could solidify his future away from the golf course.

So it was that he methodically kept his little black ledger, certain that he could cull from it information that he would use to make himself a better player. Prior to the start of his 1945 season, he reviewed his notes from '44. They told him two things— that he needed to elevate his level of concentration and that he needed to improve his short game. He resolutely approached 1945 determined to keep his mind keenly on the shot at hand and to work on his chipping around the greens. It was a testament to his dedication and dogged pursuit of perfection that he was able to discern weakness in his golf game in 1944. He had won nine of the twenty-three tournaments he entered, finished in the top three in twenty of them, and never finished out of the top ten. McSpaden won five tournaments yet spent most of the year chasing Nelson.

Nelson's notes cut away the layers of successes and exposed his shortcomings. They told him that on at least a dozen occasions he had chipped poorly, or at least not as well as a player of his stature should. He judiciously practiced his chipping in the off-season and vowed not to play a single careless shot in 1945. He had other goals as well: to lead the tour in earnings; to lower his stroke average; and to finish in the money more often than any-one else on tour. In sum, his goal was to dominate. Again.

The difficulty of doing so for a second consecutive year had intensified since victory appeared imminent in the European theater and the Japanese were beginning to reel in the Pacific. This meant that his chief rivals, who had been occupied with the war (or at least with service requirements), would return to tour play intent on tormenting him. At the outset of the year, Ben Hogan was still serving in the Army Air Corps, and he was angry. His boyhood friend had dethroned him as the best player on tour and was commanding virtually all the attention accorded to the sport. Hogan was of the mind that Nelson had been receiving accolades artificially earned by dominating a tour largely bereft of talent, notably his own. And so Hogan was eager to return and inject tournament golf with a dose of the competitive balance that he felt was missing in 1944, though he would have to await his discharge toward the end of the summer of '45 before rejoining the tour full-time. Sam Snead was also aching to return. His best golf in 1944 had been played in the company of admirals and captains. Snead's naval career ended late in 1944, curiously as the result of a back ailment. A back injury is debilitating to a golfer, yet his injury failed to keep him from playing golf and had no noticeable effect on his game.

Snead broke to the front at the outset of the 1945 tour season. He won his first start, the Los Angeles Open, by a stroke over Nelson and McSpaden. After a pair of Nelson victories at the Corpus Christi and New Orleans opens, Snead defeated Nelson in a play-off to win the Gulfport Open. He followed that with another victory, in the Pensacola Open, again at Nelson's expense. He won a third straight tournament, the Jacksonville Open, at which Nelson was not a factor, tying for sixth.

The year outwardly appeared as though it was one that would

inevitably belong to Snead. A closer examination revealed that Nelson was playing better. He had already won three tournaments, second to Snead's four victories. He had also finished second on five occasions. The tie for sixth in the Jacksonville Open was the only time in his first ten tournaments that he had not finished either one or two. Nelson was playing so well that he virtually never bothered to practice, as though taking his swing to the practice tee might be an invitation for a bad habit to infect it. He often did not bother to even hit balls before playing, instead going directly to the first tee and taking a few warm-up swings. He had such command of his golf ball that he was proving capable of calling his shots and predicting his scores. He and McSpaden frequently played exhibition rounds together between tour stops. Course officials would ask Nelson what he expected to shoot on their course. Nelson in turn would examine the scorecard, then would ask whether the printed yardage was accurate. When told it was, he'd ponder the numbers for a moment.

"I believe I'll shoot a sixty-seven," he would say finally.

When he holed his last putt some four hours later, the numbers on the card would invariably add to 67, to McSpaden's amazement.

McSpaden admired his friend's talent more than he lamented it, though it usually cost him money. On one occasion, it paid a dividend, when he teamed with Nelson to win the Miami International Four-Ball, victory number four on the season for Nelson, ending Snead's streak at three straight. The Nelson-McSpaden team won four matches, the last a thirty-six-hole affair, and never made a bogey along the way. Nelson conceded that he had been "steamed up" by his play the week before, when he had tied for sixth and had "played just horrible." He was also mildly peeved over Snead's winning streak.

The tour moved to Charlotte, North Carolina, for the Charlotte

Open the following week. Nelson won again, his victory inspired by an unfounded rumor, a note in a newspaper column that suggested that Snead had deliberately thrown the tournament on behalf of gamblers, that the fix was in. Snead was accused of bogeying the seventy-second hole intentionally, when he needed only a par to win. Those knowledgeable about the game, however, could surmise only that he had failed to par a difficult hole. His 1-iron second shot had reached the green but left him fifty feet short of the hole. From there, he required three putts to finish, a bogey that thrust him into an eighteen-hole play-off with Nelson.

The two were still tied after each shot a 69 in the play-off round, at which point Snead proposed going to a sudden-death play-off. Nelson rejected the offer, insisting that they play another eighteen holes the following day, no doubt relying on the fact that no one in the world was playing better and that his chances improved over a longer stretch of holes. His intuition was accurate; in the second play-off eighteen, Nelson shot another 69, while Snead shot 73, a four-stroke victory that boosted his confidence to a level where it had never before been. He knew that he was "in a trance," as the players called it when their swing was aligned with their focus and they played as though hitting a target was a formality.

This was evident again the following week, at the Greater Greensboro Open, when he closed with a 66 and won by eight strokes, his third straight victory. And the week after, at the Durham Open, when his final-round 65 enabled him to win by five. By now, the other players were referring to a tournament stop as "the meeting of the Nelson Benefit Society." Nelson, meanwhile, was earning new nicknames seemingly on a weekly basis. He was called "Lord Byron," "the Mechanical Man," and "the Golfing Machine." When the tour moved to Atlanta the following week, noted golf writer O. B. Keeler watched Nelson win the Atlanta Iron Lung Tournament by nine strokes, a record-setting fifth straight, and added yet another nickname, "the Great Precisionist."

The tour scheduled a two-month hiatus following the Atlanta tournament, which other players recognized was the only way in which Nelson's momentum could be slowed. They miscalculated in assuming that momentum was responsible for carrying Nelson along; in fact he had refined his talent to the point that he had developed absolute trust in his swing's ability to deliver the ball to a distant target.

This was borne out when the tour finally resumed, with the Montreal Open, and Nelson opened with a 63 that defied reason. How was it that a man could take two months off and actually improve on what had already been defined as perfection? Nelson made only a single bogey over seventy-two holes and won the Montreal Open by ten shots, his sixth straight tour win.

Number seven surely would prove more challenging. The Philadelphia Open was played in McSpaden's adopted hometown. The advantage of playing at home suggested that McSpaden had his best opportunity to derail Nelson, until his hay fever and asthma began to betray him. On the first nine holes of the tournament, McSpaden was sneezing uncontrollably and shot a 40. But then the sneezing subsided and he settled down, closing out the first round with a 33, the first of seven consecutive nine-hole scores of 33, to conclude the tournament in a remarkable display of golf by a man who at that moment was the second-best player in the world. McSpaden had rounds of 73, 66, 66, and 66, a total of seventeen-under-par 271. Were it not for the presence of Nelson it would have been cause to celebrate. Nelson hung in gamely with a pair of opening 68s, followed by a 70, to trail by one heading into the final eighteen.

On the final day, McSpaden played in the morning, while Nelson had an afternoon tee time. Nelson played the first twelve holes in four under par, an effort he assumed assured him of victory, though he was unaware of his standing and the fact that, at fourteen under par, he trailed his friend by three. At the thirteenth hole, a tour veteran, Leo Diegel, approached Nelson.

"How you doing, kid?" he asked.

"I can par in for sixty-eight," Nelson replied.

"That isn't good enough," Diegel said. "Jug is already in with sixty-six."

Nelson quickly did the math and concluded he needed a flourish of birdies to win or tie. He responded with birdies on five of the final six holes to close out a round of 63, good for a two-stroke victory and consecutive win number seven. It was a rather impolite way for Nelson to thank Jug for his hospitality that week; Nelson was staying with McSpaden at his home. Jug responded by barraging his friend with nasty names, delivered, of course, with a smile.

On deck was the Chicago Victory National Open at Calumet Country Club in Chicago. The Chicago Victory was the continuation of a tournament that had become an unofficial replacement for the U.S. Open, which had been postponed indefinitely in 1942. It represented another opportunity to topple Nelson, who was bothered by a sore back and faced the prospect of playing thirty-six holes on the final day. Nelson nonetheless limped around those thirty-six holes in 68 and 70 shots and won by seven, with McSpaden again finishing second.

"If you had not been born, I'd be known as a good player," a frustrated McSpaden told Nelson.

By now, the sporting public was taking notice, even that part of it that had no interest in golf or knowledge of the game. They understood winning streaks—in 1944, Army's football team, led by Doc Blanchard and Glenn Davis, Mr. Inside and Mr. Outside, went 9–0 and dominated its sport like no collegiate team in history. Sports fans also recognized that a streak in a quirky individual sport was more impressive than one in a team sport by a service academy in wartime. They were aware that something momentous was afoot.

The next event was a major tournament, the PGA Championship, at Moraine Country Club in Dayton, Ohio. A match-play tournament is not necessarily won by the best player. A lesser golfer on a productive day can upend a better player who might be misfiring more than usual. In the second round, Mike Turnesa was 2-up on Nelson with four holes to play. Turnesa played them in par, par, birdie, and par, which ought to have been sufficient to eliminate his opponent. Nelson, however, closed birdie, birdie, eagle, and par, to win 1-up. Moments later, Turnesa's brother Jim was eliminated, 8 and 7, by Claude Harmon. The Turnesas took their defeats in stride, even in good humor. Their double elimination required that they pay a penance, Jim decided. "Looks like we'll have to eat our spaghetti without the meat sauce tonight," he said to his brother, causing Nelson to erupt in laughter nearby. The Turnesa match was the only close one of the five that Nelson had in winning his ninth straight tournament.

The tour remained in Chicago for George May's Tam O'Shanter All-American Open, the richest tournament in golf, offering a first prize of $10,200, nearly three times the amount the more important PGA Championship had offered.

Nelson had rounds of 66, 68, 68, and 67 to win by eleven strokes over Ben Hogan, whose Army career was in its waning weeks. "Even the gaffers of the Vardon-Hagen-Jones era now admit that Nelson is the greatest golfer who ever swung a club," *Chicago Tribune* golf writer Charles Bartlett wrote.

The streak reached eleven the following week when Nelson won the Canadian Open by four strokes. But it was beginning to take a toll on Nelson, as streaks are wont to do. The longer they go, the greater the pressure to extend them. Such was the mounting stress that at one point during the streak Nelson began a round with the intention of shooting a high enough score that he could not win. He wanted the streak to end, but his pride and talent would now allow him to take a dive; he shot a 66 and continued to win. He then hoped that the inevitable bad round of golf would surface on its own. His swing was disinclined to permit it.

The streak finally ran its course at the Memphis Open, when his focus began to wane. He was in contention on the final day, trailing by two, when a 7-iron shot to the 150-yard par-3 fifth hole hit the flagstick and the ball bounded forty feet away. Four strokes later, he had a double-bogey to account for an expertly struck tee shot. His luck had turned. He eventually lost to amateur Freddie Haas, a thirty-year-old insurance salesman, by four shots, and tied for fourth, bringing the greatest streak in golf to an end at eleven consecutive victories. Nelson experienced no letdown, or even disappointment, but only relief that his manifest skill could now operate unfettered by the demands of a winning streak. The very next week, he won the Supreme Open in Knoxville, Tennessee, by ten strokes.

His year was winding down when he went to Spokane to play in the Esmeralda Open. When he arrived to check in at the Davenport Hotel, a clerk informed him that the hotel did not have a room for him, that all the rooms were being held for professional golfers. Nelson, winner of eleven straight tour events earlier in the year, quietly left and checked into a hotel next door. When the story was relayed to PGA Tournament Bureau director Fred Corcoran, he laughed hysterically, while Nelson's wife saw an opening.

"Honey," she said, "I want you to win a tournament so they know you're a golfer."

He won the Spokane tournament by seven strokes.

Nelson considered the episode a validation of his belief that the streak failed to resonate with the sporting public at large, that the game's appeal was too narrow for his streak to have generated any enthusiasm beyond the golf course. An inherently humble man, Nelson was wholly incapable of impartially placing his achievement in its proper context. It was apparent beyond the limited range of his ego that he was wrong. A few weeks later, at the Seattle Open, Nelson had rounds of 62, 68, 63, and 66, a total of 259, establishing a PGA record. He won by thirteen strokes and defeated Hogan by twenty.

"Nelson," *Life* magazine wrote, "has made golf the only sport in the U.S. that is better than it was before the war. The great Bobby Jones, who ought to know, says, 'At my best I never came close to the golf Nelson shoots.' "

His eleven consecutive victories were seven more than anyone else had ever won in a row on the PGA. His eighteen victories for the year doubled the previous record of nine, set by Paul Runyan in 1933. In the sixteen stroke-play tournaments Nelson won, his average margin of victory was 6.25 strokes. He played nineteen consecutive rounds in under 70 strokes. He averaged 68.33 strokes per round over one hundred twenty rounds, and played the final round, when the pressure was at its greatest, in an average of 67.68 strokes, each of them tour records. For the second straight year, the Associated Press sportswriters voted Nelson their athlete of the year, this time over Army football stalwart Doc Blanchard, the Heisman Trophy winner.

Nelson had captured the imagination of the sporting public in spite of subtle efforts to diminish his achievement. When *New York Times* columnist Arthur Daley wrote about golf, his subjects were stars from a bygone era, Walter Hagen and Harry Vardon, steadfastly ignoring Nelson, as though his remarkable streak was inauthentic because of the absence of depth in the fields. The evidence says otherwise. In 1945, Snead played twenty-six tournaments and Hogan eighteen, and each of them had played well. Snead won five tournaments, Hogan six, including the Portland Invitational by fourteen strokes.

Another debate that ensued was whether Nelson was the best player in history, better than Bobby Jones or Walter Hagen. "Walter Hagen could hit every shot and any shot, but this Nelson, he has more shots in his bag than any man I ever saw," said Tommy Armour. "If he just had the unrestrained temperament of Hagen, he'd never lose a tournament. Ever since I watched Nelson beat little Hogan in the 1942 Masters play-off, I thought, 'What a match he and the Bobby Jones of 1928 would have made.' He made his grand slam in 1930, but I've always thought he was only about eighty percent of the Jones of 1928. That year he was the most perfect piece of golf machinery I've ever seen. He never had an equal in his second shots."

Fred Corcoran, the PGA Tournament Bureau manager, typically resorted to hyperbole. "Jones against Nelson?" he said. "What a match it would be. It would be the Dempsey-Louis battle of golf. If they played a seventy-two-hole match, honest, I wouldn't bet a nickel on the outcome. On his record, you would have to give Jones the edge. Bobby won thirteen major titles before his retirement and was runner-up in other main events."

Nelson had played so well for so long and brought so much attention to himself that he was rewarded with a Wheaties contract. The breakfast cereal put his likeness on the back of its boxes, along with Boston Red Sox star Joe Cronin and Green Bay Packers star Cecil Isbell, under the heading "Champs of the U.S.A." In return, Wheaties paid Nelson $200 and provided him with a case of Wheaties every month for a year, more Wheaties than he and his wife were capable of consuming in a month. He kept the $200 but gave much of the cereal away.

He was more suitably rewarded by his equipment benefactor, MacGregor, which doubled his annual pay, from $5,000 to $10,000. At the time, before historical context rendered its evaluation of his streak, the money was of considerably greater importance than the victories. Nelson had his eye on a new ranch, one that would cost an imposing amount to own and operate. His mission was not an historical one but an economic one. Each week, he set out not so much to win a tournament as to add to his down payment. But in the process, he assembled the greatest year in the history of a game both royal and ancient, justifying his unwitting claim to the royalty part of the equation. He had taken a niche sport that in wartime had been decimated and elevated it to a stature it had not known since Bobby Jones was winning the Grand Slam. He was now, in perpetuity, Lord Byron.

16

THE GREATEST BOOM
OF ALL TIME

Golf, from
the War Zones to Home

The game of golf seemed to shadow General Eisenhower, as though it were another military aide, awaiting orders. Or it might have been that he was shadowing the game, determined to keep it close at hand, his most reliable ally. Either way, Eisenhower was incapable of escaping the game he loved, even in a time of war. Wherever he settled, a golf course was nearby. Once the Allies had pushed through France and to the German border, for instance, Eisenhower set up his advance command post in Reims, in the Champagne region of France. He established his headquarters in a schoolhouse, but for living quarters he opted for the clubhouse at the Gueux golf course. He and his staff took meals in the great room, which had been the nineteenth hole before the Germans occupied the region.

Eisenhower was unable to resist the urge to test his form, even in the midst of a war. Some wondered whether his preoccupation with the game was a detriment to defeating the Germans. On November 24, 1944, Alan Brooke, a British field marshal, wrote in the war diary he was keeping: "At the end of this morning's COS meeting, I cleared the secretaries out and retained only Pug [General Hastings Ismay]. I then put before the meeting my views on the very unsatisfactory state of affairs in France, with no one running the land battle. Eisenhower, though supposed to be doing so, is detached and by himself with his lady chauffeur [Kay Summersby] on the golf links at Reims—entirely detached from the war and taking practically no part in running the war! Matters got so bad lately that a deputation of Whiteley, Bedell Smith, and a few others went up to him to tell him that he must get down to it and RUN the war, which he said he would. Personally I think he is incapable of running the war even if he tries."

GOLF MANAGED TO RETAIN a level of importance even in a war zone. Devotees were often resourceful in their pursuit of the game. Among the most obsessive was Sergeant Dugan Aycock, an amiable extrovert, as well as a tournament and club professional from Lexington, North Carolina. Aycock was perpetually thinking of ways to incorporate golf into his overseas service. A special services director of his Army unit, Aycock had smuggled golf equipment into North Africa in 1943, via a shipment of kitchen equipment. He had also found a course on which to play outside Casablanca, Morocco. The course was ostensibly damaged beyond repair, though not to a sergeant with an insatiable appetite for the game. He had discovered a kindred spirit in his commanding general, who asked that Aycock restore the course to a playable condition. Aycock in turn enlisted the aid of some of his fellow soldiers and doggedly set about repairing the course. He rebuilt tee boxes and greens and cut the fairways, and eventually made the course so presentable that business flourished to the point that he had to turn customers away.

From Morocco, his unit was dispatched to Italy. Aycock was mortified that, until he reached Rome in 1945, he had not seen a single golf course in the country. In the interim, he decided to build his own course. "To be sure, the nine-hole course isn't exactly suitable for international competition," wrote Jim Burchard in *Stars and Stripes*. "It's a miniature layout, and the fairways are plain dirt mixed with oil. You could put the whole shebang in a good-sized hat. But the GIs of an ordnance battalion near Naples think it's the nuts, and they jam the Lilliputian links each evening to waggle putters and bet their bucks."

Rome presented Aycock with the opportunity to extend his largesse to tournament play. In March of 1945, he organized the Rome Open at the Rome Country Club adjacent to an ancient viaduct. He recruited players from American, British, and South African armed forces, and from Italy's professional ranks, who were no longer obligated to do Mussolini's bidding for him.

U.S. Army private Tommy Bolt, a promising and colorful amateur from Oklahoma, was among those entered. Bolt's overseas assignment was with the Army Corps of Engineers in Italy. He frequented a prestigious Italian club in Rome, which featured a course with only sixteen holes courtesy of Mussolini. Il Duce did not want Italians watching golf, so he destroyed the two holes that weren't hidden by trees. The course was popular among American servicemen on furlough, who often came to play the course and to engage in other nefarious activities organized by young Private Bolt. To supplement his Army pay, Bolt often gave them golf lessons, then fleeced them in the craps games that he organized.

Aycock's Rome Open generated substantial excitement among the golfers stationed or living in that part of Europe. Three hundred entries were received, giving the tournament too many players and not enough equipment. The size of the field and the shortage of equipment to accommodate all the players required that the first round be played over two days, with players sharing clubs and even balls. Once the first round was completed, the field would be cut to one hundred players, then to sixty for the final thirty-six holes.

The professionals among them were playing for $800 in prize money ($600 collected from the $2 entry fee each player paid, plus $200 donated by the host club). There were also two awards that would be presented in honor of a pair of fallen comrades from the world of golf. The Ben Loving Memorial Trophy was to be awarded to the low American in the field. Loving was the professional at Longmeadow Club in Longmeadow, Massachusetts, when he joined the Army in February 1944. He was a popular club professional and developing tour pro who was killed while serving with Company B of the 349th Infantry Regiment of the Fifth Army on the Italian front on January 2, 1945. The Henry Styres Memorial Cup was to be awarded to the low amateur among those serving in southern Italy. Styres had turned pro shortly before joining the Army and had also been killed in the Italian campaign.

The carnage was behind them, allowing them to redirect their attention to less important (if no less troubling) concerns, in this case the dearth of quality golf balls. On the morning of the first round, four American officers and an Italian pro commandeered a jeep and set off for the home of a woman they'd heard possessed seven new golf balls. She was very kind and understanding and said of course she'd be glad to sell them and would do so at a bargain price.

"Eight dollars each," she said in broken English. The officers pooled their money and without argument handed over $56 for seven shiny new golf balls.

New balls were at such a premium that when the tournament started, many players employed friends to dash after their tee shots to ensure that the ball not be lost in the rough. Then in the midst of the second round, word began spreading throughout the field that Sergeant Aycock had taken delivery of twenty-four dozen new balls sent from the States expressly for the tournament. They weren't precisely new, as it turned out; they were the smaller, British size (1.62 inches in diameter) that the USGA had outlawed in 1931. Aycock began wondering aloud where the benefactor could have been hiding 288 golf balls for so many years while the game experienced a ball shortage. Then it turned out that the balls weren't new by any definition; they were reprocessed, which became evident once they were hit with any kind of authority. The balls were able to withstand only a couple of belts before cracking open.

"They should have kept the balls in the States that they sent over," Aycock said. "Hell, don't they know these 1-As over here hit lots harder than the 4-Fs back there?"

Another sign of the war were the sheep that grazed on the course. With so many golfers on the course at one time, the sheep often created congestion. Several times during the course of play each day, a shepherd had to be summoned to herd the sheep away from a green or a landing area, to allow play to continue. On one such occasion, an exasperated Aycock adamantly expressed his opposition to herd them himself. "I have no intention of becoming a sheepherder, no matter what," he said emphatically.

When seventy-two holes were completed, a pair of Italian professionals, Cesidio Croce and Alfonso Angelini, had tied for first. Each of them had served with the Italian Army, Croce leaving when Italy fell to the Allies, Angelini receiving his discharge after his feet froze during the Russian campaign. Angelini won the tournament the following day in a play-off. Navy technician Al

Zimmerman finished third and was the low American, for which he was awarded the Ben Loving Memorial Trophy. Zimmerman was the popular choice of the crowd of five hundred, principally because of his relaxed manner of dress. He wore a pair of sky-blue slacks, a gray sweatshirt, and a baseball cap. Private Chester Sanok finished seventh and was the low amateur among those serving in southern Italy, for which he was awarded the Henry Styres Memorial Cup. As for Bolt, he faltered on the final day, with scores of 82 and 76, to finish sixth, good enough to win low amateur honors.

EISENHOWER, IN FACT, was minding the war, Alan Brooke's protestations notwithstanding, and was effectively doing so at that. The governments of the United States and Great Britain declared May 8, 1945, V-E (Victory in Europe) Day. Hitler had committed suicide and the Third Reich had been consigned to the pages of history. One day earlier, a representative of Germany's new chief of state, Grand Admiral Karl Doenitz, had signed an official surrender decree at General Eisenhower's headquarters in Reims.

General of the Army George C. Marshall cabled Eisenhower with his congratulations: "You have completed your mission with the greatest victory in the history of warfare. You have commanded with outstanding success the most powerful military force that has ever been assembled. You have met and successfully disposed of every conceivable difficulty. You have been selfless in your actions, always sound and tolerant in your judgments, and altogether admirable in the courage and wisdom of your military decisions."

Afterward, Eisenhower and his staff returned to his residence, the Gueux Castle, for a quiet, somber celebration that included several bottles of France's finest champagne. V-E Day and the end of the war in Europe also allowed Eisenhower the opportunity to leave Reims and return to London for a few days. "Everyone else has celebrated V-E Day," Ike said. "I think we should too." Eisenhower's driver and friend Kay Summersby, General Omar Bradley, and Lieutenant Colonel Jimmy Gault, Ike's British aide, were all invited to accompany Ike to London.

Reims, of course, provided access to an endless supply of quality champagne. Gault secured eighteen bottles to take back to London for the celebration. At customs in England, an agent informed Gault that the duty on the champagne would be exorbitant. Gault explained that the champagne was for General Eisenhower's private V-E party. Eisenhower's celebrity was at a zenith in England, where a grateful populace was willing to do anything to show its appreciation, even to overlook a tariff. The customs agent happily waved Gault through.

When Eisenhower reached London, he headed immediately for Telegraph Cottage, his English home in the war years. As soon as he walked through the door, he began to hear the sirens singing to him, luring him outside, toward the back gate, where the golf course beckoned. "Dammit, I'd like to try that thirteenth hole again," he said. His clubs were still in the closet there. He retrieved them, and he went out and replayed the thirteenth, then played a couple more holes, Ike's first postwar golf, but certainly not his last.

The game was on the cusp of a boom to which Eisenhower was positioned to be its most visible contributor. He was America's preeminent celebrity, its greatest war hero, and he was consumed with the game. The general golfing population was certain to feed on his infatuation with golf.

Its popularity had exploded in the aftermath of the First World War, as Grantland Rice recounted in an article written for the 1919 edition of *Spalding's Official Golf Guide*. Rice wrote that "with the return of peace, golf not only came back but returned with the most unprecedented rush and dash of all history.

Courses that had been deserted were soon thronged with players, old and new, while any number of new courses were started to meet the big demand."

PGA president Ed Dudley wrote, thinking back on the golf boom that had occurred in the aftermath of World War I, "It goes without saying that we stand on the brink of a new era in golf." Spectators at golf events hinted at the impending boom. The Tam O'Shanter All-American Open attracted 105,000 customers for the week, a record for a PGA event. The final round of the PGA Championship in Dayton drew 5,581 fans. Crosby and Hope, still putting on golf shows for war charities, turned out 25,000 for an exhibition at Tam O'Shanter. The tone of Dudley's article was one of optimism as well as relief. Early on in the war he was concerned that the game would vanish altogether, at least until peace returned. PGA membership had declined dramatically; courses had gone out of business; and participation had experienced a steep decline. Now, he was predicting "the greatest boom of all time."

The game that Dudley was concerned would vanish had suddenly become ubiquitous, even overseas. The U.S. Army's 16th Armored Division was ordered to leave the Czechoslovakian town of Pilsen and to move to the Czech-German border. The Special Service Force commandeered many of the hotels in the famous Czech resort town of Marienbad, intending to offer them to servicemen for rest and relaxation. Marienbad had come into existence near the end of the nineteenth century because of the mineral springs and naturally carbonated water discovered there. It was a playground for Europe's wealthy citizens and even royalty, including England's King Edward VII.

The Special Service Force was surprised to find a golf course there, albeit a woefully neglected one. When the Germans occupied the city, they had shown no interest in the game and had done nothing to maintain the course. The only way to distinguish the fairways from the greens was that the grass on the fairways had grown to knee deep, while the grass on the greens was only ankle deep. Several years had passed since the last golfer had ventured across the property.

The Special Service Force was aware that one of its own was a golf expert. Neil Martin had been a professional at Orange Hills Country Club in New Haven, Connecticut, as well as at Fort Smith Country Club in Fort Smith, Arkansas, before the war. He had also taken courses on greenkeeping at Massachusetts State College. Martin was asked to take on the task of restoring the course, to give the soldiers on leave there a place to play. When he first set eyes on the expanse, he was able to discern that beneath the weeds and overgrown grass was a superior layout, with the requisite length and character to have hosted championships. Indeed, the Marienbad Golf Club had opened as a nine-holer in 1905 and added a second nine in 1929. The renowned British golfer Henry Cotton won the Czech Open on the course in 1937.

Martin's modest goal was to return the course, if not to its former glory, at least to a playable condition. He speculated that the work would take several weeks. He asked the major in charge when he expected the course renovation to be completed.

"It should have opened yesterday," the major replied tersely.

"Yes, sir," Martin said, inherently understanding that the course was now a top priority, no doubt the result in part of the major's own interest in playing the game. Martin at least had no shortage of help. He was authorized to use as many German prisoners of war as was necessary, a number limited in scope only by the 16th Armored Division's ability to transport and feed them, as well as to guard them. Martin used as many as twenty POWs a day, though their production was limited, requiring that they be replaced by another twenty POWs each day.

Joining the crew on a daily basis was Gaston, a Frenchman,

who operated the tractor; Hans, a German civilian who was given the charge of mowing the greens; and Marion, a Pole who had been freed from a concentration camp and was employed as a translator. Two weeks into the restoration, golfers were playing the course. A month into it, only a trained eye could ascertain that the course had been out of commission for years. Corporal Lloyd Mangrum, still in Europe recovering from his war injuries, arrived to play the course. Mangrum and another golf professional, Lieutenant Matt Kowal, each bettered the par of 72, a tribute to its condition.

Mangrum had rejected doctors' prognoses that his war injuries might prevent him from playing competitive golf again, and to prove it he went from Marienbad to Paris to play in the U.S. Armed Forces Championship at the outset of August. Mangrum played seventy-two holes in nine-under-par 291 at the battle-scarred St. Cloud Golf Course to win the professional division.

The game had unexpectedly flourished in continental Europe, even while enduring the hardships of war. George Lake, president of the PGA's Southern California Section and the professional at Recreation Park in Long Beach, considered that his optimism for the future of the game was unrestricted, once he heard the stories of Danny Nowak and Earl Martin, PGA professionals who were thrust into the midst of the war. A letter that Lake wrote to *The Professional Golfer* magazine read in part:

> That golf continues to grow and become popular is a fact known to all of us in the business. We teach every day on our fairways at our respective clubs. After hearing the story I did a few nights ago, I wonder how many of us appreciate and are thankful for what we have and the conditions and surroundings that we work in. I know that one pro, when he returns from his present site, will appreciate anything with grass on it.

This man I talk of is Lt. Danny Nowak, who before the war was Marvin Stahl's assistant in Lansing, Mich., and at the Seminole Club at Palm Beach, Fla. When the war started he enlisted in the Air Force and at the conclusion of his training period, he was shipped overseas. After sixteen flights over Germany, his plane was shot down and he was taken prisoner. Following a year's silence, Marvin received word from him and he is doing as well as can be expected.

Among the few things Danny was able to say was the fact he is attempting to teach the other prisoners in his camp the fine art of swinging a golf club. He of course has no equipment, no balls, clubs, or practice fairway. But despite that his interest is there and apparently his clients have that interest, too, for they would have to have interest to attempt to learn the game under such conditions and in such a place.

As I think of this, I again wonder how many of us realize our good fortune and appreciate the conditions under which we work.

Golf has never been a very popular game in Germany, but if they leave our boys over there long enough, it will be. The story above tells us the teaching which Danny Nowak is doing in Germany, but we also have a player there who never forgets golf.

Last month I received a letter from Earl Martin, former pro at Inglewood Country Club. In this letter he told me he thought he was the first GI to hit a golf ball in Germany. Where he found the club or ball, I don't know, but he accomplished this feat in October of last year, and after retrieving the ball, sent it to Clarence Rickey of the MacGregor Golf Company.

Who says golf is not flourishing in foreign countries?

V-J Day, August 14, 1945, ended World War II, but not golf's contributions to the war effort. Touring pro Leo Diegel was the cochairman of the PGA's Rehabilitation Committee, and had written to Major General Norman T. Kirk, the U.S. Surgeon General, regarding the association's intent to build a series of golf courses for wounded military personnel, and to teach them the game. Diegel received the following letter in response:

Dearest Mr. Diegel:

In acknowledging receipt of your letter of the fourteenth of May, it would be remiss if I did not express my interest in your effective program at many of our hospitals. The Professional Golfers' Association is performing a real service to our convalescent patients in many hospitals. In all activities undertaken, your association is providing opportunities for physical recreation and reconditioning that otherwise might not have been available.

Your patriotic motive in providing this service is much appreciated.

Sincerely,
Norman T. Kirk
Major General, U.S. Army
The Surgeon General

The PGA continued its fund-raising efforts, now directed toward building the hospital courses to which Diegel was alluding. Bob Hope and Bing Crosby had played an exhibition match at Recreation Park in Long Beach, California, drawing a crowd of five thousand. For the record, Hope checked in with a two-over-par 74 to beat Crosby by three. More importantly, the event raised $1,700, the seed money for a pitch-and-putt course the PGA intended to build at the U.S. Naval Hospital in Long Beach.

Houston Press sports editor Ralph Anderson (better known as Andy Anderson) was a World War I veteran with a passion for helping injured soldiers in their rehabilitation. His own son, Ralph Junior, had been injured in the Battle of the Bulge. During World War II, Andy Anderson visited nearly two hundred veterans hospitals around the United States, helping in any manner possible. He recognized the value of outdoor sports as a rehabilitative tool for those who had lost a limb. He once devised a handle that would allow those who had lost an arm to use their prosthesis to wield a rod and reel. Besides fishing, Anderson had an affinity for golf; after the first World War, he started a golf-course construction business.

Anderson was part of a contingent of Houston sportswriters and sportsmen who formed the Houston War Sports Activity Committee. The committee approached General James Bethea, commanding general of McCloskey General Hospital, an amputation center for war wounded, and asked what it might do for the thousands of patients pouring into the center.

"Build them a golf course," the general replied.

When a general issues an order, even civilians are inclined to follow it. The committee promptly erected a nine-hole course that measured 2,200 yards and was designed to accommodate even those in wheelchairs. Money was raised by selling each hole for $500. Among those who helped secure the funds were churches, labor unions, liquor salesmen, and fraternal lodges. In three days, $7,000 was raised from fourteen groups and individuals. One evening, a local nightclub held a special party to which the price of admission was golf equipment. Seventy sets of clubs were collected for the hospital course that night. Sam Snead and Vic Ghezzi flew in to dedicate the course, giving a clinic and even lessons. The course quickly became a popular gathering spot for the amputees; as many as a hundred a day played.

"It's a sight to bring tears to your eyes to see these plucky youngsters hobbling around the links on crutches, standing on one leg for a swing, and even playing with one arm," wrote Doyle Beard of the *Houston Post*.

Among those who were moved was Andy Anderson, who postulated that with an assist those with arm amputations might have a chance to play golf. He set out to fashion a device that would allow a patient to swing a golf club using his prosthesis in concert with his remaining arm. Sergeant Norman Bromel, who lost his left arm in Germany, became his test golfer. Anderson developed a special grip that allowed Bromel to use his hook with a standard golf club. It featured a leather sleeve with a leather flap that fit around the club's grip. The flap was held in place by the working hand, while the hook was inserted into a thong attached to the leather sleeve. The first time it was tried, from 140 yards, Bromel hit a 5-iron onto the green.

War heroes weren't necessarily wearing uniforms.

Courses were springing up at veterans hospitals across the country. One was built at Oliver General Hospital in Augusta, Georgia. George J. Rommell was recuperating there when Bobby Jones came by to put on an exhibition for the patients. "Bobby looked good while I watched him," Rommell wrote in a letter. "I was able to go only two holes. I have been acquainted with the greenkeeper here who is a horticulturist from way back. The soldiers are taking a great deal of interest in golf and a great many are being rehabilitated by one-club tournaments and being assigned to these by doctors."

THE PGA WAS DETERMINED to restore normalcy to the game at its level, prompting its president, Ed Dudley, to write to his British counterpart, Henry Cotton, proposing that the Ryder Cup be resumed in 1946. Dudley even offered to send the U.S. contingent to England, though it was America's turn to host.

Dudley's generous gesture was designed to allow the Ryder Cup to jumpstart golf in postwar Britain.

Cotton politely declined, citing the need for more time to allow Britain's players and courses to recover from the deleterious effects of a long and costly war. "We must allow our players and course to recover from six years of total war," Cotton wrote in a cablegram sent to Dudley. "We will let you know when we are ready."

It was not a popular decision in the States, for two reasons. One, the British Open and British Amateur were scheduled to resume in 1946; if the courses and players were up to the challenge of individual events, why not a team competition, particularly in light of the postwar popularity of Americans and the enthusiasm their appearance would generate? Second, as PGA Tournament Bureau manager Fred Corcoran pointed out unnecessarily, the U.S. had been at war too.

A painful reminder appeared in a United Press story that listed those from the world of sports who had lost their lives in the service of their country. "The Professional Golfers Association service flag carries eleven gold stars, including those for Ben Loving, Bill Harmon, and John Shimkonis," the story read. "Among the outstanding amateur golfers who were killed was Johnny Burke, former national intercollegiate champion from Newport, R.I."

It was a reminder that the game itself was not a casualty of the war, that considering it as such was trivializing the meaning of the word. The game had simply encountered obstacles in its pursuit to continue. Morton Bogue, the outgoing president of the United States Golf Association, addressed the obstacles in the annual report he wrote on the state of the game. "We are hopeful that the golf clubs will be able to get sufficient labor material and equipment to rehabilitate their courses which have had to stand neglected to a great extent because of the war," he wrote. "We are also hopeful that golfers will be able, before the end of the year, to get golf clubs and golf balls of the pre-war type. . . . We noted with regret the growing tendency during the war to drift away from observance of the rules of the game. We hope that this era has passed and that the game will go under the rules which have stood the test of time. We hope the program for the rehabilitation of our wounded may be aided by golf clubs and golfers generally. The Professional Golfers' Association of America has already rendered valuable assistance in this program."

The Rules of Golf had taken a beating during the war. In 1942, the Chicago District, among other golf associations, recommended that winter rules be used for the duration of the war, and referred to them as "war rules." Winter rules violate one of the bedrock principles of golf, that a golfer is required to play the ball as it lies, but had been invoked to accommodate the deterioration of the turf from neglect.

As for the ball shortage to which Bogue alluded, golf had survived its scare, to a large degree as a result of its resourcefulness. Reconditioned balls kept the game going at the local level while professionals had hoarded the quality prewar balls. At the Dallas Victory Open in 1945, Don January, a fifteen-year-old amateur golfer determined to star as a professional one day, paid the entry fee that would enable him to play alongside his idols Nelson, Hogan, and Snead. He was thrilled with the prospect, but his anticipation was greater over the possibility that he might secure some prewar balls. He had played enough of the reconditioned balls to conclude that they were not of the quality that new balls were. They often split at impact, with the two halves fluttering off in different directions. January viewed his entry as an opportunity to scour the lakes for the pros' misguided Spalding Dots. He found an ample supply, as it turned out.

THE PGA CHAMPIONSHIP at Moraine Country Club in Dayton, Ohio, had shed light on the strength of the game and the cause for optimism. It was identified, appropriately, by a Scotsman, Kerr N. Petrie, the longtime golf writer of *The New York Herald Tribune* (and *The New York Herald* before that). Born in Carnoustie, Petrie had come to America in April of 1908 to visit another Carnoustie man, Alex Smith, who had emigrated to America in pursuit of a job as a club professional. Smith, who won the U.S. Open in 1906, had landed at the Nassau Country Club in Glen Cove on Long Island toward the end of the nineteenth century. Petrie decided to stay on as well and ended up at *The New York Herald*. Petrie took away from the PGA Championship an appreciation for the efforts golf and golf professionals had made and were continuing to make on behalf of the war effort. He was sufficiently moved to write an article of appreciation for *The Professional Golfer,* the house publication of the PGA of America. It read in part:

> After Dayton the Professional Golfers' Association of America must feel glad it did not hide its head in the sand. Not only did the 1945 Championship at Moraine Country Club provide an added vote of confidence for the action of the P.G.A., but it fired our august professors on the faculty with a new zeal, or should have, at least, showed them that Golf (with a capital "G") really was a wartime asset instead of a liability, a snake in the grass, or a festering sore on the honest face of patriotism.
>
> For a long time after Pearl Harbor golfers felt jittery about carrying their clubs about. Several prominent golfers have confessed to feeling like "heels," this despite the fact that they were over age for military duty and merely continuing to make their living in the only way they knew. What a pity every member of the P.G.A., every one of its detractors or critics of sport in wartime,

could not have been at Moraine. They would have seen the fairways, greens, and tees lined with soldiers in steel helmets pulling
ropes as marshals and enjoying it, hundreds upon hundreds of
officers and men from Wright Field and Patterson Field mingling every day with the citizenry of Dayton. They would have
seen something much more reassuring. They would have seen
jeep loads of wounded veterans in their plum-colored fatigue
uniforms rolling up and down the hills of Moraine after the
matches and having the time of their lives. . . .

Ed Dudley, your president, together with S. C. Allyn, president of
Moraine, and other P.G.A. and golf club officials went out to Wright
Field the morning after the final and handed over for rehabilitation, both at Wright and Patterson Fields, a check for $51,515.26. I
have been told this latest contribution sends the indicator for P.G.A.
rehabilitation flashing towards the second hundred thousand. I
have been told also that the ball has only started to roll. . . .

Arriving back home I find no letters excoriating me for taking
an interest in sports or telling me I still should be under the hedge.
Why, I believe I have courage enough now to carry a bag of clubs
openly through the crowds of soldiers and sailors in Times Square.

General Dwight David Eisenhower would be among those saluting
him for doing so, surely. Incidentally, Eisenhower's headquarters
for the American postwar occupation of Germany were in Frankfurt, in the I. G. Farben Building, an eight-story, six-hundred-
thousand-square-foot office complex that somehow survived
Allied bombs. For his residence, he chose the palatial Schloss
Friedrichshof, also known as the Kronberg Castle, built by Em-
press Frederick outside Frankfurt, Germany, in 1889. As early as
1914, golf had been played on the park grounds surrounding the
castle, further evidence that Ike and the game were inseparable.

17

WORTHY CHAMPIONS

The Masters and U.S. Open Resume

The black man in the white coat, waiting tables and shining shoes, cut a familiar figure in the clubhouse, a comforting sign to the membership there that business as usual had returned to the Augusta National Golf Club. The war was over, the Masters was set to resume, and there was Beau Jack, flitting around once more and working for tips.

Gene Tunney gave him one. Tunney was a former heavyweight champion of the world and an Augusta member, whose shoes Beau Jack was in the process of buffing to a reflective sheen. "Keep your left jab shorter," Tunney said. "Don't reach out so far with it."

It was a tip that exceeded in value the two bits Beau Jack might otherwise have received for a shoeshine. He had become an accomplished boxer in his own right, one who had been weaned on the fight racket in his hometown of Augusta in the late thirties, a protégé of Bowman Milligan, Augusta National's head steward. Milligan was responsible for providing nightly entertainment for the club's out-of-town members, and he often did so by putting together a boxing card at the Bon Air Vanderbilt Hotel in town. The last fight of the night typically was a battle royal, featuring six fighters, each of them blindfolded, engaging in a free-for-all. They were equipped with oversized boxing gloves and at the opening bell would begin swinging wildly (and blindly), hitting ring posts, ropes, air, and, of course, chins, this being the point of the excessively barbaric exercise. The last man standing was declared the winner.

Beau Jack, fifteen at the time, was among Milligan's most spirited contestants in the battles royal, despite his diminutive size—135 pounds or so, including the twenty-two pieces of buckshot that were imbedded in his chest area by his father's shotgun in a hunting accident when he was nine. When Beau Jack won one such battle royal for the Augusta National members, he earned a thousand-dollar payday and a job as a shoeshine boy and caddie at the club.

Meanwhile, his local boxing career continued, under the management of Bowman Milligan, who doubled as his boss at the Augusta National. Beau Jack could neither read nor write, but he had an engaging personality that endeared him to the members there, including Bobby Jones. When Beau Jack decided to pursue boxing as a profession, Jones stepped up as his benefactor, raising the money required to send him to New York. Jones collected $50 from each of fifty members at the club, then topped that with his own $500 donation. Beau Jack took his $3,000 stake and went to Massachusetts, where he lived on a golf course while he trained for his professional debut.

He accumulated a 42-6-2 record before winning the vacated New York World Lightweight Championship by knocking out

Tippy Larkin in the third round on December 18, 1942. The fe-
rocity with which he fought earned him stardom in New York,
even when he lost. He became among the most entertaining
boxers New York had ever seen, and one of its marquee stars. In
three Madison Square Garden bouts in March of 1944 alone,
56,622 fans paid $332,579 for the privilege of watching him
work. Two weeks after losing his New York World Lightweight
Championship to Bob Montgomery in a fifteen-round decision,
he won a ten-rounder from Al "Bummy" Davis at the Garden, a
bout that drew the largest boxing crowd of the year, 19,963, and
the year's largest gate, $132,823. Among his most ardent fans
were members of the Augusta National Golf Club. Each time he
fought, usually at the Garden, a contingent of Augusta National
members would join the crowd cheering on one of boxing's
favorite pugilists.

Beau Jack was flush with money (an Atlanta sportswriter called
him "an incipient millionaire"), a fact not lost on Augusta's
members welcoming him upon return for the '46 Masters. When
Beau Jack delivered a round of drinks, someone invariably joked
that he was a little light today, could he cover him? The truth was
that Beau Jack had earned more money with his fists than most
of the golfers in the Masters field had earned with their clubs, yet
there he was, back on steward Bowman Milligan's staff, back on the
second floor of the clubhouse, shining players' shoes and delivering food and drinks to Augusta members.

"As long as I can get around on my feet I'll be right here," he
said. "This is where I love to be."

The atmosphere at Augusta National in the spring of 1946 was
magnetic, pulling in anyone with even a remote association to golf
or the club, including a well-heeled black boxer who was willing to
shine shoes and wait tables for the opportunity to be a part of the
unofficial grand reopening of professional tournament golf.

The successful suppression of the German and Japanese threats elevated the collective spirit of the nation, its people buoyed by the long-awaited return to normalcy. The impending start of the first postwar major championship also heightened anticipation in Augusta and magnified the importance of the Masters beyond what it had been before the war.

"It's like the United States Open, only more so in a way," the old golf pro Walter Hagen said.

A return to normalcy was relative. There were painful reminders of the savagery of the war that was now behind them. One of them was Army lieutenant George Poschner, a former University of Georgia football star who had played in the Orange Bowl in 1941 and the Rose Bowl in 1942. Poschner had lost both his legs below the knee and part of his right hand in the European theater. From his wheelchair perched by the eighteenth green, Poschner watched practice-round proceedings and greeted each player as he came off the course.

Record crowds were predicted for the week. The course again was manicured to perfection, though the colorful flora of which it had once boasted was still recovering from the damage inflicted by that ill-conceived herd of cattle that had roamed the course during the war. The field of fifty-one players was the largest ever, boosted as it was by the benevolence of the tournament committee, which wished to accommodate many of those who had been on active duty. The field included five players who had been awarded Purple Hearts for war injuries. Lloyd Mangrum was the most prominent among them; he received two Purple Hearts, one for injuries on D-day. Johnny Palmer had sustained injuries during the course of the thirty-two missions he flew over Japan. Rod Munday received shrapnel wounds while serving with the Army's 84th Division in the European theater. Al Zimmerman was wounded while serving with the Navy off the coast of Anzio, Italy, and Buck White was wounded while serving with the Army in Italy. Other warriors included Jones, Clayton Heafner, who was a front-line medic with the Army's 87th Division, Augusta National member Charlie Yates, who served on a Navy cruiser for the better part of four years, and Herman Keiser, a sailor who had served aboard the USS *Cincinnati*.

The press was less interested in battlefield stars than golf stars. The Masters was the first major roundup of the game's elite since the '42 PGA Championship. "The stage is set," wrote *The Atlanta Constitution*'s Jack Troy breathlessly. "Will it be Hogan, Nelson, or Snead? The Augusta National has a blueprint for everything but the winner of the famous event. There was a final dress rehearsal today. The tension mounted. The gallery gets in on some of the pressure. For even the followers can't feel carefree in following matches where every shot counts."

Bookmakers established Hogan and Nelson as cofavorites, at two to one. The gap separating Nelson from a sure thing had widened considerably in recent months. Earlier in the year, he had had his streak of sixty-five consecutive tournaments in the top ten ended at the Pensacola Open. He had begun searching for a new ranch to buy, when a friend from Denton, Texas, phoned him and asked him to look at a place. Nelson inspected the property just before leaving for Pensacola. He then played the tournament with his mind elsewhere, home on the range, as it were. The distraction brought to an end one of the great streaks in golf history. He tied for fourteenth, his worst finish in four years. He later purchased the ranch.

Bobby Jones was also entered, though his appearance was largely ceremonial, an obligation he felt as the tournament host. At forty-four, Jones was no longer prepared to play competitively, and instead, he was forced to rely on diminished skills and instinct to get around the course without embarrassment.

The stars may have been cast, but when play began Herman Keiser was not following the script that had Hogan, Snead, and Nelson in the leading roles. Keiser had one career victory to his account, in 1942, and was largely unknown beyond the confines of the USS *Cincinnati,* on which he had served thirty-one months during the war. The *Cincinnati's* most prominent achievement was intercepting and destroying the *Annalise Essberger,* a German blockade runner, taking all sixty-two German crew members prisoner before the ship sank.

Keiser was playing as though his ship was about to come in, and there were those at Augusta National who deemed it unacceptable that a petty officer was threatening to upend the captains of their game. His mien failed to convert those whose interest gravitated toward the stars. Keiser was called the Missouri Mortician, his grim demeanor suggesting that he was more likely making his living with holes that were six feet deep. Still, Keiser was a coleader after the first round, then opened a five-stroke lead after thirty-six holes, a margin he maintained heading into the final round.

Keiser was certain that there were those at the club who did not want him to win, notably high rollers whose money had been wagered elsewhere. He claimed that Grantland Rice, the legendary sportswriter and Augusta National member, had sidled up to him on the fourteenth hole of the third round, and, without introducing himself, told him to pick up the pace or he'd face a two-stroke penalty. Keiser threatened to take a swing of another sort.

If Rice indeed was the culprit, he at least was correct in his assessment of Keiser. His pace of play was slower than a southern drawl, which failed to endear him to the crowd. *Atlanta Journal* sports editor Ed Danforth wrote that his playing partner, Byron Nelson, "had to stand for endless minutes while Herman studied his drive, took wind and tide readings on approach shots, and plotted the longitude and latitude of every cup on his putts."

Keiser also accused club officials of changing his third-round tee time without informing him, forcing him to rush to the first tee, where he was provided the use of a thirteen-year-old caddie who was unable to tote the heavy bag more than a single hole, before he took to dragging it along behind him. Keiser demanded a stronger, more experienced caddie, yet club officials told him none were available.

The nature of a golf fan without a vested interest in the outcome is to root for the best story. Hogan was an established star, which made his winning more appealing than a Keiser victory, the latter's war resume notwithstanding, a Keiser who had helped bring down the Kaiser, as one press wag had noted. His cause was further diminished by the back-door nature of his having qualified for the field (the top thirty finishers from the last Masters and the last U.S. Open played, in 1942, were extended invitations).

Resentment was palpably building on Sunday. "It just won't do for Keiser to win the Masters," a fan said, echoing what most in the crowd of 7,500 were surely thinking. There was a modicum of hope circulating throughout the crowd (and the press) that Keiser understood his place in the golf hierarchy. Only a few weeks earlier, he had unwittingly yielded to Hogan's superiority at the Phoenix Open, by losing to him in a play-off. Maybe he would politely do so again.

Hogan was Keiser's closest pursuer. Through seventeen holes of the final round, with Keiser uncomfortably waiting in the clubhouse, Hogan erased four strokes from the five-stroke lead. Then at eighteen, Hogan hit his second to within twelve feet of the hole.

"Well, I hope that he gets either a three or a five," said Keiser, who became queasy at the prospect of another play-off altercation with a man determined to establish himself as the best in golf.

Hogan missed his putt to win, but left himself a two-and-a-half-foot putt to tie Keiser and force an eighteen-hole play-off the following day. A putt that was shorter than the odds on him winning inexplicably scooted past the hole, giving Keiser an improbable victory in the Masters.

"Herman Keiser was a painful surprise as the winner," Danforth wrote in the *Journal*. "He was a long shot. He was to this tournament what Donerail was to the Kentucky Derby, a hundred to one. Ben Hogan was the people's choice. They chose Hogan before the tournament started and invested heavily in his chances. You know how people are about golf. Hogan carried the sentimental and/or the material interest of nearly every man and woman in the gallery of 7,500."

Keiser could have told him that in fact he was a twenty-to-one shot. These were the odds he had received when he wagered fifty dollars on himself, a bet that provided him a return of $1,000 for his prescience, running his take for the victory to $3,500. Moreover, he did not consider his victory a surprise. He explained that those in the service returned to civilian life in the best condition of their lives, giving them a muscled leg up on their competition that had not been in the service.

Entirely overlooked was the certain harmony about the outcome, a feel-good quality, that of a man stepping off a warship that had contributed to the Allied victory and winning the most important postwar tournament to date. The stars were indeed aligned—behind the winner, as it were. Hogan finished second, while Snead and Nelson tied for sixth.

It was also a small victory for the baby boom that was under way following the end of the war. Keiser's wife had been anxious to start a family, but he insisted that he win an important tournament first. Within a matter of days after his Masters victory, the Keisers were pregnant.

THE UNITED STATES GOLF ASSOCIATION was eager to resume its national championship schedule, including the first playing of the U.S. Open since 1941. The organization had no regrets about its decision early in 1942 to suspend its championships for the duration of the war. USGA president Morton Bogue issued a statement defending the association's position: "The number of amateurs and professionals who joined the colors and fought in the Mediterranean, European, and Pacific theaters has borne out our view that no tournament during the war could have produced truly representative champions and has fully justified the cessation of national championships during the war."

The 1946 Open was assigned to Canterbury Golf Club in Cleveland, which only six years earlier had hosted the tournament. The '40 Open had been won by Lawson Little, but its legacy came courtesy of Walter Hagen's Canterbury tale, an Open curtain call that was a microcosm of his career. Hagen was renowned for playing as hard off a course as on one, and accordingly he was bleary eyed and running late for his 10:35 A.M. third-round tee time. He finally arrived at the first tee in a cab, just after his playing partners had teed off. He struck his tee shot, then playfully admonished the starter for not recognizing that his bag had one club too many, a Canadian Club, as it were. He pulled the bottle of whiskey from his bag, a remnant from a party at the Hollenden Hotel the night before. At the end of his round, Hagen was notified that he had been disqualified, and he never played in another Open.

The '46 Open at Canterbury came through with another memorable incident, this one eventually having a bearing on the outcome. Byron Nelson's caddie that week was Eddie Martin, who prior to joining the service had worked for Nelson. A soldier stationed in Panama, Martin had received a furlough and was using it to again caddie for Nelson, an opportunity he relished. After Nelson hit his tee shot on the thirteenth hole, he and Martin made their way down the fairway, along with an overzealous crowd that was held back only by the thin gallery rope the marshals were holding. The crowd began surging toward Nelson's ball, nearly overtaking it, unbeknownst to Martin. When he finally ducked under the gallery rope, he inadvertently kicked Nelson's ball. A USGA rules official, Ike Grainger, was consulted, and it was agreed that Nelson would have to incur a one-stroke penalty. Nelson took the penalty in stride, even telling Martin that it was not his fault. Martin, nonetheless, was on the verge of tears. The press, always helpful, checked in with a suggestion on preventing similar episodes from occurring: "They say that peacetime refinements develop from innovations produced by wartime necessity," columnist Arthur Daley wrote in *The New York Times*. "Hence the idea is respectfully offered to the U.S.G.A. to borrow a leaf from the British book. The Prestwick course over there was dotted with land mines during the war, each land mine being encircled by a ring of barbed wire, and a ball which popped within the wire was generously termed an 'unplayable lie,' and thus could be removed without penalty—or explosion. The only way to hold spectators in check is to string the fairways with barbed wire—this a horribly macabre suggestion—charged with electricity. Nothing else ever could stem the thundering herd."

The crowd, large and rambunctious, was indicative of the renewed interest in the game, as well as reflective of the perpetually shifting leader board that had everyone confused. In the press room, a telegraph operator who was assisting the writers with the filing of their stories, suddenly shrieked, "He wins!" A giveaway ought to have been the *Daily Racing Form* protruding from his pocket. The assembled press, largely unaware of the progress on the course, turned to him in anticipation of his delivering the news for which they were waiting. "Who won?" one of them asked breathlessly.

"Assault wins," the telegraph operator replied. "Yeah, Assault wins the Dryer Stakes."

Assault had been a two-to-five favorite to continue to dominate his sport. His winning was no surprise, other than to a roomful of golf writers.

The penalty stroke absorbed by Nelson became a pivotal one. By the end of play on Sunday, Nelson, Lloyd Mangrum, and Vic Ghezzi were tied, requiring an eighteen-hole play-off the following day. A waiting photographer greeted Nelson coming off the eighteenth green, "Hey, Byron," the callous photographer asked, "how about a big smile?"

"Why should I?" Nelson replied, pondering the notion that he now had to scratch and claw to win a tournament he'd have already won were it not for an unfortunate error on the part of his caddie.

The play-off was equally dramatic. Former baseball great Tris Speaker was there, rooting for Nelson. When he encountered Nelson's wife, Louise, near the clubhouse, he told her, "Now, don't worry. I'll worry about Byron and you quit. No sense in both of us worrying."

Each of the three players shot 72, requiring a second eighteen-hole play-off in the afternoon. The tournament came down to the eighteenth hole, a hazardous one in any tournament, more so in this one. Lightning was crackling overhead and rain was falling. Mangrum was one ahead of Ghezzi, two ahead of Nelson, who no longer could win. In the end, Ghezzi needed to make an eight-footer at eighteen to force yet another play-off round. Ghezzi missed and Mangrum was the winner.

Renowned broadcaster Bill Stern asked Nelson for his thoughts on losing a tournament he might have won had his caddie not booted the ball in the third round.

"Bill," Nelson replied, "just give me one of those things you're advertising and I'll cut my throat."

The radio broadcast was sponsored by Gillette, maker of fine razor blades.

In his report for the United Press, Oscar Fraley introduced some battlefield allusions to the play-off proceedings. "The former corporal [Mangrum] was just another G.I. Joe again for a minute," Fraley wrote. "His cream-colored sports shirt seemed to turn to khaki and to him it no longer was a golf course. That rumble was too familiar and it meant trouble. And that's when Mangrum looked up at the flashes, laughed, and really started to go then. The pressure which he had unloaded seemed to settle on the shoulders of the other two."

Mangrum himself had previously noted that combat experience should alter one's perspective of the importance of a crucial shot, saying, "I don't suppose that any of the pro or amateur golfers who were combat soldiers, Marines, or sailors will soon be able to think of a three-putt green as one of the really bad troubles in life."

Unlike Keiser at the Masters, Mangrum was a popular winner. He was debonair, a Hollywood star seemingly cast in the role of a golfer, a cigarette usually dangling from his mouth, even while he executed a shot, the epitome of cool. Arthur Daley wrote in the *Times,* "It was Lloyd Mangrum, the slight and dapper fellow from Los Angeles, wearing the Purple Heart for wounds received in the Battle of the Bulge. Every inch a worthy champion!"

The exclamation point was a fitting conclusion to the first

U.S. Open played in five years, and the first since war's end. It's tough to script a golf tournament, but this one, the national championship, begged for a war hero to prevail in the end. Mangrum, a staff sergeant with the Third Army, a man who had landed at Omaha Beach on D-day and had fought with Patton in Germany, took the cue and delivered the most riveting and remarkable performance of his life.

DWIGHT EISENHOWER WAS a general with five stars, none of which gave him the authority to command a golf ball. He could move armies thousands of miles in a prescribed direction with a single order, yet a small dimpled ball declined to acquiesce to his elementary expectation that it go straight for two hundred yards on occasion.

He was never much of a golfer, but he was a soldier par excellence. Indeed, Eisenhower was among the most decorated soldiers in American history, the recipient of the Distinguished Service Medal with four Oak Leaf Clusters, the Navy Distinguished Service Medal, the Legion of Merit, and a plethora of service medals. Similarly, the international community generously accorded him many of its highest honors, including France's Grand Cordon of the Legion of Honor and the Croix de Guerre with two palms, and Great Britain's Knight Grand Cross of the Order of the Bath and the Order of Merit.

His military work was recognized in another fashion as well. Renowned golf clubs began bestowing honorary memberships on General Eisenhower, creating an interesting dichotomy for the man who only ever wanted to be a soldier: He derived pride from the medals, certainly, symbolic as they were of an important job well done, but the golf honorifics, well, they simply gave him greater pleasure.

Eisenhower had the soldier's understanding of the nature of war, that good could come from it, but never joy. The medals encouraged looking back at a success that was tempered by its ghastly cost in human life. The golf memberships provided Ike with something he could look forward to, a standing invitation to play some of the finer golf courses in the world.

Eisenhower was overjoyed upon receiving the news, in December 1945, that the Royal and Ancient Golf Club of St. Andrews had extended to him a lifetime honorary membership, "in recognition of your great service to mankind." Great Britain, naturally, could tender no higher honor to a friend with a passion for golf than to share the game it had founded by including him in the second-oldest golf association and granting him access to the oldest surviving course, the Old Course at St. Andrews. The Brits were so appreciative of Eisenhower's efforts on their behalf that anything less would have rung hollow.

British prime minister Winston Churchill was offered the same lifetime honorary membership, though he politely declined. "As I don't play golf anymore, I do not feel I can avail myself of this kindness, and in this I hope you will excuse me," he wrote to the club.

Eisenhower, of course, gratefully accepted the membership, fully intending to avail himself of this kindness at every opportunity. His acceptance letter, dated December 21, 1945, read:

Dear Mr. Secretary,

I am more than complimented by my election to honorary life membership in The Royal and Ancient Golf Club of St. Andrews. I deeply appreciate the honor you have bestowed upon me and sincerely hope that some day in the not too distant future I shall be able to take advantage of your hospitality. I trust that my performance as a golfer will not be publicized to my Scottish friends as they would disown me at once. I had thought that Scotland had already exhausted every possibility of further kindness to me. Your invitation shows me my mistake.

Please express my deep and sincere gratitude to all of your members for the honor they have so graciously accorded me.

Sincerely,
Dwight Eisenhower

Ten months later, the not-too-distant-future arrived. On October 9, 1946, Eisenhower went to St. Andrews to accept the honorary life membership and to play a little golf on the Old Course with the new captain of the club. Two weeks earlier, Roger Weathered had "driven in" as captain, according to tradition. The incoming designee, although preselected by committee, is entered into a competition for the captaincy, though there are no other competitors. He is declared the winner after hitting a drive from the first tee, usually done in view of past captains and a small crowd. The members call the ritual "driving in."

Eisenhower was playing in a five-ball match with Captain Weathered, John Inglis, Michael Lindsay, and Sir George Cunningham, and a large crowd had gathered to watch the war hero play his first shot as an honorary member. Originally, they were to play three holes out, then three holes in, but the day proved so enjoyable to all involved that they played six holes out and six holes in. All except General Eisenhower, who elected not to "drive in" on the first tee. After Weathered struck his tee shot down the middle, Ike took a couple of practice swings, then began striding down the fairway without taking a real swing, much to the surprise of the large crowd that had gathered to watch him play.

"If I whiffed on the first at St. Andrews," Eisenhower said, "I'd never live it down."

Eisenhower allowed Weathered to hit the second as well, the ball coming to rest eighteen feet from the hole. At that point, Eisenhower took over, holing the eighteen-foot putt for a "team" birdie.

His first-tee fears notwithstanding, Eisenhower was genuinely pleased with his reception at St. Andrews. "Simply wonderful and something really memorable," he said. The fact that he was so smitten with the game that the Scots had gifted the world with elevated him to virtual sainthood in the town. Eisenhower had a home in St. Andrews, literally: The Scots rewarded him with a suite of rooms at Culzean Castle in Ayrshire, which conveniently was just a short drive from the links at Turnberry.

The Scots likely would have given him anything he requested in their postwar euphoria, such was his popularity there. St. Andrew himself had never been in Scotland, not when he was alive, at any rate. His remains, however, were buried there for a long enough time that he became Scotland's patron saint. On the reverence scale, he was without equal, at least until Eisenhower entered their realm. St. Andrew gave a Scottish town his name, but Eisenhower defended its freedom, and the Scots' appreciation knew no bounds.

He was a soldier, one of the finest, but he was also a golfer. It was a convergence that proved irresistible in the auld country, where a kindred spirit with a passion for the game they loved stepped forward to deliver victory in a war for their survival.

EPILOGUE

A Sunday-morning tee time on December 7, 1941, near Pearl Harbor introduced golf at the beginning of the war. Arthur Seyss-Inquart, a Nazi party official on trial at Nuremberg, invoked it at the end of the war. Seyss-Inquart was attempting to avoid the hangman's noose for his war crimes, some of them committed in a Dutch concentration camp under his command. "The inmates of the camp played golf," he said, pleading his case in vain.

Between Pearl Harbor and Nuremberg, golf kept resurfacing, in both likely and unlikely places, a demonstration of the game's endearing quality and enduring nature. It not only survived the war but exposed its benevolent side in the process.

Golf may not have saved Seyss-Inquart, who was one of ten Nazi war criminals hanged, but it proved a reliable lifeline for many others, including Pat Ward-Thomas of the Royal Air Force.

Ward-Thomas was among the thousands of airmen imprisoned at Stalag Luft III in what is now the Polish town of Sagan. From having written brief reports for the camp newspaper (such as it was) on the golf matches played on the rudimentary course the prisoners had built in Stalag Luft III, he took a shine to the craft and began pondering whether he might have a future in writing about games, provided the war allowed him a future at all.

The thought stayed with him, and when the Allies finally prevailed and he had recovered his freedom, he began pursuing a career in writing about sports, particularly golf. Over time, Ward-Thomas developed into one of the finest golf writers of his generation, on either side of the Atlantic, one who commanded equal respect among the players ("one of the great writers of all time," Jack Nicklaus said) and his peers ("one of the finest golf writers of all time," wrote Herbert Warren Wind in the forward to Ward's book *Lay of the Land*).

"On balance," Ward-Thomas wrote in another of his books, *Not Only Golf,* "being a prisoner of war was a lucky break because in my youth I could never have anticipated a more rewarding life than that which has been my fortunate lot these past thirty years."

Curiosity is among the writer's most valuable assets. Ward-Thomas always wondered how the golf balls that he'd cobbled together from scraps during his incarceration in Stalag Luft III would perform for a preeminent player. Two of his handmade golf balls had survived, and shortly after the war, he asked a pair of former British Open winners, Reginald Whitcombe (1938) and Alfred Perry (1935), to test his handiwork. Each ball traveled about two hundred yards.

Ward-Thomas was only temporarily satisfied with what he had learned. When Jack Nicklaus came along in the sixties and began overpowering the game in a way no one ever had, Ward-Thomas's curiosity began to stir anew. One day he brought one of his handmade golf balls to Nicklaus, explained its humble beginnings, and asked him to hit a drive with it. Nicklaus at the time could crush a golf ball. "Pat," he said, "I would be afraid I might break it." He politely declined from a concern that he would destroy an historical artifact. The ball belonged in a museum, Nicklaus said, and indeed, one of Ward-Thomas's golf balls found a permanent home in the United States Golf Association's museum in Far Hills, New Jersey. The ball represented only one of golf's many enduring gifts that emerged from an otherwise somber period.

The memory of John Burke, the Rhode Island amateur killed in North Africa, has been preserved through the benevolence of the Rhode Island Golf Association. In 1946, the association established the John P. Burke Memorial Fund for the purpose of providing scholarships to caddies from around the state. "The John P. Burke Memorial Fund was established by the Rhode Island Golf Association as a tribute to all its members who served our country during World War II, and in particular as a tribute to those of them who did not come back," its literature explains.

The fund has provided scholarship assistance to more than five hundred students and has had the support of all Rhode Island golf courses, as well as the two most prominent golfers from Rhode Island, PGA Tour players Brad Faxon and Billy Andrade, who are corporation members of the John P. Burke Memorial Fund.

Dale Bourisseau was too durable to erode in a pool of self-pity for an extended time. The part of his leg that he had sacrificed at the Battle of Monte Cassino in Italy was not going to grow back. He reconciled himself to that fact and got on with his life. His daughter, Joie Bourisseau, never knew her father with two complete legs. She was born three months after a land mine had redirected his course in life. In 2000, Joie wrote of her father's metamorphosis: "[He was] lying in that hospital bed, month after month, recuperating, rehabilitating, and reorienting himself and his life priorities. Dad decided that being an invalid was not a valid option for him. He began to meet other war veterans who, like himself, had lost a limb or two. Many felt hopeless and despondent. Dad decided that what they all needed was an outlet; they needed a vehicle where they could move their bodies to feel vital again, a place where they could commiserate and laugh with each other over their recently acquired inadequacies, and a forum where they could share their stories. . . . In 1947, on a small public course in Aurora, Ohio, Dad gathered together his war-strewn cronies and sprouted those seeds full bloom into the first national golf tournament for amputees."

The National Amputee Golf Association was born from that gathering, the product of Bourisseau's vision and his desire to reintroduce productivity into his life and the lives of others. Today, the NAGA has more than 2,500 members from around the world, playing in a variety of regional, national, and international tournaments.

"It became my dad's life," his son John Bourisseau said. "It was his identity. He was extremely dedicated to it. The people involved were amazing people."

In 1958, Bourisseau was awarded the Ben Hogan Award, presented by the Golf Writers Association of America "to an individual who has continued to be active in golf despite a physical handicap or serious illness."

Before Palmer, Nicklaus, and Player came along, the Big Three were Nelson, Hogan, and Snead, who collectively gave the war years a prominent place in the history of the game. Byron Nelson in fact did retire to his Texas ranch following the 1946 tour season, as he had hinted that he might amid his remarkable

1945 run. He made only ceremonial appearances after that, but managed to add one more victory to his career total of fifty-two—the Bing Crosby Pro-Am in 1951. Sam Snead enjoyed a long and distinguished career, eventually winning eighty-one tournaments, the last in 1965. Ben Hogan found immortality by winning the U.S. Open four times in six years (1948, 1950, 1951, and 1953). He would never be forgotten in other ways as well.

More than three years after the war ended, John Searcy, his body on the mend, finally learned more about the skilled instructor from whom he had learned golf while he was recuperating at the Army convalescent hospital at the Don Cesar Hotel in Pass-A-Grille, Florida. On February 2, 1949, Hogan was involved in a near-fatal automobile accident on a back road of Texas, thrusting him onto page one of the newspaper.

"At the time," Searcy said, "I didn't think Hogan was that well known. When he had the accident and it was reported in the news, I said, 'Hey, he was my golf instructor.'"

Initially, Searcy had viewed those sessions with Hogan in the summer of '45 as little more than a renewable day pass to escape the dreariness of the hospital, his ticket outside and into the sunshine. "I didn't really care that much about golf," he said. "I wound up playing the rest of my life."

Every week that weather permitted for more than half a century, Searcy took to the first tee the lessons that Captain Hogan had given him. His association with Hogan continued indirectly throughout his life; by chance, he began his postwar golf using Hogan-brand clubs and by design always replaced them with newer Hogan-brand clubs.

In 1945, Lance Anderson also took lessons from Hogan, for whom his affection was immediate. So was his devotion to the game. "Sheer smartass ego led me to try my hand, and every shot that advanced the ball beyond my shadow or stayed on the shorter grass thereafter dragged me further into the abyss," he said. Anderson, like Searcy, also played golf the rest of his life, and he attempted to do so with a facsimile of Hogan's swing. "For years, I hit the ball as exactly as I could to the way Hogan hit the golf ball," Anderson said. The results, he noted, weren't always the same.

The injuries he had incurred that had landed him in the 14th Regional Convalescent Hospital and in the company of then-Lieutenant Hogan may have worked as a detriment. Anderson prefers to think it was the equipment's fault. "It is certain my scoring improvement would have been more precipitate without the three woods purchased from a permanently crippled fellow patient," he said. "They were as flexible as buggy whips. The suggestion from the Lieutenant (Hogan) to 'always hit it as hard as you can off the tee' took many hours of really dogged play to develop timing sufficient to stop those slices from hitting me in the rear. Eventually, I was able to hit those K-28's (Hogan's choice, naturally), fade, draw, or straight, a country mile."

WHEN THE APPROACHING RUSSIAN ARMY forced the Germans to evacuate their prisoners from Stalag Luft III, the emaciated men, bracing for a long march in bitter cold, left virtually everything behind. One of them, Robert Laubach, took from the camp only an affinity for golf. "I had no game up until then," he said, his only knowledge of golf gleaned from his days as a caddie at Crystal Downs Golf Club in Frankfort, Michigan. His experience with golf in the POW camp "got me into the game," he said.

For Laubach, once he was in, there would never be a way out. The game consumed him. Eventually he became the director of the Golf Association of Michigan, as well as a vice president of the Arizona Golf Association. He was a rules official for the United States Golf Association and was a longtime member of the USGA's Green Section Committee. He served on the USGA Sectional Affairs and the U.S. Senior Amateur Championship committees and was awarded the Piper and Oakley Award for his long and meritorious service to the USGA Green Section.

Golf did not relinquish its hold on Oliver Green either. Another veteran of Stalag Luft III, Green spent his working life in and around the military, eventually becoming Britain's military representative to NATO. But he never ventured far from the game. Henry Longhurst, the legendary British writer and BBC golf commentator, sponsored Green's membership into the Royal and Ancient Golf Club of St. Andrews. Green later oversaw the construction of two golf courses on the Woburn Estate in Woburn, England, at the behest of the duke of Bedford. The Woburn Golf and Country Club has hosted the British Masters and Women's British Open, among other events.

The game did not serve William Powell to the same degree that he served the game. When Powell returned home, he found an America that had not appreciably changed with regard to its treatment of blacks. He wanted only to play golf but discovered his options limited by the color of his skin. He solved the problem by building his own course, the first in America ever designed and owned by an African American. The Clearview Golf Course in Canton, Ohio, became Powell's enduring legacy, his gift to a game that was disinclined to respond in kind.

Only a Hollywood director might conclude that the story of the Japanese attack on Pearl Harbor required tweaking to make it more compelling. The film *Pearl Harbor* accordingly took liberties with the whereabouts of Admiral Kimmel on December 7,

1941. The film showed him already on the golf course. In fact, he was only preparing to leave for the course when the attack began, a minor point, but one worth noting to spare him further indignity. It should be a moot point at any rate. On May 25, 1999, the U.S. Senate overturned the Roberts Commission finding that Kimmel and General Short had been derelict in their duties. The Senate exonerated them, declaring that they had performed their duties "competently and professionally."

A SHORT TIME BEFORE HIS DEATH in 1971, Bobby Jones, confined to a wheelchair and suffering from the debilitating spinal disease syringomyelia, was the guest of honor at Merion Golf Club in Ardmore, Pennsylvania, which was installing a fairway plaque to commemorate Jones's having won the fourth and final leg of the Grand Slam there in the U.S. Amateur in 1930. He was approached by a man he only faintly recognized at first.

"Burt," the man said by way of reintroduction, though he was unable to get the second name out before Jones intervened.

"Etherington," Jones said, completing the man's name for him.

In 1943, Burt Etherington and Bobby Jones had attended Army Air Corps Intelligence School together in Harrisburg, Pennsylvania. One afternoon, at Jones's urging, the two of them escaped for a round of golf that Etherington never forgot. Neither, apparently, had Jones.

Etherington, then the vice president of Merion, asked Jones to sign three programs, one for each of his three sons. He handed a pen to Jones, whose loss of muscle control required that he clutch it with his entire hand. He was in apparent pain, yet he signed the first program. Etherington immediately recognized his faux pas—asking the ailing Jones to sign three programs. He thanked Jones, then began reaching for the pen.

"But you said you had three sons!" Jones said, before painfully affixing his signature to the other two programs for a grateful old friend to whom he had been bound, so many years before, by a mutual passion and a shared purpose, bound by golf and war.

ACKNOWLEDGMENTS

My late uncle, Leonard Spencer, of Everett, Washington, was wounded in the Battle of the Bulge, leaving him with a permanent limp that never succeeded in keeping him from his appointed rounds at Legion Memorial and Walter E. Hall golf courses over the next fifty-plus years. I need not have looked any further for inspiration than to Leonard and the other men in my life from that remarkable generation, including my father, William Strege, a former Marine Corps lieutenant and an octogenarian who twice a week renews his quest to squeeze a few extra yards from his driver; my father-in-law, Harry Hoelzel, a former Army Air Corps lieutenant, who piloted B-17s; and my friend Bob Mericle, a Navy electrician.

One of the first interviews I conducted in researching this book was with General Louis Truman, who was ninety-four and living in Buckhead, Georgia. General Truman, second cousin of

President Harry S. Truman, was gracious enough to rummage through his storehouse of memories and share what he recalled of the golf he was scheduled to play near Pearl Harbor on December 7, 1941. Alas, General Truman died in December of 2004, at ninety-five.

It was a privilege to have gotten to know Joseph Burke, twin brother of John Burke, the former national collegiate champion. Joseph was kind enough to recount the details of one of the sadder chapters of his life, the death of John, who was killed in North Africa in 1943. My thanks as well to Dale Bourisseau's family—children Joie and John and brother Zane.

Those who assisted me with research have my deepest appreciation. They include Patty Moran at the United States Golf Association; Heidi Wegmueller at the PGA of America; Emma Jane McAdam at the Royal and Ancient Golf Club of St. Andrews; Cilla Jackson at the University of St. Andrews; Herb Pankratz at the Eisenhower Presidential Library; Sid Matthew, the foremost authority on Bobby Jones today; Robert Conte, the historian at the Greenbrier in White Sulphur Springs, West Virginia; Dave Mann in Atlanta; Vanessa Gomez in Miami; Avery Holton in Fort Worth, Texas; and the unfailingly friendly and helpful staff at the Ziffren Library in Los Angeles, the best sports library in the country.

Thanks to those who generously shared their stories, including Larry Etzkorn, former USGA president Sandy Tatum, Byron Nelson, Jack Snead, and former POWs Robert Laubach and Oliver Green. My appreciation as well to the staff at Gotham Books—including publisher William Shinker, Brendan Cahill, and Patrick Mulligan—for its professionalism, enthusiasm, courteousness, and helpfulness.

And as always, many thanks to my agent and friend, Freya Manston, who won't let me rest.

INDEX